Words for Today
2010
Notes for daily Bible reading

IBRA
INTERNATIONAL BIBLE READING ASSOCIATION

Words
for today ■■■■■ *2010*

Edited by Nicola Slee

International Bible Reading Association

Words for Today aims to build understanding and respect for a range of religious perspectives and approaches to living practised in the world today, and to help readers meet new challenges in their faith. Views expressed by contributors should not, however, be taken to reflect the views or policies of the Editor or the International Bible Reading Association.

The International Bible Reading Association's scheme of readings is listed monthly on the Christian Education website at www.christianeducation.org.uk/ibra_scheme.php and the full scheme for 2010 may be downloaded in English, Spanish and French.

Cover photograph: Emma Riddell
Editor: Nicola Slee

Published by:
The International Bible Reading Association
1020 Bristol Road
Selly Oak
Birmingham B29 6LB
United Kingdom

Charity number 211542

ISBN 978-1-905893-17-1
ISSN 0140-8275

Designed and typeset by Christian Education Publications
Printed and bound in the UK by Mosaic Print Management
www.mosaicpm.com

Contents

Editorial

This year's cover shows the church in an urban setting – as it happens, St Martin's in the Bullring in Birmingham city centre, but it could be any major city, more or less anywhere in the world. There has been a church in this place for centuries, witnessing to the love of God while the city around it has changed dramatically through the forces of war as well as peacetime, times of prosperity and recession, decay and regeneration.

The church – the body corporate of those who seek to follow after the way of Jesus, however haltingly – is called to relate and respond to the world as it is, not as we might want it to be or remember it was in times past. Where might we find living 'words for today' to speak into such a context and to challenge and encourage those who are looking for meaning to live by? This is one of the underlying questions that motivates the team at International Bible Reading Association and all the writers who contribute to *Words for Today*.

It is not enough to continue to repackage old, well-worn words and concepts – these will not speak to a generation unversed in scripture and untutored in the knowledge of Christian tradition. We are after new words, new ways of saying old things, new things unearthed from familiar places – and if this often makes for comment that takes our readers out of their comfort zones and into a place of wrestling with the things of faith and working hard to rethink their discipleship, then that is precisely the kind of Christians the world has need of.

As you read, ponder, pray and seek to put into action this year's readings, may you be equipped to engage with the worlds you inhabit and know with all the resilience, realism and passion that are hallmarks of the Spirit of God. And as you do so, may you find refreshment and renewal.

Nicola Slee
Editor

Prayers

O God, make me real
and ready to hear you speaking in the lives
of the people I shall meet today and the places I shall go to or hear about.

Nicola Slee

Lord, help us to let go of whatever hinders us
from seeing things from your perspective
and help us to recognize the signs
that show your kingdom
is even now actively at work in our midst.

Edmund Banyard

Lord God,
we believe that your revelation comes to every nation
in its real and concrete situation;
Help us to see you more clearly in our tradition and culture.
Lord God, we believe that you have called us
to be your hands and feet in this land.
Help us to be living witnesses
of your love and grace to all people . . .
May your justice and peace reign among us.

Charles Klagbo, Togo

May God give us new visions,
to take advantage of new possibilities,
to go out and reach new people.
May the Holy Spirit empower us to do this work.

Josef Ceruenak, Czechoslovakia

You are the Way we shall walk.
You are the Truth we shall take into ourselves.
You are the Life we shall enjoy for ever
and share with all.

Donald Hilton

How to use a 'quiet time'

Pay attention to your body Take time to slow down, consciously relax each part of your body, and listen to your breathing for a while.

Use silence to relax and empty your mind of all that's going on around you. Know that God's loving presence encircles you, your family, your community and the world. Learn to enjoy God's presence.

Have a visual focus – a cross, a plant, interesting stones, pictures or postcards. . . Create a prayer table on which to display them with other symbols.

Read the **Bible passage** for the day several times, perhaps using different translations, and then the notes. Allow the words to fill your mind. Try to discover their message for you and the world around you.

Listen Remember that the most important part of prayer is to hear what God is saying to us. God speaks to us through the words of scripture, the daily news, and often through people around us.

Include the world Hold the news of the day in your mind. Enter the situation of those you hear or read about and try to pray alongside them and with them.

Pray without ceasing Prayer is not only 'the quiet time' we set aside. It becomes part of the whole of life, a continuous dialogue between God and ourselves, through all that we do and think and say: a growing awareness of the loving presence of God who travels with us and never leaves us.

Acknowledgements and abbreviations

GNB   *Good News Bible* (The Bible Societies/Collins Publishers) – Old Testament © American Bible Society 1976; New Testament © American Bible Society 1966, 1971, 1976.

NIV   Scripture quotations taken from *The Holy Bible, New International Version* © 1973, 1978, 1984 by International Bible Society. Used by permission of Hodder & Stoughton Limited. All rights reserved. 'NIV' is a registered trademark of International Bible Society. UK trademark number 1448790.

NJB   Taken from the *New Jerusalem Bible*, published and copyright 1985 by Darton, Longman and Todd Ltd and Doubleday & Co. Inc., and used by permission of the publishers.

NSRV   *New Revised Standard Version* © 1989, Division of Christian Education of the National Council of Churches of Christ in the United States of America.

REB   *Revised English Bible*© Oxford University and Cambridge University Presses 1989.

RSV   *The Holy Bible, Revised Standard Version* © 1973, Division of Christian Education of the National Council of Churches of Christ in the United States of America.

BCE   Before the Common Era. BCE and CE are used by some writers instead of BC and AD.

Readings in Luke

1 The coming of the Messiah

Notes based on the New International Version by

Jonash Joyohoy

Preparing for the week

Luke's first two chapters appear to be a concise introduction to the teachings and earthly ministry of Jesus Christ. The series of readings emphasises the connection between Jesus Christ and John the Baptist and explores the early foundations of Jesus' ministry of holistic salvation – that is, a salvation which addresses the whole person, mind, body and spirit, and the individual within community – within the local and global context in which Christ's coming was historically situated. These narratives, leading to the climax of Jesus' birth during Rome's first imperial census, suggest a kind of pattern of problem solving at a global level. When read critically and theologically from the context of mass movements in the Philippines, striking parallels may surface between Luke's time and our own, along with some challenging reflections. Such parallels and reflections may also be illuminating for other places and contexts where, under the impact of globalisation, the modes of domination and exploitation are very similar.

For further thought

- The world's Messiah was born in the context of intensifying global and imperial domination; how might that help us to think about our current global crises?

- If the world's greatest miracle, the birth of Jesus, happened through a natural process, should we then cease to believe in supernatural miracles?

The Revd Jonash Joyohoy has been a priest for sixteen years, based in the Philippines. He served as a parish priest in the Philippine Independent Church for five years before working as a community organiser and human rights advocate for more than ten years now. Through a scholarship from the Church of England's USPG, he came to the UK and was awarded a Birmingham University MA in Applied Theological Studies in 2007 from the Selly Oak Centre for Mission Studies at the Queen's Foundation for Ecumenical Theological Education, Birmingham.

The family background of John the Baptist

Luke 1:1-25

Zechariah, the father of John the Baptist, was a temple priest in Jerusalem. Serving in the most influential Jewish institution and belonging to the priestly class, Zechariah must have been a prominent figure in Jewish society. His only son John, later known as the Baptist, grew up in what we might call a middle-class context, privileged to have acquired formal education, inheriting the credibility and prominent identity of his father. More importantly, John seems to have also inherited the religious qualities of his father and mother Elizabeth, of 'observing all the Lord's commandments and regulations blamelessly' (verse 6). This family background was part of what moulded him into becoming the 'forerunner' and 'introducer' of Jesus Christ.

In the Philippines, it is not uncommon to hear of good parents like Zechariah and Elizabeth who work in the church, in government, or in the corporate world. Middle-class and in the social mainstream, people regard them with honour and respect. As good parents they dream of their children becoming even more successful in the future, teaching them good values and sending them to top universities. From such contexts may emerge individuals like John the Baptist who, despite their comfortable upbringing, yet chose to live simple lives in order to serve as forerunners and pioneers of the common people's struggle in order that all may find holistic salvation.

We thank you, dear Lord, for the kindness of your grace. May we be among the company of your servants who use what has been given us in our upbringing for the welfare of others.

Jonash Joyohoy

Mary the mother of Jesus is of undistinguished origin. Coming from the countryside town of Nazareth in Galilee, neither she nor her family's roots are known except that Luke tells us she was a relative of Elizabeth. Joseph's bloodline to King David is of little significance, as he was not the biological father of Jesus, and Mary was already pregnant by the Spirit before marriage. Though Joseph the carpenter was not his biological father, however, Jesus grew up in his house. Is this significant, and if so, why?

There is an obvious contrast between the family backgrounds of John the Baptist and Jesus of Nazareth: John comes from the middle class and social mainstream while Jesus comes from the working class at the margins of society. This contrast was surely providential; it certainly laid the ground for their distinctive roles as 'forerunner and introducer' and as 'Messiah and saviour' respectively.

The diverse class origins of the 'forerunner' and the 'saviour' become more significant when seen from within the mass movements in the Philippines. Here, individuals from the social middle class serve as excellent articulators of social realities. Hence they also serve as 'forerunners and introducers' to the common people who themselves are the 'liberators' or main force in the struggle for liberation and social change.

The family background of Jesus Christ

Luke 1:26-45

Enlighten and embolden us, O Lord, so that with confidence we may count ourselves among your workers in the world.

A common ground for unity

Luke 1:46-56

The song of Mary points strongly to social equality as a condition God seeks for his people. It emphasises the primacy of the 'Mighty One' over the 'rulers of the time' and reveals God's bias towards the humble and materially poor over the rich and proud. This revolutionary song is the longest and most significant articulation of the vision of holistic salvation that we find in the early chapters of any of the gospels, presenting a striking alternative to the realities of the time.

The Magnificat also provides a common meeting ground for both the God-fearing middle class and the oppressed lower classes at the margins of society (represented by John and Jesus respectively). Through this song, people of diverse class origins with varied interests see each other at the same level and agree on a common vision for the future.

This radical equality may come as a challenge to people in the present time. Can those separated by great differences agree on a shared agenda for the good of people and the future of the world? Is it possible that the usual divides of colour, nationality, class standing and faith be placed secondary to the common longing for world peace, justice, poverty reduction and environmental protection? The Blessed Virgin Mary in today's reading gives an assurance that this is possible.

How would you distinguish the working from the middle class in your community and at the global level? What are their distinctive characteristics?

Clear our conscience of inequalities, dear God, so we can see and act according to your priorities.

Through another song Zechariah announces that his son John is 'a prophet of the most high' (verse 76) – highlighting the role of John as the Messiah's forerunner and introducer. When John later baptises and recognises Jesus as the Messiah, this must have accorded the Nazarene teacher the needed acceptance and 'mainstreaming' in the Judean capital Jerusalem and in other Jewish communities, without which he might have struggled for recognition. Thus John effectively prepared the way of the Messiah along accepted social terrains and across cultures, races and classes.

Note, too, how Zechariah's Jewish and nationalist understanding of the coming of the Messiah is expressed in the Benedictus. In his song, he refers to the Messiah as 'the God of Israel, because he has come and has redeemed his people . . . to rescue us from the hand of our enemies' (verses 68, 74). Nevertheless, as the gospel of Luke unfolds, we will see how such a Jewish understanding of salvation evolves into a salvation that is inclusive and global. The coming of the Messiah is for all, not only for the Jewish people.

Historically, participants of mass movements in the Philippines also underwent an evolution in terms of their perception of freedom and liberation. In the 1896 revolution against Spanish colonialism, the concern was limited to national liberation. In the present time, the vision is wider, and the struggle for national liberation is interdependent with the movement for international solidarity and global emancipation.

Dear God, we humbly ask you to enable us to discern the purpose behind your actions in history and in our own time.

From local to global

Luke 1:57-80

Readings in Luke   Jonash Joyohoy

Political and economic realities as pointers

Luke 2:1-14

The linking of the Messiah's birth to Emperor Caesar Augustus' first census 'of the entire Roman world' (verse 1) is more than a historical reference and authentication of the birth of Jesus. The first global census, being a major political action aimed at systematising domination over imperial subjects, demonstrates the universal significance of Christ's coming into the world.

This significance can be seen in the following emphases. First, the passage presents a pattern of problem and solution wherein the Messiah is the 'Mighty One' who 'shine(s) on those living in darkness and in the shadow of death' (Luke 1:79a, see also Matthew 4:16). Second, the coming of the Messiah at the time of the first global census suggests that the Messiah is the global saviour – and moreover he is the saviour born into a context of rising global domination.

From these two emphases can be drawn two conclusions. One supports the position common among liberal theologians, that political and economic liberation is inherent in Christ's salvation. The other suggests the need for Christians to be critically aware of the realities of any given context in which we are seeking to proclaim the gospel. If it was out of a context of global domination that there emerged the understanding of the global Saviour, so in our time, social realities which may seem wholly negative may nevertheless serve as pointers to Christians to discern the work of the Spirit.

We need to learn to read the signs of the times in order to know how to respond appropriately to what the Spirit is doing.

Guide us always through your ways, dear Lord, so we can live our lives according to your will.

The brief narrative of the birth of Jesus tells of the natural processes the Messiah underwent from birth to childhood and into maturity. Being born in a manger after his parents' rejection by the inns in the neighbourhood illustrates the revolutionary nature of the saviour's birth. Yet equally significant is the fact that history's greatest miracle, the coming of the Messiah, happened according to a natural process of being born through a human mother and growing up according to Jewish customs. There was nothing magical involved in this greatest miracle; every process the Messiah went through from birth to adulthood was consistent with the laws of nature. This supports the position of many biblical scholars that apparently miraculous or supernatural narratives in the gospels and in other places in scripture are more literary or theological devices than a literal narration of historical facts.

So we should look critically at claims in our own day for miracles that are magical or contrary to the laws of nature and science. Similarly, in mass movements such as those in the Philippines and elsewhere, genuine transformation happens not by supernatural or extraordinary spiritual agents, but according to the ordinary laws of social change. Liberation may require extraordinary courage and effort, but these are only possible through natural and scientific processes.

How would you reconcile the miraculous narratives of the Bible with natural processes of working for liberation and justice?

Loving God, give us a true appreciation of the beauty of your creation and the inherent laws you placed within it.

The greatest miracle by natural processes

Luke 2:15-24

Jonash Joyohoy

Coming together of lay people, priests and prophets

Luke 2:25-40

The narrative tells of a devout lay person, Simeon, foretelling that the Messiah will 'cause the falling and rising of many' (verse 34), and of the prophetess Anna relating the child Jesus to the redemption of Israel. Their pronouncements confirm the words of Zechariah that we read about earlier in the week.

Simeon, Anna and Zechariah represent the three major sectors of Jewish society, namely the lay people, prophets and priests. All of them were present to witness to and proclaim the coming of the Messiah, the Saviour of the world. All three share the same understanding that, in the coming salvation, there is no distinction between economic and political salvation on the one hand, and spiritual salvation on the other.

In mass movements in the Philippines, a parallel to the above can be seen in the joining and working together of three important sectors. These are: first, the activists who resemble the biblical prophets; second, the religious sector who are similar to the biblical priests; and third, the usually uninvolved majority who resemble the biblical laity. Here is another example of unity, in addition to the coming together of the people in the middle and lower classes which we spoke of earlier.

In your own context, what are the usual reasons for the coming together of activists, religious and lay people?

Thank you, dear God, for the diversity of people coming together and working hand-in-hand for the attainment of a better world for all.

Growth in wisdom and stature

Luke 2:41-52

The last verse of today's reading tells of the boy Jesus growing 'in wisdom and stature, and in favour with God and men' (verse 52). Getting flak for 'eating and drinking', Jesus in another setting taught that 'Wisdom is proved right by (her) actions' (Matthew 11:19). Wisdom, which is invisible, can only be proved by correct actions. Correspondingly, correct actions embody wisdom.

In this passage, 'stature' may mean the positive perception by the public of a person (or group): hence the words 'in favour with God and men'. Wisdom shown by correct actions may therefore be the main criterion for 'stature' or the people's acceptance. This suggests that the people's acceptance of Jesus from boyhood onwards was earned through correct actions, not given by external status or others' approval.

Growing in wisdom and stature, as the Messiah did, may also characterise liberation and mass movements in any country. It is a great challenge for the leaders of such movements to earn people's acceptance by means of correct action. Philosophies and ideologies vary, and all may sound good. However it is always the people, the victims of domination and exploitation, who have the last say and who make the lasting judgements about which actions are correct and are worthy of their acceptance, solidarity and co-operation.

How do you discern the saving and inviting hands of God at work in your day-to-day living?

Draw us to your work of salvation, O God, and allow us to see the needs to which we should respond.

Readings in Luke   Jonash Joyohoy

The economy of God

1 The economy of grace

Preparing for the week

Oikonomia (economy or plan) is from a group of related words that includes house, household, inhabited earth and ecology. The word is used in the epistles to refer to God's offer of salvation in Christ. While the economy of the world is materialistic, divisive, atheistic and idolatrous in its dogmas and behaviour, the economy of God is all including, uniting, generous, justice making and life affirming for all. The economy of God works with different ground rules, is motivated by love and grace, and is extremely generous. While the former asks, 'What have you done on earth to increase the GNP?' the latter asks, 'What have you done to the least of these our sisters and brothers?' The logic of the latter stands in sharp contrast to the illogic of the former.

Grace is at the heart of the economy of God in Christ. It is not earned, yet it is costly (Bonhoeffer). Here the liturgy of abundance (not scarcity) is celebrated. This is characterised by a lifestyle of thankfulness, love, generosity and self-emptying.

For further thought and prayer

- How would you characterise and contrast the economy of the world and the economy of God?

- Pray for grace to live your life according to God's economy rather than the world's.

Sunday 10 January

Notes based on the New Revised Standard Version and the *Good as New* Bible by

Mike Holroyd

Mike Holroyd is currently a part-time doctoral student at Aberdeen University research-ing the importance of the lived experience of disabled people in the formulation of disability theology. He also works for a disability organisation in the area of advocacy and project development, based in Bristol. 'Theology is a strange thing,' says Mike. 'Sometimes it illuminates the way, and sometimes it gets in the way.' Nevertheless, Mike hopes that his research and work will play a small part in encourag-ing the church and society at large to be more organically inclusive of people on the margins – whether this be social minorities or economic majorities.

We can't have it both ways – either we get to God by being good, believing all the right things, going to church three times on a Sunday, or ... we don't. Either God's grace is sufficient or it's not. So two thousand years of Christian history has tried to compromise – we like the idea of God's grace, but we need a few rules to make sure that we're ready to receive it. Even the first few verses of this chapter of Ephesians can set off in us an avalanche of righteous thoughts – 'I used to be like that, but now I am a Christian . . . ' This is futile on two counts. First, I know from my own experience that, even though I try to identify as a Christian, I'm rather less perfect than I might like to think. And second, even if I was perfect, that would be an even bigger problem because it's not my perfection or lack of it that has anything to do with God's grace.

God's grace is for all, and has always been intended thus (verse 10). The most important thing is for us to know in our hearts that we can do nothing to earn God's love and approval – and if I can do nothing, then neither can any of my 6.5 billion neighbours.

And so let us together sing – 'Amazing grace, how sweet the sound'. Over and over again – God's grace is a gift, not a theology.

God's grace is sufficient

Ephesians 2:1-10

The economy of God   Mike Holroyd

Economics of thankfulness

Philippians 4:4-9

Many of us used to think that saying please and thank you was a sign that we had made it in civilised society. To say thank you is a kind of moral obligation, perhaps a way of paying back for kindnesses received. But thankfulness is not so much a moral duty as a way of being. We often find it difficult to think of things to say thank you for because we're looking in the wrong places. The gift of life is amazing, the human sparkle that we find in strangers and friends is tremendous, the richness and diversity of our planet is breathtaking.

One day I was walking down the road with my long cane (because I have a visual impairment) and I overheard someone say to her friend, 'Isn't there something they can do for him?' Leaving aside questions of dignity and human decency, I was saddened that these people could not experience the gratitude that I feel for the unique gift of visual impairment that God has blessed me with. Like most gifts from God, it comes with its challenges as well as its joys, but I have a choice and, whilst being realistic about the pain and sometimes despair in life, I give thanks for who God has made me.

So how about you? What will you give thanks for today?

Self-emptying economics

Philippians 2:5-11

Our modern experience of economics can sometimes point us in the wrong direction when we try to understand passages such as this one. We tend to read it as a formula – the more I empty myself, the more God will love me, or some such. But rather than an economics of transaction we have here the economics of transformation.

Father Richard Rohr often talks about 'getting ourselves out of the way'. This is not an attempt to say that in ourselves we are not valuable and loved beyond all understanding, but rather an invitation to enable the fullness of God's presence to enter every part of our being. Self-emptying can of course suggest a variety of techniques to help us to live more simply, but more than that, it is about making space for the fullness of God's presence in our cluttered minds and hearts.

Belief, morality and even belonging can, if we're not careful, be part of our economics of transaction. These things are indeed important companions on our spiritual journey, but we need to allow them to lead us to the deeper place of transformation where we are more content to behold the things we don't understand than believe the things we do. The work of Jesus on the cross is a model of transformation for all of us; we don't need to understand it so much as enter into it.

O God, may I behold the mystery that the more I become empty, the more there is space for your Spirit to fill me beyond all measure.

The economy of God   Mike Holroyd

Generous economics

2 Corinthians 8:1-15

We're being reminded in our readings this week that this wonderful gift of grace that comes from God is the energy behind transformation. If we allow ourselves to be touched by the grace of God, then we will slowly experience the permeation of this grace into every area of our lives.

What we do with the things we have is a critical question, especially for those of us who live in the West – and the question can never simply be tackled in an individualistic way, but must have social and political implications. Alan Jones, previously Dean of Grace Cathedral in San Francisco, talks of the way in which the accumulation of stuff has a negative impact on us. Sharing our possessions, financial or otherwise, is a gospel imperative on both a micro and macro scale. It's an interesting paradox that often the more stuff we have, the harder we find it to share our love and time with others.

We live in a physical world which we should cherish and enjoy. But more than this, we must strive for a more just economy where the resources of the earth's household are shared. It is in such an economy that grace will flourish – again, not a transaction but a transformation.

O God, as I give thanks for the resources I have, show me how to enable them to be ours rather than mine.

Economics of love

1 John 3:16-24

What does it really mean to love and be loved? How can we embrace this most Christlike of characteristics? As I read through this passage my mind is full of questions – sometimes the language feels a little uncomfortable. The concepts are concerned with laying down our lives and living in obedience. Yes, it's the language of old-time religion, but in a radically new context – the context of Jesus' transforming love on the cross. The way of Jesus is not to blame someone else, or pay back evil for evil, but to transform pain into love and hurt into forgiveness. This is the life-changing power of Jesus – that he opens up the way to reverse the whole of human history. René Girard has highlighted the way in which the scapegoat mechanism has been played out through history. James Alison, amongst others, has written concerning the way in which Jesus puts an end to the scapegoating mechanism.

To be obedient to the way of Jesus is to believe in a transformation that, by the grace of God, is able to deliver us and the whole of creation from the scapegoating mechanism. This is the real power of love, and the biggest threat to the way of the world as we know it.

Loving God, to love freely is often difficult, and to be loved is even harder. Show us the way in Jesus again and again, that our hearts may explode with love, and our lives embody your love in the world.

The economy of God   Mike Holroyd

Timeless economy

1 Peter 3:13 – 4:6

It's all here – those who have passed away (the past), those who are being addressed by this letter (the present), and even the angels (the future). But is that not a rather linear way of looking at it? We often see God's judgement and reconciliation as events marked out by chronological time, unfolding in a historical context. However, it seems apparent that God sees things rather differently without the constraints of the human clock.

Part of our challenge today is to learn to live in the present – we are too often tempted to live by our diaries or our Outlook calendars, and we can spend all our time looking forward without learning to live in the present. If we allow ourselves to be controlled by our desires, then we are always wanting more, new levels of excitement and an ever-increasing diversity of experience. Desire, of course, is not always bad, but to be controlled by it means that, rather than living in and for the moment, we miss the moment completely. If we learn to live completely in the present then we will start to sense God's judgement, yes. But we will also be aware of God's constant invitation to receive God's grace and live according to God's way.

O God, let me not be so consumed by the future and the past that I miss the present. Help me to find ways of participating in your economy of grace in Jesus' name.

The economy of God

The economy of God

2 The economy of fools

Notes based on the New Revised Standard Version by

Sandra Pollerman

Sandra Pollerman is a story-teller and spiritual companion currently living in Suffolk. Sandra is also a founding member of Holy Fools, UK (www.holy-fools.org.uk), and has enjoyed clowning for God nationally and internationally.

Preparing for the week

Unusual life choices have been characteristic of holy people since early days. In order to come close to God, and to show others a possible path, women and men in many countries and locations have chosen to live a life of poverty and solitude, focusing on prayer and self-denial. For many, a feigned madness and seemingly foolish behaviour was a way of avoiding honour.

In Christian times holy fools have been particularly important. The Russian Church has a special term *yurodivi*, meaning 'holy fools' or 'fools for Christ's sake'. One of the most famous was Basil the Blessed who lived as a vagrant and wore only a loincloth. Many also recall the practices of Francis of Assisi who talked to birds, tamed a wolf and walked unarmed across the Egyptian desert into the sultan's camp seeking a non-violent resolution to the conflict raging due to the Crusades, when thousands of Christian soldiers had taken up arms against the Muslims.

Such 'fools' were scorned by those whose social and economic standards honoured wealth and power. Such 'fools' were followed by those who heard and saw people making choices based on the economy of God.

Through the readings this week, may we come to recognise the ground rules of this economy of God and make our choices based on them. May we also extend gratitude and respect across denominational borders in this Week of Prayer for Christian Unity.

For further thought and action

- In what ways do you consider Christian faith to be foolishness or madness?
- Find out more about Francis' life and exploits through a search on the internet or your local library.

Monday 18 January

Fools to follow

1 Corinthians 1:18-25

In 1948, my Hungarian refugee father-in-law and family were invited to relocate in North America. After re-qualifying, his medical skills and experience continued to be useful and his practice developed well. He was a loving man and cared for his family. They could have lived very comfortably indeed.

None the less, he and his wife made some clear choices. Growing out of their faith and gratitude, they continued to live frugally, using a good percentage of their resources to support their extended family overseas. Medicines were sent, and used clothing (worn once by their own family, since new clothes wouldn't clear Customs). They invested savings in education for their children, and for Hungarian nieces and nephews. The next generation, and the one after that, continued to grow and thrive.

My father-in-law did save some things for himself: cardboard boxes, used paper, and *many* bars of soap – he never wanted to run out of soap again! And he did have some indulgences: summer driving holidays with his wife and eight children (all in one car) and sugar – three or four teaspoons in each cup of tea or coffee. When his estate was settled, many bequests were uncovered: each one labelled with the names of one of his eight children or one of his grandchildren.

In my experience there have been few who have lived out the foolishness of God's economy with such grace.

Loving God, may we recognise and follow those 'fools' who show us ways to live out the wisdom of your ways.

Sandra Pollerman

The economy of God

Paul's cheeky game of 'I'm better than you are' always draws me in. I can almost see his rising tower built of gifts and accomplishments suddenly crumble and fall as he declares all this rubbish. He changes the ground rules dramatically! This holy foolishness of Paul challenges those around him to recognise and consider what they value in their own situations.

It's challenging for me as well and, in a strange way, very encouraging. It gives me heart to reclaim these rules of the game and, once again, to leave the past behind and turn ever towards the future in response 'to the heavenly call of God in Christ Jesus' (verse 14). Especially when times are tough, and economic and political events drain away resources and make things difficult, it is important to recognise the opportunity to live out the hard sayings of Jesus and allow the heavenly light of God's love and grace to shine out through all we do.

If you were going to play the game like Paul, with what gifts and accomplishments would you build the tower? And how easy is it to be hopeful and recognise God's love and grace shining through real difficulties?

Loving God, may we continue to hear your heavenly call and press on towards the goal in the company of Christ Jesus.

Ground rules

Philippians 3:4b-14

The economy of God

Sandra Pollerman

Faith of fools in action

James 5:13-20

The end of this reading is in effect the beginning and a real challenge for the faithful. It makes me think of the clowning ministry of Roly Bain. He is for ever falling down to raise folk up. Roly tells the stories of Jesus and invites people to trust in God. In his baggy trousers and big floppy shoes, Clown Roly goes through the process of setting up a tightrope wire, climbing up to it and attempting to carry a cross from one side of the wire to the other. He always makes it, but there are a variety of falls and unexpected incidents in the process! Theologically what Roly has to say is deep and challenging as he calls people to return again and again to the loving ways of God through repentance, prayer and praise.

By the time he finishes, everyone around is usually laughing and smiling – but the thoughts they've absorbed along the way can be life changing. Roly's visit to one of our deanery churches increased attendance and encouraged more active participation in everyday affairs. One woman, who has since become a leading contributor to our pastoral outreach, still speaks of her gratitude for Roly's words and the good humour that brought her back.

Loving God, we pray that we may have the grace and trust in you to offer to those around us an opportunity to return to your forgiveness and protection.

The process of redemption and transformation is quite a mystery. The economy of God's promise is not that our world will be ended and started over again, but rather, that as we wait with hope and move with the Spirit, the whole of our bodies and our known environment will be renewed.

It may seem foolish to many to trust in a promise, in an ending and a glory that is not even visible and really quite hard to imagine. Yet through the gift of the life, death and resurrection of Jesus, who was the Holy Fool for us, and trusting in the Spirit, we can move ahead with the confidence that God's promise will be fulfilled.

In order to encourage this ongoing process, we need to come even closer to God in prayer, and strive to make choices that will help the world and those around us to come even closer to the loving economy of God.

Is there one small thing that you can choose to do today which will enable you to enter the mystery and join the whole company of 'fools for Christ' – for your good and for the good of all?

Loving God, help us to not to be afraid of the unknown as we become 'fools for Christ' and move forward with the hope of your promise spilling out into our actions.

Transforming economics

Romans 8:22-27

The economy of God

Sandra Pollerman

Economic reversal

Luke 16:19-31

Getting through to the scoffing Pharisees was not easy! In this passage, Jesus is really getting down to the hard core of his message: we are put here now to learn reality, to distinguish good and evil, and to adopt and apply God's economy. This really puts the spotlight on our daily choices and illuminates the topsy-turvy nature of this world – and the next! The rich man's story gives us the view that the greatest torment of the dead might be that the dead cannot warn the living! Salvation is not possible if repentance and change comes too late.

The real punchline of this story might be that we are one of the five brothers. It is sobering to realise that we have had someone come back from the dead, and indeed, we still don't act on the economy of God. In times of increasing growth in poverty, sickness, and decline in quality of life, we really could turn the economy of things upside down by investing our gifts in the poor and needy.

What one gift, foolish or otherwise, could you give today that would confirm your renewed commitment to applying the economy of our loving God?

Heavenly Father, thank you for accepting our repentance and renewed commitment to walk more truly in your way. We pray for the grace to live out your ways in our communities and in the world.

In this reading, Paul is not forecasting the end of the world: that is, its destruction. Rather, he writes that as the result of God's saving work in Christ, the rule and culture (or economics) of the present world would give way to the economy of God. In this inside-out pattern of living, Paul is really talking about detachment. He spotlights how dominating and obsessive the necessities of daily life can become. He is reminding people that all things must be kept in perspective and that detachment is the appropriate spiritual practice for the way ahead. God and the good news of Jesus Christ are the most important. The stress and concerns of daily existence should not get in the way of that priority.

Though a great deal of time has passed since Paul wrote, we are called, still today, to put the cares, routines and demands of our daily lives in context. We also need to practise discernment and to remember what is truly the most important. Our daily living, with all its stress, should not get in the way of living out the seemingly 'foolish' economy of God.

Can you take time some extra time this weekend to come closer to God and to place your life's stresses in God's hands?

Loving God, may we have the grace and discernment to recognise and to put your good news first in our lives.

Passing away of the present order

1 Corinthians 7:29-31

The economy of God   Sandra Pollerman

Readings in Luke

2 Beginnings

Preparing for the week

In this week's readings from Luke's gospel, we consider the work of John the Baptist in preparing the way for Jesus, we recall Jesus' baptism and temptations in the wilderness, and the beginning of his teaching and healing ministry in Nazareth.

In his mission statement in the sermon in the synagogue at Nazareth (Luke 4:16-27), Jesus becomes the herald and agent of liberation to the poor, the one who puts the content of their hope into words and then devotes his life to its fruition. We are called to share in this mission – requiring us to become 'poor in spirit', willing to let go of worldly power and status and identify ourselves with those who are marginalised and commit ourselves to their liberation. Poverty is not good in itself, but where it leads to a deeper dependence on God and coexists with generosity it can be a rare grace – remember Jesus marvelling at the widow's mite (Mark 12:41-44). This week, we are invited to consider both the poverty that must be resisted and that which must be embraced.

For further thought and prayer

- Does insecurity make me more self-seeking and less caring about the needs of others, lessening my humanity, clouding my sense that people matter more than money?
- Or does our current worldwide turmoil strengthen my compassion and fuel my commitment to God's kingdom?

Notes based on the New Revised Standard Version by

George Wauchope

The Reverend Canon George Wauchope is tutor in World Mission Education at the Queens Foundation, Birmingham. He was an anti-apartheid activist in South Africa, was detained a number of times by the regime there and fled the country for Zimbabwe in 1989. He was ordained priest in 1996, was Dean of Studies at Bishop Gaul College in Harare and later became a parish priest in Botswana in 2002 before coming to the UK in January 2007.

No VIP treatment

Luke 3:1-14

In Africa, when a head of state visits another country, an advance party is sent to that country for security reasons. The party checks to ensure that the suite in which the head of state will sleep is not bugged, that there are no explosives there; and they also book themselves into strategic rooms next to the head of state in order to ensure his protection. They go to the places he is going to visit to make sure all is well. The advanced party is trained in what is called 'VIP protection'. A lot of money is spent on this, money that could otherwise be spent on alleviating the problems of the poor. And, incidentally, the security budgets for the countries that embark on this expensive exercise are usually three times the budget for health and education in those countries.

Well, the forerunner of the Prince of Peace is a 'maverick' called John the Baptist whose security concerns are the cleansing of the sinners through a baptism of repentance. For Jesus there is no VIP treatment. There is no room for him in the inn; he is born in a humble stable and is meek and mild. Does he need tight security? No! In fact he has come to lay down his life for the salvation and redemption of humankind. Compared to the heads of states referred to above, Christ is the Prince of Peace and of his reign there shall be no end.

Lord, help us fix our earth-bound longings on peace and justice in this world.

Salvation for the whole person

Luke 3:15–22

Luke begins his account of the public life of Jesus with a long introduction to the political and the religious leaders holding power at the time. He says: 'In the fifteenth year of Tiberius Caesar's reign' (verse 1). This would already be enough to arrive at the date, but he goes on giving the names of other important people: the governors of Palestine and of neighbouring territories, the high priests Annas and Caiphas. These VIPs played prominent roles during state functions and sat in prominent places for all to see.

Why all this detail? Luke wants us to keep clearly in mind that he is not about to tell us a nice fable, a myth, a legend, fruit of the extravagant imagination of some dreamer. The events he is about to write about are concrete history. God has intervened in the history of humankind at a clearly identifiable time and in a very definite place. God has sent his son to bring salvation to all humankind.

But the salvation brought by Jesus Christ must reach out to the whole person, to include every moment of our lives. It is this society, this community, this family, this concrete person that must be transformed. Thus the only true religion is the one that changes this world, that produces new relations among people and yields fruits of peace, love, justice and sharing where now there is greed, corruption, selfishness, oppression and injustice. Whenever we think of the reign of God, we should associate it with love, joy, peace, justice, righteousness and mutual respect.

In whatever we do, Lord, help us remember the fruits of the Spirit – love, joy peace and the rest.

George Wauchope

Readings in Luke

In South Africa, we say: *'umntu ngumntu ngabantu'*. Translated literally it means 'a human being is a human being through other human beings'. What it means is that each one of us only comes into being in and through our connections with others – both those who came before us and those who will come after us.

Ubuntu also means that we share in each other's joys and sorrows in life here and now. When there is cause for celebration we all rejoice; when there is cause for sorrow, we all mourn. When there is a wedding, every member of the community is obliged to attend. This may sound contradictory, but no one is compelled to attend. It has to come from within and it always does. The women will bake, cook and brew African beer, whilst the men's role will be to slaughter a beast. Similarly, when there is death, the whole community mourns. The women will help with the cooking and the brewing of African beer, whilst the men will dig the grave and slaughter the beast.

Jesus, as one of us, is no different. He was connected to his community, his tradition and his people, and emerged out of those connections. The genealogies that the gospels provide are important because they assert that Jesus was a real human being rooted and grounded in community. He did not come down out of heaven from nowhere. He was born out of a long line of patriarchs and matriarchs, forefathers and foremothers. He was born out of deep connection, and he exemplified that deep connection to others and concern for others throughout his life.

Ubuntu

Luke 3:23–38

Let us remember before God our foremothers and forefathers and give thanks for them.

Readings in Luke

George Wauchope

Living in the wilderness

Luke 4:1-15

The reign of God begins in the wilderness, the place so laden with remembrances and deep emotional echoes for the people of Israel. In the wilderness they had experienced the power of their God. There, devoid of all human support, they had learnt to trust God.

At the time of Jesus, those who wanted to flee from the hypocrisy of a religion turned into formal and exterior practices had run away into the desert; and there too had gone those who refused to share the corrupt life of the unjust and oppressive society that had taken over Palestine. The prophetic vocation of John the Baptist, the forerunner of Jesus, reminds us that we all become anonymous in the wilderness with neither fame nor status.

We are told that John was not a man to wear the white tunic of the priests of the Temple. He wore coarse clothes, like the Prophet Elijah (2 Kings 2:13-14); he did not feed on the town products but what he found in the wilderness.

Like John, Christians too, though in the world, should live in the 'wilderness', foreigners in their own country. Among so many who speak of war, violence, oppression and feuds, they must utter words of peace and forgiveness; in a world where happiness is founded on money, often obtained by exploiting or enslaving others, they must proclaim the beatitudes of love and service to the poorest and the sharing of goods.

Lead us, good Lord, into the wilderness where we may be more deeply in touch with you and with your truth.

Good news to the poor

Luke 4:16-30

Jesus' mission statement, his manifesto as it were, is found in this passage. He is anointed by the Holy Spirit and sent by God his Father to proclaim good news to the poor. The only news that can be 'good' to the poor is the eradication of their poverty and its causes. And poverty means the lack of basic needs such as food, clean running tap water, clothing, shelter, health care and education.

Why is it that Africa is poor and cannot look after its own? The answer is colonialism, with its evil corollaries of military conquest, racism, economic and political subjugation, exploitation of cheap labour and the transportation of raw materials. In his book, *How Europe Underdeveloped Africa*, Walter Rodney explains in detail how this was done.

What really surprises me is that African leaders who sacrificed their lives in order to liberate their countries are the ones who behave like the shepherds that Ezekiel alludes to who do not eat and clothe the sheep but grab the resources of the land for themselves (Ezekiel 34:2b-4). How can close to two thousand people die of cholera in Zimbabwe today, a disease that is easily preventable? How can the sewage pipes burst with no money to repair them? How can a sane leader boldly state that there is no cholera when the death rate is increasing by the day? The man who placed his life in danger by fighting for the liberation of Zimbabwe has successfully run down that same country so that it is now on the edge of complete chaos.

Lord, may your message of good news transform the whole world and bring joy to those who are the most damaged members of our society.

Readings in Luke

George Wauchope

True freedom

Luke 4:31-44

In March 1977, after spending 297 days in solitary confinement, my captors (who accused me of instigating the 1976 students' uprising in Soweto) told me I was free to go. I received the news with mixed feelings: feelings of joy that I was free to go home and feelings of anger that the apartheid regime had wrongfully incarcerated me in the first place. The second reason for my anger was that it was unlawful for my wife to tell people that I had been detained. Many people disappeared without trace, as is still happening to members of the opposition in Zimbabwe today. There are many other oppressive regimes that do the same to their citizens. But for me, the good news that I was free from captivity took precedence.

The various stories of deliverance and healing in today's passage show Jesus freeing people from disease, from oppression, from powerlessness and from uselessness. Focusing on the poor in Latin America, Sobrino states that in Jesus the poor, the oppressed, the captives and the blind see the one who liberates them to the very depths of their being. He delivers them from their anguish, their resignation, their individualism, their desperation. In Jesus they see the one who conveys to them an interior strength that transforms them, personally and collectively, from terrified human beings into men and women who are free – free to hope, to unite, to struggle. In Jesus the poor see the one who carries on a practice calculated to transform an oppressive society into a communion of sisters and brothers, a society of justice in conformity with the ideal of the reign of God.

Pray for the equal distribution of the gifts of God and for true freedom for all.

Clothing

2 Clothing our nakedness

Notes based on the New Revised Standard Version by

Rachel Mann

Rachel Mann is an Anglican priest and poet based in South Manchester. Her writing has appeared in magazines, journals, books and newsprint. She likes lazing in bed, wasting time and has recently discovered the joy of painting. After a period of major ill health, she is looking forward to enjoying more of the good things of life again.

Preparing for the week

Clothes are not merely about comfort or keeping warm or hiding one's modesty. They are things we use to reveal or conceal identity. Perhaps in all societies, but certainly in the countries of the political North, clothing is a signifier of power, status, and who we are. Clothes are so significant that some cultures have strong codes about who can wear what, and transgressors are subject to ridicule, punishment or rejection. These reflections and meditations adopt a range of perspectives and voices, some quite disturbing, as well as drawing on the author's own experience in Jamaica. What unites them is the power of clothing as a place of both revelation and vulnerability, of both exposure and safety – whether chosen or forced, good or as the result of victimisation.

For further thought and action

- What things do you use to 'clothe' your identity or protect yourself from uncomfortable realities? How can you live more simply and confidently in the company of God?

- If you have the skill, try taking on a creative project involving the arts of sewing, weaving, knitting or other handicrafts. Consider taking up a course in creative handicrafts.

- If you have surplus or unnecessary clothing, dispose of them generously – donate to charity or try recycling the wool from a garment and making something new with it.

- How can you and your community become more practically involved in supporting those who have been stripped naked of their dignity and hope?

A mother's provision

1 Samuel 2:18-21

My husband was delighted with those words – 'May the Lord repay you with children by this woman for the gift that she made to the Lord' (verse 20). Right and proper he called them. A blessing to us. For me, seeing the child and bestowing the garment was enough. For these men don't know of a mother's love. They do not know how love can be woven into clothes of linen. They do not know how to pray each thread, how to embed the weave with faith and hope and love. They do not know how these garments continue my song for the fulfilment of God's promises.

When my heart exults in the Lord, I weave that love into these clothes for my beautiful boy. And I trust that in his heart he shall hear them. Let the men rejoice in the promise of their blessings. But I too have known God – God the weaver, God the mother, God the maker of love. If they heard me talk so, I fear the men would have me stoned for blasphemy. But surely it is never blasphemous to weave love deeper into our lives. Clothe our fear with love, O Lord.

O God the weaver of love,
spin your hope into our hearts,
and bring faith into the tangle of our lives.

A cloak taken in pledge

Exodus 22:21-27

When you have to run away from your homeland to another what do you expect? When I ran away to Britain – a rich land, a fair land – I did not expect this.

Where I grew up it was dangerous to be different – dangerous to be political or stand up for your rights. I have always been different. Since I was a little girl I have not followed the path my society set out for me. I like women, you see. In my country you can be killed for being a lesbian. When they came for my partner, I ran. It was so hard to escape: I used all my money, I did not want to leave my partner, my friends, but all I could do was save myself. In England I knew I would be treated right – right?

The British authorities suspected me right away. Said I was just after a better life and job. They detained me for weeks. When they let me go I was sent north, given vouchers to live off. Then they took them away too. I was told it was safe for me to go back. I was told that I had to go and no one would support me. So I went into hiding. I can get no money, no job. I've lost everything. They might as well take my clothes.

Without my few friends I would be on the street. All I wanted was a chance to live and be me. But they have taken everything. I miss my partner so much. Some days I think I should end it all. Just to be with her again.

Refugee God,
help us to resist the forces of this world
which strip people of their dignity and hope.
Travel with us when we are lost and alone.

Clothing

Rachel Mann

Stripping as humiliation

Isaiah 3:18 – 4:1

Out of the night they came. They always came out of the night. The machete men. In those days no one remained a child long. There was no room for children, not for the machete men. I will not say how young I was that first time. Or how many there were of them. It happened so quickly. Behind their shouts I heard the sound of a scream. And I realised it was me shrieking, shrieking as if I wasn't myself. I heard the tearing of cloth, a vast rip across my back, a sound so terrible it might have been the world's end. His hands all over me, ripping my naked skin and forcing me to the floor. And the laughter and the eyes gleaming by the torches of the night. Dozens of greedy laughing eyes watching. And me no longer knowing what pain was.

I have heard a hundred explanations of what was done during those times: the fortunes of war, the sinfulness of man and so on. I no longer care. I only want to feel clothed again, deep down in the core of my soul. To feel warm, just for a moment. I'm afraid I shall feel naked for ever.

God of hope,
dress our wounds with peace and justice.
Clothe our nakedness with hope.

Acts of mercy

Matthew 25:31-40

The roads were hot enough to burn the soles of your feet. You could drink bottle after bottle of Ting and still you'd thirst. Yes, Kingston was always sweaty and hot. And down in Constant Spring, everything was as it always was: bustling and noisy with rich and poor, black, mulatto and white, shopping and jostling side by side. Street traders shouting and the trucks down from the hills belching fumes in every direction. And the reggae, always the reggae pumping.

Nothing unusual until I saw her: a woman, surely still in her teens, wandering about in the middle of an extremely busy road. She was totally self-absorbed, ignoring the angry horn beeps of the drivers. But that wasn't the truly startling thing. She was completely naked, with cuts and mess all over her body. She was ranting and raving, snatches of scripture mixed with gibberish. She was clearly so ill and in so much danger. But everyone ignored her. The drivers only cared that she got in their way. Everyone else just got on with their shopping. I could have gone to her. I could have offered her something to wear. I could have done something, anything. I watched and then I did what everyone else did – I turned away. I carried on shopping. I tried to forget her. I never have.

God of the lost,
forgive us when we turn our faces from you;
enable us to stand by you in your hour of need.

Clothing

Rachel Mann

Jesus stripped and humiliated

John 19: 23-24

Jesus has been stripped and humiliated not just at Golgotha, but on endless occasions throughout history: in the abuse of countless innocent victims, in the persecution of God's people. Across the world, there are countless places of murder and humiliation. The following poem is a response to the butchery in Europe during the Second World War, but it could easily be set on any continent, at any point in the last hundred years.

Special treatment

*Finally, we arrive at a clearing – a halo
of stripped birch glistening around a pool,
its sheen the sheen of the prepared dead.
Everywhere silver trunks stained green, and outcrops
furred with moss, fungi melting to a sickly yellow.
This is a place no one has seen for a hundred years.
I swear I see spirits on our breath.*

*We have been told to expect food, but no longer
know what to believe. We could be the last
rotten children
of the earth; we could be her first failed attempt
at rebirth.*

*An officer says we must dig pits: supposedly,
shelter for the night.
Beneath our feet thousands of fiery damp leaves
crushed back into the ground from which they
joyously came.*

Murdered and humiliated God,
forgive our indifference and betrayals.
Make us faithful to the call of your love.

Rachel Mann

Clothing

If we are wounded, whether that be physically or emotionally, we want protection and healing. Depending on the seriousness of the wound, we might apply a bandage, a plaster, get it stitched. But sometimes, if we travel honestly with God, we discover that our wounds may be places where we find our true selves and feed others. We sometimes discover that our true selves are indeed our wounded, vulnerable selves and the 'bandages' we cover ourselves with are not for healing, but for keeping God and others out. We clothe ourselves with ever more layers. On top of the 'bandages', we slide layers and layers of 'clothing' to act as insulation. We hide ourselves from the world and forget we are called to share and be generous.

As you reflect on the Bible passage for today dare to take time to reflect on the layers you might use to insulate yourself from the world and others, and even God: the possessions, if you have many, or the defence mechanisms to keep others out. We all need to protect ourselves from time to time, and there are some situations which are toxic for us, but what are the things which are really necessary for you to both survive and flourish? And how can you be more generous with your wounded, vulnerable self?

Vulnerable God,
Help us to be unafraid to share our true selves;
May we discover your hope in the midst of our wounds.

Be generous, like God

Matthew 5:38-42

Clothing

Rachel Mann

Clothing

2 Robed in honour and glory

Preparing for the week

Clothing that has a special significance in our public service, either in the church or in society, is a recurring theme this week. Clothing may be used to distinguish a role, or as a sign of honour.

Honour brings with it both recognition of commitments made and a response through our service. For believers this is expressed both as an affirmation by others of their commitment to Christ and a desire to live out their faith as wholeheartedly as possible.

For further thought

- Think about how clothes, special clothing in particular, shape our minds and responses.
- Think too of how you live out the commitment to Christ you made in baptism.
- Pray for increased faith to remain true to that consecration of your life.

Notes based on the New Revised Standard Version by

Sister Christine South SLG

Sister Christine South is a member of the Anglican Community of the Sisters of the Love of God, in Oxford, England.

Anyone who has ever held public office knows how significant the regalia are; each item holds special meaning. The office of High Priest was no exception, each garment representing some aspect of his privileged task. This High Priest also bears a name famous in Israel's history. The first Joshua led the people over Jordan into the promised land. This Joshua is an exile from Babylon returning to his homeland. Those who had not been deported and who had done their best to maintain true temple worship believed that an exile marked those so taken as unclean. To appoint one of them High Priest was offensive, though politically expedient. Zechariah metaphorically describes to the opposition how the foreign, suspect clothing is being replaced with garments specially blessed in heaven – 'festal apparel'. It is the prophet who ensures that the outstanding mark of office, the turban with the ornament engraved with the name of God, is also a divine gift.

We all remember garments worn to celebrate an important event: a wedding, a graduation ceremony, taking up public office, receiving the signs of ministry. For me it was the reception of the nun's habit. With the joy of receiving new public apparel comes the duty to live out the meaning of what we wear. The garments are a sign of God's call, and reflect our intention to live according to God's law and commandments.

Divine regalia

Zechariah 3:1-5

Thank you, Lord, for the signs of your favour to me. May I show forth your love through them.

Clothing

Christine South

Purple, the highest honour

Daniel 5:1-7

Terror can induce us to make some very rash promises. Belshazzar might have regretted his words if anyone less upright than Daniel had come forward to interpret the words written by the ghostly hand. The rewards are the best he knows of, but as nothing when the final interpretation is made. However, he is a man of his word, so does not withdraw his promise. But with the reward come duties and obligations to Belshazzar's kingdom.

Purple-dyed garments were the most expensive in the ancient world; it is recorded that 10 000 shellfish of the murex genus were needed to make one Tyrrian-purple toga. It was normally only royalty who could afford this attire. To be given a robe of such quality, especially when the interpretation of the message was unfavourable to the king, was indeed a high honour. However, it is unlikely that it changed Daniel's service of God, especially as the temple vessels which had been set apart for the worship of God had been desecrated at the banquet. Because of his belief in the one God he was able to serve in a polytheistic society with integrity and without fear.

A day in your courts, O Lord, is better than a thousand elsewhere . . .
No good thing does the Lord withhold from those who walk uprightly.

Psalm 84:10-11

Christine South

Clothing

Second-hand garments of grace

2 Kings 2:9-14

For someone who wears a monastic habit this story has a particular resonance. Many of our clothes, especially our habits, are hand-me-downs from other members of the community who have either died or left. We go to this store first when a habit needs replacing. It is more than a way of expressing our vow of poverty. The sister who previously wore the habit brought her own contribution to the community life; as we don her habit, we can look back to her living of the vocation and all that was given to us through her life. Like Elisha we hope to appropriate the best of someone's relationship with God. Through Elijah's distinctive piece of clothing, his mantle, Elisha inherited more of the prophet's spirit than he expected. God empowered him to re-enact the dividing of the Jordan by Joshua when the Israelites entered the promised land. God's power is with him, and the covenant made with Abraham tacitly reinforced and renewed. He can be a prophet with confidence.

It is good to reflect on what it means to wear other people's clothes, especially if they represent signs of commitment and service. It is an honour; but it is also a comfort that others have travelled the same road and known that God's grace is with them on the journey.

Lord, give us confidence in your saving power and abiding presence.

The tyranny of unconditional love

Matthew 22:1-14

It is difficult to know whether the man unsuitably dressed for the banquet is one of those gathered from the streets who has been picked upon as an example; or whether the others had had time to change and he tried to gatecrash, hoping he would be admitted as he was. Whatever the facts, he is not properly dressed to celebrate a wedding, nor to honour the bridegroom at this joyous feast.

Because this is a parable, there is a message relevant to us to be teased out. Here is a call to persevere in the Christian life beyond our first commitment in baptism. We have been admitted into the kingdom of heaven, but it is easy to be so lured into the self-gratifying aspects of life that we forget our first fervour. When we are suddenly brought up short by a further invitation to participate in the life of the kingdom we discover that we are quite unprepared.

The king appears to be an unfeeling tyrant, but he shows us what God requires of a believer. We may be unconditionally loved by God, but that does not mean that we can live a life of sin once we have set out on the Christian way. Christ, the bridegroom we serve and represent, is worthy of our best.

May I serve you, Jesus, with all my heart, with all my mind, with all my soul and with all my strength.

It is not surprising that the rough lives of soldiers bored with keeping an uneasy peace far from home should encourage them to humiliate and torture someone on trial. Their mockery of the trappings of royalty and parody of respect to the 'King of the Jews' give them brief amusement. We shall never know where they got the purple robe from: it would not be of royal purple. In the ancient world 'purple' covered a multitude of colours, so it might have been a piece of rough indigo-dyed cloth, or one of the scarlet cloaks the Roman legions wore.

Pity, if you can, the soldier who had to sacrifice his cloak, and the one who pricked his fingers making the crown of thorns. They did not know they were clothing the true King, the long-expected Messiah who would rule the world in true righteousness and justice – which is the love of God in action.

Jesus does not need kingly attire to rule our lives with power and authority. And we in turn do not need special recognition to participate in this kingdom. We may have to undergo taunting and mockery for our faith, be roughly treated, and badly clothed into the bargain. But we can take comfort from the fact that Christ has been there before us and is with us in whatever suffering and misunderstanding we have to endure.

Praise be to you, O King of eternal glory.

The lesser purple of kingship

John 19:1-7

Clothing

Christine South

No room for complacency

Revelation 3:1-6

In the colour spectrum true white is as difficult to find as true black; any dyer, householder or sacristan will tell you this. The additives in modern washing powders accustom us to a brightness that is not present in natural fibres unless they have been sun-bleached. A store of old linen or cotton is usually more yellow than white.

Whatever standard we use for 'white', it is always a distinctive, eye-catching colour. In some cultures it is a sign of mourning, but in the ancient world it signified both purity and victory (although it was also the colour of leprosy and therefore a symbol of death). White is the epitome of attainment; every colour of life is absorbed into it. For Christians, white is the traditional colour of baptism, showing that we are now one with Christ and members of the kingdom of heaven.

Although we are assured of membership of the kingdom, we must always be on the alert for the coming of Christ. We can never be complacent Christians as the people of Sardis seem to have been. Sometimes we catch unexpected glimpses of the thievish return of Christ, which force us to assess what is most important in our lives and to renew our baptismal commitment. For these let us give thanks.

We ask and urge you in the Lord Jesus that, as you learned from us how you ought to live and to please God (as, in fact, you are doing), you should do so more and more.

Thessalonians 4:1

Readings in Genesis

1 In the beginning

Notes based on the Hebrew Bible (Jewish Publication Society) by

Sylvia Rothschild

Sylvia Rothschild serves as Rabbi of Wimbledon and District Synagogue in a job share with Sybil Sheridan. She has been a congregational rabbi for 22 years, and writes new liturgies for life events.

Preparing for the week

The book of Genesis deals with a number of deeply complex human questions: Why are we here? What is my life about? With whom do I share? For whom am I responsible? In a few stories we are brought face to face with creation and destruction, with love and betrayal, rivalry and hatred, with possibility beyond imagining and with narrow self-seeking lives. God is omnipresent in Genesis, but we focus mainly on the growing up and learning of human beings – this, primarily, is *our* story. Yet God too learns as God's creation is learning, and that is one of the kinder aspects of the book.

God learns to moderate the need for justice over mercy, and both we and God begin to see that human life will always be a compromise, a mixture of love and hate, of desire and containment, of good deeds and bad. And with this admixture of different qualities, humanity comes to understand the richness we have been given by God – that we can hate and also forgive, that we can do and also imagine, that we can live with pain and not be destroyed by what could have been. The book of Genesis is a book about growing up together – us and God, and learning to forgive each other for who we are, while helping each other to become better for each other. By the end of the book, both human beings and God have learned and changed and are ready to go on learning and changing in relation to each other.

For further thought

- How do you respond to the idea of God changing? Does this alarm or excite you?
- How have you grown with God?

Starting something new

Genesis 1:1-19

We imagine that the Bible opens with absolute beginning. As if history starts here. Yet the first word, *bereishit,* is much more complex a statement. Rabbinic tradition tells us that the Bible opens with the second letter of the alphabet (*Beit*) to remind us that there is a first one already present – the *Aleph,* also signifying the number one. It weaves stories around the shape of the letter *beit* which looks like the opening of a bracket, closing off what came before and what lies above and below so that we are forced into reading onwards into the future, yet aware that on the other side of the boundary there exists – something.

The word *bereishit* is better translated as 'in the beginning of'. The narrative is really telling the story of 'the beginning of God's creation of heaven and earth' rather than the beginning of everything. Implicit here is that there is more we are not privileged to know. Effectively, we are shown God starting something new, adding to what God already creates. 'Even God starts again' seems to be the thinking behind this strange word, 'there is always the possibility for innovation'. And if God can make a new start, then so can we, drawing a line between then and now, moving forward into the future. In the words of the Hebrew blessing over a new event: 'Blessed are You, Sovereign God of the Universe, who has kept us alive and sustained us and brought us to this time'.

Let us think about what we may be starting afresh, as we continue our journey through our life.

Creating meaningful rest

Genesis 1:20 – 2:3

In this first story of Creation, God creates humanity in the image of the divine, and God's first act then is to bless these people and to set a series of obligations for them. They are to be fertile and increase and fill the earth, taking stewardship over all the flora and fauna in existence.

A whole system has been set up that works together in harmony at this point, something that God sees as 'very good' – but this ideal moment cannot last much longer than the moment of creation itself. So one more task is given to human beings: while stewardship may tip into control and selfish abuse, and while the ideal biblical state of vegetarianism will descend into carnivorous hierarchy, people are obliged once every seven days to try to recreate this ideal moment, to 'make' Shabbat – the wholeness and completeness that is frequently traduced the rest of the week. More than the absence of activity, to fully achieve a restful and healing state we have to create the right conditions. Shabbat, the rest created by God, is something made at will and explicitly, something that, because we do it, makes us truly human beings. It takes concentration and deliberate action, but for those twenty-five hours of time away from the weekly grind, when we are given the opportunity to reflect on our essential purpose, making Shabbat is one of the best pieces of work we do.

What will I do today to help create meaningful rest in the world?

Blessed are you, Eternal God, who allows for the sanctification of time.

Readings in Genesis   Sylvia Rothschild

Making moral choices

Genesis 2:4-25

The Bible tells us we are formed from the earth. What animates us is the breath of life given us by God. And that gift is temporary – when it leaves us we will become once more simply dust of the earth. What must we do while we have the breath of God within us? In the garden of Eden God planted two trees – the tree of life and the tree of moral discrimination. The tree of knowledge of good and bad was explicitly forbidden us – but why would God put such a tree in our environment if we were truly not supposed to eat from it? Once we ate and understood moral choice we were liberated from the enclosed childish world of Eden, born into the world of finite mortality. Here the breath of life within us reminds us that the moral choices we make are real, that life will end and so each decision is of importance in the ultimate weighing of our lives. Death is inevitable but it is not evil, nor is it punishment. Instead it gives shape and meaning to the choices we make and turn our lives into works of art.

Dust and breath is what we are – the two most common and humble qualities – yet we use them in miraculous ways.

We pray to be able to understand each day that we are ourselves simply dust and breath, and from our confidence in that understanding, create something truly special.

Expulsion from Eden is like expulsion from the womb. To the child going through the event it must seem like a violent and hostile act, yet awaiting that child is a life of possibility. I have always liked the fact that in the middle of the violent expulsion God makes some amazing acknowledgments: the ground will be cursed, yet the people will be able to fend for themselves and feed themselves from it. Man and woman will be able to create life – something only God has been able to do so far. And finally God made garments of skin for Adam and Eve, and clothed them. It always seems such a protective parental thing to do – 'before you go out, put on a warm coat'. Providing for human continuity and sustenance becomes God's prime concern as they leave the garden and enter the adult world. Moral judgement takes a back seat to practical support. Human beings will have to create their own way of being in the world, but God is there to help them. Leaving the womb may be scary and cold, but the world out there is worth the agony of the transition.

I call heaven and earth to witness against you
this day, that I have set before you life and
death, blessing and curse; therefore choose life.
(Deuteronomy 30:19)

Blessed be God, source of all life, who gives us the many possibilities to choose life.

Self sufficiency – with a little help from God

Genesis 3:1-24

Readings in Genesis

Sylvia Rothschild

Whose responsibility?

Genesis 4:1-16

We cannot pretend that people, having been given freedom of choice by the Creator, will not sometimes choose the wrong option – as we see in this story. And it is clear that God holds Cain responsible for the murder of his brother – but is that the whole story? There is a tradition in Judaism that Cain continued his speech, saying to God in effect 'You are God, You created humankind so You have some responsibility for us. If I made wrong choices, You held back from preventing me.'

It is a radical view of the text. The Bible is telling us that human beings, having acquired moral discrimination, are responsible for their actions, but there is that question of God's silence when challenged. We still have difficulty with God's silence in the face of much evil in the world. Why doesn't God prevent genocide or natural disasters? Why does God seem to stand silent at the murder of the innocents, again and again?

It is surely legitimate to challenge God who gave us freedom of choice and then somehow stood back to watch what would happen. But in challenging God we should not forget that we share responsibility with God – that while we may be distressed when God is not obviously around at times of crisis, we are around, and must do all we can to make life better for our fellow human beings.

Blessed is God, who shares responsibility for the world with all those who are created.

I've always wondered about Mrs Noah. Noah is described as a man who was righteous for his generation. Is this damning by faint praise, suggesting that he was pretty awful but at least better than the violent murderers and sinners around him? Or maybe he was a shiny-souled saint who kept his integrity even in such difficult circumstances? Either way, I get the feeling it was Mrs Noah who kept him on the straight and narrow. Why else do she and her three sons survive to become, in effect, the ancestors of all living peoples? The Bible tells us that we can all trace ourselves back to Mrs Noah.

Noah blithely obeys God's instructions in the full knowledge of imminent destruction of the world. I'd like to think Mrs Noah would not have been such a creature of unquestioning faith, that she would have thought about all the innocents who would have been swept up in the catastrophe. Like Mrs Lot generations later, would she have been unable to resist a connection with those being destroyed? Would she have shown her agony in the face of the annihilation and looked at what was happening? And would such a sense of connection with the others have changed her behaviour?

Surely the test of a divine message must be its compassion, and if such a quality is missing, surely we have a right to question its authenticity and its validity. Some people seem to believe that they have been directed by God to do terrible things. In such a case we must challenge them and instead hold to the values of love, empathy and compassion, which are the hallmark of true revelation.

Blessed are you, God, who has taught us to love our neighbour as we love ourselves, for you are the God of all peoples.

Noah, Mrs Noah, and the need to challenge God

Genesis 6:5-22

Readings in Genesis

Sylvia Rothschild

Readings in Genesis

2 The great flood

Notes based on the New Revised Standard Version by
Tom Arthur

Tom Arthur is a recently retire minister of the Presbyterian Church (USA) who for the pas twenty years or so has been serving in mission with the United Reformed Church in the UK. He continues to live i Cardiff, Wales, writing, teaching and painting.

Preparing for the week

The stories of Genesis are told as foundation stories for the great drama of the liberation we meet in Exodus, which itself was compiled as a means of self-understanding for a people in exile in Babylon, and as a means of hope for new life. Stories of God carrying life through the experience of great loss, like Noah's story, or stories like Abraham's that follow God's promise away from the predictability of the past towards a new future that will be lived as a blessing for generations yet unborn, are stories for people who live in longing hope. Such a hope is ultimately not so much hope for our own wellbeing but a hope for the wellbeing of others, and all life. In a world so threatened by the kind of economic and environmental collapse that comes as the inevitable consequence of self-serving, short-term goals, surely such a larger hope as we find here is what is needed today.

For further thought

- Where do you look to find stories of hope?
- In what ways do you look to have your own ideas enlarged by reading Genesis?

God's big family

Genesis 7:1-16

They say this is one of the essential Bible stories people ought to know, and, indeed, it is one of the most popular. There are innumerable books and toys devoted to this story. Children flock to it as the animals do to the ark. With no coercion, without having to be rounded up, the animals simply come into the ark, two and two of every flesh in which there was the breath of life (verse 15). As I write, we are celebrating Darwin's bicentenary. Children take a natural delight in the parade of animals, perhaps sensing the genetic kinship we have with 'all flesh in which there is the breath of life'. We're all family.

When Genesis was being written there were probably as many versions of this popular story as there are today. Those who put Genesis together collected two of them and wove them together seamlessly. In one version the 'clean' animals who are to survive the flood come not in pairs but in groups of seven, so that there will be enough of them to sacrifice to God in thanksgiving when dry ground appears once more. There is a dark side to this story. Not only are these clean animals slaughtered at the end of the journey, but the journey begins with an act of un-creation. The boundaries and limitations that were put in place in Genesis 1 are loosened. Life is destroyed on a massive scale.

Today we don't need God to undermine what sustains life. With interminable war, environmental devastation and economic collapse, we are doing a fine job by ourselves, as if we had no family relationship with creation, as if we had no concern for our world's future.

What does it take to recapture Noah's vision today?

Eternal Father, strong to save

Genesis 7:17-24, 8:1-5

The flood deepens and all living things not on the ark die. Then a wind passes over the water as in the original Creation story. A process of re-creation begins that is echoed throughout biblical literature, a process illustrating the Christian conviction that new life can follow the bitterness of death.

One of the innumerable retellings of the Noah story is the sci-fi movie *Deep Impact*. Life on earth is threatened with extinction by the imminent impact of a large asteroid. Everything will die, except for a chosen few who are gathered in well-provisioned caves, along with a parade of animals that clinch the reference to Noah's ark. But in this version of the story, 'all flesh' is saved by the self-sacrificial action of Robert Duvall and a crew of astronauts who choose to lose their own lives to save the life of the world. A passing reference is made in the movie to Mark Twain's *Huckleberry Finn*, who is warned by his Christian aunt that he will burn in hell for ever if he helps a slave escape. He decides to help his slave friend Jim escape anyway, even if it *does* mean an eternity in hell. This is the real Christian alternative, Twain implies, not to seek our own salvation, but that of our neighbour. And this is the alternative wisdom that saves the day in *Deep Impact*. Surely we need such a vision that seeks the world's survival as a greater good than our own flourishing. If we grasp to hold on, the gospels teach, we lose. If we let go, we win.

Theologian Dorothee Soelle once told an interviewer that we can only understand God's grace once we have died. 'Have you had this experience?' she was asked. 'Yes', she said, 'in my divorce'. Do we only understand life once we have experienced death? Does something have to die in order for something new to be born?

Tom Arthur

The dove returns to the ark carrying an olive branch, signalling the end of divine wrath. But the real sign that the ordeal has come to an end is when the dove doesn't come home at all. It's like the bird that leaves the nest, and Noah and his crew just have to let go.

The sacrifices Noah offers were also a form of letting go. In offering sacrifice like this, Noah is acknowledging that life is not our own. Life did not belong to Noah, but to God. Life itself is received and given as gift, not possession. It seems to me that this is a lesson God himself comes to learn in this story. The story begins with cataclysmic punishment for those who have been wicked, and rewards for Noah's moral rectitude. The story ends with God responding to Noah's giving away in sacrifice what has just been saved from the flood. Now, in an amazing change of heart, God decides his former ways will not do. He will bless his creation even though he knows deep down that human beings are inclined to evil from the moment they are born, and there is just not much you can do about it.

Life doesn't need to be deserved. It does not come as a reward for good behaviour. It comes as a gift. There will always be seasons. Fertility will endure. Blessing will prevail. Giving is what the Giftie is all about, and what we need to be all about. As my wife likes to say, 'Don't give until it hurts, but give until it feels good'. When giving feels good we know that the wrath of God has truly come to an end.

A change in the weather, a change in me

Genesis 8:6-22

Doing Noah

Genesis 9:1-17

In the days when the Noah stories were first told, warfare was conducted with bows and arrows. So when God says he is putting his bow in the sky it is a gesture similar to hammering spears into pruning hooks. Thomas Pynchon's book, *Gravity's Rainbow*, plays with a similar juxtaposition, between the arc made by a missile and the arc made by the traditional emblem of peace. The rainbow is to remind God of the covenant he has made.

I remember learning from some Hasidic Jews in Chicago that we are all, Jews and Gentiles together, under the covenant of Noah by virtue of our basic humanity. Very little is actually required of human beings, other than to respect life – that is, to be like God. We are not to kill one another, and when we eat we refrain from blood as a way of reminding ourselves of this command.

So God isn't the only one obligated under this covenant. The covenant obliges us to engage in acts that overcome the ways we undermine the sustainability of life on earth, and further God's blessing. This is the kind of work I saw being undertaken when we held a celebration of Operation Noah at the Lightship, the Welsh ecumenical centre anchored in Cardiff Bay. Operation Noah, a UK-wide organisation, pro-motes environmental concerns, animal welfare and concern for creation in general. The children assembled for the celebration, all made up like animals, were having a whale of a time, as they used to say in days when whales weren't so threatened.

The Noah story is a story we need to *do*, not just listen to – to live out, to organise for. That's what covenant life is all about.

Lost in translation

Genesis 11:1-9

In 1951 there was a riot in the northern Dutch province of Friesland when a judge refused to hear a case in Frisian, a language he didn't know. Today, linguistic identity and difference is not considered a curse but a blessing. They say Barcelona is in danger of becoming a more provincial city than it should be because its people are more keen to learn Catalan than Castilian Spanish.

The confusion wrought in the Babel story still comes as a natural consequence of our celebrated diversity. Here in Wales we have bilingual road signs, for instance. One went up recently in Swansea that said 'No entry for heavy goods vehicles. Residential site only.' Below the English was the Welsh: 'Nid wyf yn y swyddfa ar hyn o bryd. Anfonwch unrhyw waith I'w gyfiethu.' The sign maker obviously didn't realise that the email he got back from Swansea Council's in-house translator was not, in fact, the translation, but an out-of-office notice: 'I am not in the office at the moment. Please send any work to be translated.'

The pride we take in our native tongues bears with it an awareness of the precarious status of such languages, which disappear from use in the same way that the biodiversity so necessary for a healthy planet is shrinking. English has become the lingua franca of international business, pop music, computer technology and airline travel, not just science, in the same way that the human footprint is stamping out a diversity necessary to its own survival. The pride of the people of Babel that muscled cities and skyscrapers from the windswept plains of the ancient Middle East remains a cultural conundrum.

How do we attempt to learn to listen to difference and care enough about good translation to communicate with strangers?

Readings in Genesis   Tom Arthur

To be a blessing

Genesis 12:1-20

I first heard Jean Vanier, founder of the L'Arche communities, at an evening lecture at Chicago's Metropolitan Cathedral. Just to be there that night filled us with a sense of hope for the world. The theme of Vanier's visit, proclaimed in large banners, was 'To Be A Blessing', a phrase taken from our Abraham story. Vanier's vision was that Christians should live as a blessing for others, particularly for those most 'un-blessed', as a way of making God present in the world.

This was to be Abraham's vision, too, when he left the security and predictability of home – in the same way that the dove left the shelter of the ark. It's as if the Abraham story picks up where the ark story leaves off. Abraham may have set out to find his fortune, but his real fortune, he discovers, is to be a blessing for a future generation.

What we have in this story touches on the theme of rebirth and new possibility that lies at the heart of so many religions. The teller of this tale wants us to link Father Abraham with the Exodus story of a *people's* rebirth, the main story of the Pentateuch, coming later. Abram and Sarai anticipate the journey Jacob's sons make, going down to Egypt to escape famine. Whatever the deeper significance of this strange little domestic comedy, Abraham has got himself into trouble, God gets him out, and somehow God still has confidence in him.

Once when Haiti was in deep turmoil Jean Vanier was asked to speak to a group of Haitian young people on the theme 'What is my hope?' His hope, he said, was in each one of those gathered, in their hearts, in their capacity to overcome their bitterness and be a blessing for others. Every one of us can change. That's the gospel.

Readings in Genesis

3 God's covenant with Abraham

Notes based on the New Revised Standard Version by **Susan Hibbins**

Susan Hibbins is an Anglican, a freelance writer and editor. She is especially interested in choral music, and in her spare time is secretary of a local community choir of 50 people.

Preparing for the week

The readings for this week show us God's dealings with Abram, soon to be renamed Abraham, and Sarai, who would become Sarah. The story reveals how, step by step, God's covenant with Abraham – that he will become the father of a people so great that they cannot be counted – will become reality. We think of Abraham as the first great example of a man of faith, who set out from Ur not knowing where he would end up, but putting all his trust in God to get him there. Perhaps we feel that his faith was so firm that he never looked back or wavered; but these passages tell us of two people who are much the same as ourselves: one day full of faith, the next full of doubt, believing God's promises while at the same time trying to force the pace by meddling in God's plans. For us today, the miracle is that, no matter how feeble our faith, no matter how many times our foolishness diverts God's purposes, God's patience and belief in us never falter. The same God who guided and cared for Abraham, Sarah, Hagar and Ishmael still guides and cares for us today.

For further thought

- In what ways do you struggle to exercise faith?
- What helps to strengthen and increase your faith?

Not part of the plan!

Genesis 13:1-18

Have you ever started a new project that you felt God was calling you to do, only to find that it turned into something completely different? Sometimes we set out in faith, as Abram had set out from Ur, convinced that our plans are in place, and that we are going in the right direction. If we are working with a group of people we may form committees or write mission statements to keep our aims in focus. For a time things work out as we hoped they would, we feel on top of the situation and satisfied that we are doing what God has asked us to do. As the project becomes more complex, more people may become involved, with all the organisation that entails. More paperwork, reports and financial statements might be necessary.

Then perhaps something happens that was not in the plan, that temporarily throws us off course, making us realise that our direction may not be the right one after all, that we have become bogged down in the detail. Lot had to leave Abram and go his own way before God was able to show Abram the land that would one day belong to his descendants. In the same way we need to be flexible, to allow God to show us the way we are to go.

Where is God leading me today? Am I facing in the right direction?

Last year I was made redundant from a job that I loved and did not want to leave. The reassurances I received that I would soon find other work and that everything happens for a reason did not, if I am honest, make me feel better, and for a time I sank into feelings of sadness and something approaching helplessness as I fought to stay positive. One afternoon I went for a walk feeling that I was losing my battle. A young woman with a little girl passed by me; they had a young puppy in tow which was doing its best to trip them up as it darted towards every exciting smell in its path. It was impossible not to smile at its antics and as I drew level with them, the little girl gave me a dazzling smile of her own as she rejoiced in her new puppy and the happiness it gave her. I felt unexpectedly blessed as I went on my way.

Life may sometimes tip us into unpleasant and unwanted experiences that sap our energy and faith. Like Abram, we are forced into situations we do not want but nevertheless have to deal with somehow. Yet I believe God wants us still to remember his presence with us, in the smile of a child, in an unexpected blessing that Abram received from Melchizedek, in a sunbeam that lights up a cloudy day.

Unexpected blessings

Genesis 14:13-24

Loving God, help us to remember that, however difficult our circumstances, you still have blessings in store for us.

Readings in Genesis   Susan Hibbins

Daily trust

Genesis 15:1-16

Abram is held up to Christians as the great person of faith, setting out on his journey from Ur, putting his trust in God, believing God that one day he would become the father of a great nation whose members would be greater in number than the stars of the heavens or the grains of sand on the seashore. Perhaps the name Abram conjures up for us the kind of faith we will never be able to emulate. Yet as we read Abram's story we realise that his faith was not, as it might appear, a cut-and-dried affair. Like us, he had constant doubts; like us, he felt he had to remind God about his situation in case God had forgotten about it. When God reassured him, he was reassured – for now.

Somehow, in the midst of his doubts, however, Abram 'believed the Lord' (verse 6). It was this ability to believe that what God promised would become reality that kept Abram moving forward, and it is this simple act of faith that can keep us in step with God's purposes for us, too. We may never be asked physically to leave our homes and journey to far countries, but spiritually we may be asked to journey just as far. Can we too step out in faith, believing that God's way for us is the right one?

Dear God, you know how we struggle to move forward in faith. Help us to put our trust in you daily, to believe that your promises to us will be fulfilled.

Susan Hibbins

Readings in Genesis

In stark contrast to Abram putting his trust in God, this passage shows human nature at its frailest as Abram and Sarai decide – as we have all doubtless done – to take matters into their own hands and leave God out of their plans. Desperation for some sort of result drives Sarai's actions, and while she achieves what she wants, she also unleashes all the human emotions that naturally accompany such an arrangement: envy, jealousy, anger and strife. Abram will take no responsibility for a situation he helped to create, and the outcome is near catastrophe for Hagar and her child. God's care ensures their survival, but nobody comes out of this well.

There were lessons to be learned for Abram and Sarai: and for us too. While we might sympathise with Sarai's plight, to embark on a course of action that we know in our heart is wrong, even though we feel justified, is to invite trouble. God's timing is not ours, and though we sometimes might wish God would fit in with our plans for our lives, it is part of our loving relationship with God that we trust God with our present and our future too.

Where am I trying to force the pace in my life decisions? Take time to reassess priorities, placing all that perplexes you into God's hands.

God's time, not ours

Genesis 16:1-16

A promise for all time

Genesis 17:1-22

If you're anything like me, there are times when you feel that God is not listening to your prayers, and that however much you pray about a situation, nothing seems to change. The old problems that beset us for years are still there; the old weaknesses and difficulties drag us down. Next time I feel like this I will try to remember the wonder found in this passage: despite the past, despite the fact that Abraham views God's promise of a son with scepticism, God places the whole future of Israel, and its relationship with God, in Abraham's hands. What untold riches God has in store for Abraham and his descendants – and the greatest gift of all, the promise of God's presence with them for all time.

The impossible – God's promise of a son – is to be made possible, despite the obstacles that stand in the way. Sometimes when we look at the world, with all its sorrow, strife and seeming preference for the darkness instead of the light, it can be hard to hold on to the idea that the promise we have of God's presence holds good for us as it did for Abraham. Yet this is the truth. Can anything ground our faith more surely than that?

Loving God, when our faith in the future wavers, help us to hold fast to you, and to remember that you will never fail us, that your promises to us are sure.

Susan Hibbins

Readings in Genesis

Abraham and Sarah come alive for me in this passage. Sometimes the great characters of the Bible seem remote to us, separated by vast distances of time and culture. Yet here, in this domestic scene, we can feel the heat of the day, sit with the three strangers and rest, smell an appetising meal being cooked. Hospitality is an important part of our Christian witness. Referring to this incident Hebrews 13:2 reminds us that Abraham and Sarah 'entertained angels' without realising it, and they brought an incredulous Sarah the message that she would soon bear Abraham their longed-for son.

What do we think about angels? Are they still in our mind's eye the winged messengers from the Christmas story, or are there modern-day angels who bring us messages from God today? Perhaps we feel God only speaks to us in church or through the Bible. But have you ever had a conversation with a stranger on a train, not knowing who that person was or anything about them, and felt blessed by something they said to you? Maybe we need to be open to chance encounters, and aware of our God working through them; to be alert to God's messages for us in our daily life.

Lord, help us to show hospitality to all we meet, and to be aware that you speak to us at any time, anywhere.

Entertaining angels

Genesis 18:1-15

Readings in Genesis   Susan Hibbins

Readings in Genesis

4 Abraham, Lot and Isaac

Notes based on the New Revised Standard Version by **Renato Lings**

Preparing for the week

This week's theme is Abraham, Lot and Isaac. These names represent some of the Hebrew patriarchs whose lives take up a large portion of the book of Genesis, although the Bible does not present the patriarchs in the same way. Lot, nephew of Abraham, is not generally regarded as a patriarch in tradition. However, Lot's life is inseparable from that of his uncle. For this reason it makes good sense to place the two men under the same heading. Abraham's cherished son Isaac is certainly regarded as a patriarch. Yet Isaac's story is almost reduced to being a mere hyphen between the eventful sagas of his father Abraham and his own son Jacob.

Thanks to their presence in the very first book of the Bible, the stories included in Genesis have paradigmatic force – that is, they have taken on the status of enduring models or myths. Their mythological character makes the central issues discussed in them relevant for all generations, including our own. Major themes in this week's texts are knowledge, migration, outsiders, refugees, exile, vulnerability and children.

Kjeld Renato Lings is a Danish translator/interpreter. He holds a PhD in theology from the University of Exeter (UK). Renato's doctoral thesis 'Restoring Sodom: Towards a Non-Sexual Approach' (2006), proposes a fresh, language-based interpretation of the biblical drama. Renato currently lives and works in his native Denmark. His main occupations are teaching, translating, interpreting, lecturing, writing and singing.

For further thought

• When you consider the idea of the 'patriarchs', what associations and assumptions come to mind?

• How are we to learn from people and stories from a very different time and world?

God and knowing

The covenant between YHWH and Abraham is expressed through the haunting phrase 'I have known him' (verse 19). Such recognition requires Abraham to practise the virtues of justice and mercy. As the subsequent passage reveals, he fully rises to the occasion as soon as he realises the nature of the divine fact-finding mission to Sodom.

Genesis 18:16-33

I have always found the graceful hospitality and passionate intercession put on display by Abraham immensely appealing. Deep down I understand that to be 'known' by God has to do with welcoming the stranger and being concerned for the wellbeing of others. At the same time, I am uncomfortably aware of moments in my own life in which I have failed to live up to this ideal.

The second 'knowing' in this passage occurs in verse 21. By saying 'Let me know', YHWH makes it clear to Abraham that a proper investigation of the situation in Sodom is under way. This is why two messengers are dispatched to the city. In Jewish legal tradition it takes two concordant witnesses in the courtroom for a testimony to be valid.

Abraham hailed from Mesopotamia, which today is called Iraq. The recent history of this country highlights how terribly wrong things may go when a proper investigation is not carried out. Despite an international clamour for restraint, the punishing invasion of Iraq in 2003 was launched before the alleged crimes had been verified. The outcome has been catastrophic.

Eternal God, teach me to be generous like Abraham. Kindle in my heart the passion to know your truth.

Knowing the stranger

Genesis 19:1-14

Can we ever know what God is up to? Is it for human beings to proceed with violence towards the divine? Such questions emerge from this famous passage in the story of Sodom and Gomorrah. Here the king of Sodom and his officers demand to 'know', i.e. investigate, the divine messengers (verse 5). Ironically, they are themselves being investigated or 'known' by the visitors, as announced by YHWH (18:21).

I have often meditated on the relevance of the story of Sodom to the modern world. One interpretation that makes sense is to focus on Lot, the vulnerable immigrant with no rights. As he carries out what he regards as his ancestral duties of hospitality, the city authorities raid his house. No one listens to his arguments. Indeed, Lot is treated as a non-entity. Even his dramatic offer of handing over his under-age children as a pledge, in an obvious gesture of loyalty, is to no avail. Instead, he himself is on the verge of being arrested (verse 9).

I am reminded of the multiple obstacles to integration faced by thousands of immigrants in my own country. Their adherence to ancestral traditions from other parts of the world is causing friction with the host society. In recent years the legal rights of immigrants and refugees are becoming curtailed. The driving force among the majority population seems to be ignorance, fear and a desire to control those who are different.

To what extent does your community welcome outsiders?

Creator of the universe, enable us to face our own fear and prejudice. Teach us to trust our immigrant neighbour.

The first refugees described in the Bible are Lot, his wife, and their two daughters. Lot the immigrant is in deep trouble. For reasons that are not entirely clear to him, his house has been raided late at night by the local authorities, and he himself has narrowly escaped being arrested. The divine visitors urge him to face reality: his situation in Sodom has become untenable. The only solution available to Lot and his family is flight. A painful overnight journey into the wilderness ensues. Lot's wife does not survive the trauma.

The narrative style of the story of Sodom is minimalist, i.e. some essential information is barely hinted at. In modern times, the plight of these refugees from Sodom is re-enacted in the lives of millions. For example, the endemic violence in Colombia and Central Africa is uprooting people from their homes. Day after day, individuals, families and entire communities are forced to flee for their lives. Many are injured along the way. Others never make it to safety.

I often wonder about the nature of the forces that are causing such widespread human misery. Most media reports are minimalist in the sense that they focus on the military and political aspects of conflicts and the suffering of victims. Unfortunately nothing is said about the industries and countries making a profit. I wonder why such background information is missing. Is warfare allowed to continue because it is good for business?

O Eternal, give us the courage to examine the financial causes of warfare.

Refugees from Sodom

Genesis 19:15-29

Diversity and privilege

Genesis 21:1-20

I was born in a country situated comfortably on the privileged side of the divide between poor and rich nations. I am reminded of the 1950s and 1960s when London and Paris became popular tourist attractions. Upon returning from those cities, many Danes would enthusiastically share the amazing experience of walking down major shopping streets amid throngs of people from all over the world.

During the industrial boom of the 1960s, immigrants from northern Africa, the Middle East and southern Asia arrived in Denmark. Initially they were welcomed, thanks to the gaps they were filling along the assembly lines. The situation might be likened to a marriage of convenience. As a growing number of immigrants stayed on, however, the national mood changed. By the 1970s, street crowds in major Danish cities were becoming increasingly cosmopolitan. Intriguingly, this colourful scenery was not greeted with enthusiasm. Unlike previous generations, a growing number of Danes have been responding to the sight of non-Western clothing in our streets with criticism.

Similarly, in today's Denmark the important languages brought to our country by various immigrant communities are regarded as a problem rather than an asset. Instead of integrating this tremendous resource into our education system, it is turned into a source of friction and discrimination. Like Sarah in Genesis, many Danes are determined not to share our privileges with Hagar and Ishmael.

In what way(s) do you respond to ethnic diversity in your community?

Loving God, open my eyes to the inspiration brought by immigrants and refugees. Let me share with them the water of my well.

Is there a special child in my life? Would I be prepared to let go of this child if it were required of me?

Children at risk

The book of Genesis explains how God brings about the miracle of Isaac's birth. All their lives Abraham and Sarah have been waiting for the fulfilment of the promise of a son. When Isaac finally arrives, their joy is complete. They become deeply attached to the boy. The thought of losing Isaac is total anathema to Abraham. For this reason, the binding of Isaac is one of the most haunting stories in the Bible. Apparently without hesitation, Abraham obeys the divine command. At the same time, he must have been plunged into despair.

Genesis 22:1-19

The seemingly outlandish idea of handing over or giving up one's own child (or children), if required, is not unheard of in scripture (see Genesis 19:8, 22:9, 33:2, 43:13; Judges 11:35; 1 Samuel 1:24-28). Some modern readers feel scandalised at the 'callousness' of parents in ancient times. But what happens if we apply the binding of Isaac to present-day scenarios?

In the media, cases of child abuse, child labour, child pornography and child prostitution surface regularly. All of this is going on as I write, in many parts of the world. Who is responsible? And how can you contribute towards making this world a safe place for children?

Gracious heavenly parent, make us aware of the unprotected children in our midst.

Readings in Genesis   Renato Lings

Saturday 13 March

Parents and blessings

Genesis 25:19-34

Can only one sibling be blessed? In the world of Genesis, the fierce rivalry between Esau and Jacob, which is a fact even before they are born as twins, seems to point in that direction. The rivalry extends to their parents: Isaac loves Esau, who becomes an expert on outdoor activities, whilst Rebekah favours Jacob who takes an education in domestic science.

Within my own family circle, my elder brother was my father's favourite. As a child he was unruly and often punished. As he grew up, my father became immensely proud of him. Like my father, my brother enjoyed hunting. He went on to become a banker, a military officer, and a politician. He married and raised a family. Between him and my father the chemistry was excellent. No doubt my father blessed this brother.

As a child I was quiet and had academic inclinations. I did not take to hunting. Later I chose a career that my father found totally foreign. In addition, my political views diverged from his. During my teens I realised I was gay. Following a long struggle, I came out of the closet at the age of 24. My father found all of this difficult to deal with. But my mother accepted me. Her support was a blessing.

Are you able to bless members of your family who differ from you?

God of all nations, remind us that all children were created in your image.

Readings in Genesis

5 Jacob

Notes based on
the Hebrew Bible by
Rachel Montagu

Rachel Montagu teaches biblical Hebrew at Birkbeck College's Faculty of Continuing Education. She has worked as a congregational rabbi and for the Council of Christians and Jews. She is particularly interested in women's interfaith dialogue.

Preparing for the week

Jacob's name means 'heel' and 'a heel' sometimes describes his behaviour towards his brother! Later he is named Israel which becomes a name for all his descendants as they continue to wrestle with God. He and Esau are presumably affected by their parents' relationship: Rebecca and Isaac's marriage seems to have deteriorated from the time when they first met. Then she literally fell in love with him, toppling off her camel, and her love comforted him for the death of his mother (Genesis 24:64-67). Each loves one of their twin sons whose characters differ completely: this does not sound like an emotionally united, happy family (Genesis 26:8). Puzzling questions arising from these chapters: did Isaac realise what Jacob had done and go along with it because he felt Jacob would be a more responsible custodian of the covenant with God? Or was he really deceived? Rebecca ensures the birthright blessing goes to her beloved Jacob but then must send him away to save him from Esau's anger, depriving herself of his company.

For further thought

- Do you find it comforting or shocking that God can use 'heels' to work through?
- In what ways is your own family dysfunctional? How might God be at work there?

Fathers and sons

Genesis 27:1-17

In this chapter Rebecca speaks to Jacob and Isaac talks to both sons, but Rebecca and Isaac never communicate. Isaac feels it is time to pass the birthright to his firstborn, even though Esau's marriages to Hittite women had distressed his parents and even though a while earlier Esau had casually sworn to transfer his rights as firstborn to Jacob in exchange for a bowl of lentil stew (when he arrived home hungry and exhausted from hunting – see Genesis 25:30-34). Did the twins' parents ever learn about this transaction? Even if 'the hunted food in his mouth' explains Isaac's love for Esau (Genesis 25:28) and perhaps admiration for his son's physical strength and skill, by insisting that Esau earn his blessing, rather than simply giving it to him, Isaac makes possible Rebecca's plot. Did Rebecca encourage Jacob to lie to his father because she thought he would use the birthright better? Or because she loved him more? Or because she believed she was fulfilling the prophecy she received while pregnant (Genesis 25:23)?

Can believing your actions will make things better for everyone in the end, ever justify deceiving your family?

As well as ensuring that you have an up-to-date will which distributes your financial assets to your family and friends, write a letter suggesting who should receive items of sentimental value and giving last affectionate messages to those you love.

Eternal our God, let us sing your praises and let your teaching enlighten us.

Isaac thinks the bringer of delicious game sounds like Jacob because he praises God for his successful hunting – presumably something Esau didn't do. Perhaps this chapter should warn parents never to categorise one child as the one who shows any characteristic in case they block their other children from feeling able to do that too.

Esau's complaint in verse 36 is a word-play that does not survive translation – firstborn-rights is *b'chorah* in Hebrew and blessing *b'rachah*.

Not only is Isaac's sight limited, it seems that his imagination is also. He struggles to find a second blessing for his beloved Esau. Although his eyes are weak, Isaac uses hearing, touch, taste and smell to give him pleasure and information.

One of the most important teachings here is that parents should bless their children explicitly. Here and in Genesis 48:13-16 fathers bless their sons and grandsons before they die. Jacob says, 'My soul will bless you' – the blessing comes from the deepest life source within him. That makes a blessing before death an appropriate last gift, but later Jewish tradition said parents should bless their children each Friday evening as part of welcoming the sabbath into the home.

If you are a parent, consider when and how you might regularly bless your children, perhaps using the words from Numbers 6:24-26 and a few words about your hopes for them that week. If you are not, who are the children you could bless?

My soul will bless you

Genesis 27:18-38

May the Eternal bless us and protect us; may the Eternal enlighten us and give us grace; may the Eternal grant us wholeness.

Readings in Genesis   Rachel Montagu

The deceiver deceived

Genesis 29:16-30

Early Jewish commentators who lived under Roman rule linked Esau and Rome – Roman soldiers wore red, Esau's colour. Their comments on Esau show their hatred of Roman oppression; they suggest Leah believed she was destined to marry Esau and weakened her eyes by weeping at this horrid prospect.

Laban married off both daughters in eight days and got the promise of seven more years of labour from his nephew – presumably even he didn't dare suggest Jacob wait seven more years before he married Rachel. Because Jacob deceived Isaac by pretending to be Esau, he could hardly object when Laban tricked him by marrying him first to Leah, not his beautiful, beloved Rachel. Genesis 29 and 30 show that this arrangement may have suited Laban but was sometimes hard on the sisters, one loved by her husband, one not, one blessed with children, one not.

A rabbinic legend tells how, after Moses and Aaron and many others pleaded unsuccessfully with God to end Israel's exile in Babylon, Rachel challenged God. If she could overcome her jealousy of Leah and not tell Jacob Laban's plan, so sparing her sister the embarrassment of being revealed as the wrong bride on her wedding night, then surely God should not be jealous of the idols the Israelites had sometimes worshipped? Sticks and stones could not threaten God as Leah had threatened her. God relented and redeemed the people from exile.

These chapters teach the need for employers and employees to deal honestly with each other. Do we?

Blessed are you, Eternal our God, Redeemer of Israel.

After leaving Laban with the colossal flocks created by his selective breeding programme (Genesis 30:32-43), Jacob is afraid that Esau will still be angry with him for taking the birthright/ blessing. He sends Esau an enormous gift of animals to propitiate him. Angels had appeared to Jacob on previous journeys (Genesis 28:12, 32:2). Just as 'men' appeared to Abraham and gradually it became apparent that they were more than passing travellers (Genesis 18:1-15), so Jacob wrestles all night with a 'man' and gradually realises that this is another divine encounter. Because of this night-long wrestle, Jacob is linked in Jewish tradition with prayer that involves a wrestle with God and/or the evening service – as distinct from Abraham who got up early in the morning to obey God and is the exemplar for morning prayer and for obedience, and Isaac who meditated towards evening and so is the role model for the afternoon service and for meditative prayer.

Rabbi Arthur Waskow wrote at length in his book *Godwrestling* (Schocken Books 1978, p.10) about the significance of this wrestle with an angel and what it means for Jacob and Esau, Rachel and Leah, himself and his brother to wrestle and for us all to struggle with our angry impulses. He says, 'It is Jacob's Godwrestling that frees him from his life-long necessity to wrestle Esau . . . It is Jacob's Godwrestling that lets him turn his deadly headlock on his brother into a kiss, a hug.'

Happy are we whose help is the God of Jacob and who hope in the Eternal, Jacob's God.

Battling our worst fears

Genesis 32:22-32

What do angels look like?

Genesis 33:1-11

Jacob's example of poor parenting skills is used by Jewish commentators as a warning against favouring one child over others; here the sons by the handmaidens, Leah and Rachel, are all left in no doubt whom Jacob most cares for and wants to protect.

The angel he wrestled with is often assumed in Jewish interpretation to be Esau's guardian angel: Jacob names their wrestling place Peniel, face of God, and now when he sees Esau he says, 'I see your face, like seeing God's face' (verse 10) – meaning that Esau resembled the angel he had wrestled with. The night of wrestling with his brother's angel resolves Jacob's feelings about their last encounter – or perhaps is what helps Esau respond graciously now when they meet.

It seems that Esau, although fierce-tempered, does not bear a grudge. The Masoretes, who added punctuation to the biblical text in the Middle Ages, were not convinced Esau was sincere in warmly embracing his brother and added dots above 'and he kissed him' to express their doubts. In our days, this phrase has been used by Rabbi Tony Bayfield as an analogy for the reconciliation of Jews and Christians who are at last learning to embrace dialogue with each other.

In verse 11 Jacob describes his gift to Esau as a *b'rachah*, blessing, perhaps intending it to be some material compensation for the birthright/blessing he had tricked Isaac into giving him.

How good and pleasant it is when brothers and sisters dwell together as one.

Idols out, monotheism in

Genesis 35:1-14

Jacob vowed that the pillar he set up to commemorate God's appearance to him would become a 'house of God' (Genesis 28:19-22). It is interesting to consider whether it was difficult for Abraham's family to make a complete transition to belief in one God without any physical form. Rachel robbing Laban of the teraphim (Genesis 31:19-35) suggests that she at least combined monotheism and idol-worship – at least when the idols were treasured family relics. The preparations for a new idol-free life parallel the preparation for the new covenant at Mount Sinai (Exodus 19:10). The repeated marriages with Abraham's original family may have brought repeated infusions of Mesopotamian ideas, and perhaps that explains the mention of Rebecca's nurse Deborah at Alon-bachut, the oak of weeping. Her death coincides with the end of the Mesopotamian paganism she may have brought along with Rebecca's clothes and possessions.

God blesses Jacob again with the new name given after his Godwrestling. Whereas Abram became Abraham and the old name was never used again, Israel and Jacob continue to be used interchangeably.

'El Shaddai' is usually translated 'God Almighty' (verse 11). There may be a link to the Hebrew word *shaddayim*, breasts – multi-breasted pagan fertility figures are found in the ancient world. Once the Israelites discarded their idols, they transmuted their names into attributes for the one God: El Shaddai is often used to refer to the nurturing and protecting activities of God.

The eternal God of the heavenly hosts is with us, the God of Jacob is our protection.

Readings in Genesis   Rachel Montagu

Readings in Luke

3 Confrontation in Jerusalem

Notes based on the *New Testament Study Guides* 'freshly translated' by Nicholas King (Kevin Mayhew 2004) by

Helen-Ann Hartley

Revd Dr Helen-Ann Hartley is Tutor in New Testament at Ripon College, Cuddesdon, and curate in the parish of Littlemore, Oxford. In addition to her college and parish duties, she is a frequent broadcaster for BBC Oxford and BBC Ulster.

Preparing for the week

The ministry of Jesus is, in so many ways, a story of journeying. Because we know the beginning and ending of the story, we expect the events that unfold. It's inevitable that Jesus will die, inevitable (at least to us) that he will rise again at the end of the story. Part of the difficulty with the end of the story is that its familiarity leads us into complacency. Luke, who wrote his gospel towards the end of the first century AD for a predominantly gentile community, was keen to stress the universal nature of God's salvation through Jesus. Central to this was the death, resurrection and ascension of Jesus. It was these dramatic events that brought a new hope to all, but especially to those whom society marginalised. This brought about a new community expressed through the idea of the kingdom of God, an idea which brought with it outreach, but also embrace to all people. The 'good news' meant a reversal of fortune for many, and it is helpful not to forget the radical nature of this gospel message, nor the implications for our contemporary faith. The events of Passion Week, as presented by Luke, are perhaps best described as a journey to transformation, a journey in which all participate as children of God.

For further thought

- In what ways do you see yourself and your community needing transformation?
- What is your prayer as you begin the journey of Holy Week – for yourself and for others?

All four gospel writers record the events of Jesus' arrival into Jerusalem, but Luke has some distinctive features. One of the most interesting is that the joyful reception of Jesus takes place on the top of the Mount of Olives itself, just as Jerusalem is coming into view. If there's one thing that is certain about Jesus' ministry, it's that there was always something different around the corner, or as in the case of today's passage, up a mountain. In the Bible, mountains are frequently places of revelation, and this passage is, in many ways, about finding out more of who Jesus is. Mountains too can represent a shift in perspective; things look different from the top, and perhaps we feel different too once we are 'up there'.

An unexpected entry

Luke 19:29-40

People cope in various ways when bad things happen, but one thing that most people need to do is to be able to tell their story. That might take some time, but it is often in the action of speaking out loud that we come to terms with what has happened to us. That is the point at which transformation may take place. Christians believe that the ultimate transformation takes place beyond this life, and this is the story of Easter itself. In Western culture, which doesn't 'do' mystery and wonder very well at all, all this business of resurrection seems completely unbelievable. But that's the whole point of Passion Week. The drama is unexpectedly shocking, and Luke begins as he ends – with an unexpected turn of events.

God of our journeying, help us to prepare to welcome Christ as we travel with him through the events of this week. May we meet him in the places and people that we encounter.

Readings in Luke   Helen-Ann Hartley

And they rejoiced?

Luke 19:41-48; 22:1-6

Jesus weeps over Jerusalem, whilst others looking to capture him rejoice. The scene is set for the events that rapidly begin to unfold. The description of Jesus weeping over Jerusalem has been influenced by the laments of Hebrew prophets, as well as the descriptions of the destruction of the Temple by the Jewish historian Josephus and others. Whereas Luke elsewhere expands on Mark's version of events, when it comes to the driving out of the sellers in the Temple, Luke's account is terse. For Luke, the Temple's importance lay much further back in the story, when the elderly Simeon proclaimed Jesus' birth from within the Temple. Now Luke wants to move events on beyond the bounds of the Temple.

The second part of our passage moves the story on further, with the shocking news that it is from amongst Jesus' closest associates that betrayal is located. People in power struggles often need a 'mole' on the other side, and in Judas they find one. Judas agrees to the plan which, in the Greek, is the language of confessing. The irony runs deep: rejoicing and confessing. The reality of the situation couldn't be further from that truth.

What difference can your faith make to the situations of power struggle that you encounter?

God of weeping and rejoicing, you share in our trials and sorrows. Be with us always, that we may know the light and peace of your presence when we feel most alone.

A meal and an argument

Luke 22:7-23

The apparent ordinariness of sharing the Passover is both transformed and shattered by Jesus' actions. Jesus has clearly looked forward to sharing this meal with the disciples before he must 'suffer'. There is a close similarity in the words for 'Passover' and 'suffer' (in the Greek, *pascha*), and we are surely meant to pick up on the word-play. For Luke, Jesus' story is one that we all share in, and this part of the narrative emphasises the importance of participation. Luke is not so focused on the complexities of what Jesus' death meant in itself. Rather, through the very act of sharing in the meal, we are all participants in God's kingdom, that's the point of it all.

Meal times can be points of celebration, sharing in news, coming together as a family at the end of a busy day. But meal times nowadays are most often disparate and hurried affairs. Too many other things compete for our attention, we just don't have time to sit and eat together. The disciples receive the dreadful news that a betrayer is in their midst. What follows is predictable: an argument. 'It's not me!' You can almost hear the conversation. The story of Judas teaches us not to be naïve, either about ourselves or about those around us who call themselves Christians.

Have you ever been betrayed by someone? What did that feel like?

God who suffered, forgive us when we deny that we know you or when we reject your presence amongst us. Help us to be mindful of the needs of others, and never to be so complacent that we stand by when others are scorned in your name.

Helen-Ann Hartley

Jesus? Never heard of him

Luke 22:24-38

Luke continues his gospel theme of the reversal of fortunes with the first part of our passage for today. The houses in which Christians met for worship were designed architecturally to reinforce the social status of the owner, who would recline comfortably and be served by slaves. The idea of the greatest becoming like the servant would have been incredibly offensive and shocking.

Another shocking turn of events follows, with the news of Peter's denial. The structure of Jesus' words both emphasises Jesus' own prayer for Peter, and Peter's faith. At this point, the contrast between Matthew's and Luke's narratives is interesting: after Peter denied Jesus, Matthew never mentions his name again, but Luke goes on to recount Peter's speech at Pentecost. Peter is every inch the example of someone who is redeemed after a terrible act of rejection.

The final part of the passage picks up on the instructions about travelling that Luke has already mentioned much earlier (in chapter 10). But the picture has apparently changed somewhat, and the previous instructions are to be ignored. The reference to the 'two swords' seems odd, but what seems to be presented is a classic Lukan image of fulfilment. Here the reference is to the 'Suffering Servant' passages in Isaiah 53. Perhaps Jesus' farewell discourse is pointing to a future tension between Jesus' successors and society?

When do we deny Jesus?

Hear us, Lord, as we turn to the events of your death. As the mood turns to darkness, may we catch glimmers of hope and light.

In this passage Luke concentrates on Jesus' prayer rather than the failure of the disciples to support Jesus in his hour of need. The fact that Jesus twice tells his disciples to pray is significant. Jesus' struggle is then supported by the presence of an angel. Although we should note that verses 43 and 44 appear to be a later textual interpolation, there is good reason for Luke to have included these verses as a proper understanding of the struggle that Jesus endured at this point, rather than understanding it simply as an experience of 'agony'. Interestingly too, Luke omits the name of the place in which Jesus prayed. There is no mention of 'Gethsemane'. The use of the language for 'sleeping' is best understood as metaphorical language which Luke uses to emphasise the cosmic nature of the unfolding drama. This is not just a human story, but it is God's story too.

Notice how Jesus takes steps to prepare the disciples for the future; it is Jesus who takes the initiative in addressing Judas. Furthermore, even in this most desperate of times, Jesus continues his ministry of healing. There is much irony in Jesus' words when he questions those who try to arrest him as a robber. Significantly, Jesus seems to be in control of events at this point. Everything he has done has led up to this point, and the prophetic words of Isaiah, that Jesus would be arrested with the lawless, are being fulfilled here in this passage.

Why me? Why now?

Luke 22:39-53

Lord, we pray that during this time of struggle, we may find strength and compassion to accompany you as you accompany us throughout our lives.

Readings in Luke

Helen-Ann Hartley

Bitter tears?

Luke 22:54-71

It is hard to imagine how Peter must have felt at this point. Given his earlier protestation that he would never deny knowledge of Jesus, for this to happen was devastating. Luke's remark that Jesus 'turned and looked' at Peter is a pivotal point in the story. Luke again highlights Jesus' prophetic presence as Peter remembers the word that the Lord had spoken. The reaction is a weeping of bitter tears.

Although in Luke's account the council meets formally in the morning when the examination of Jesus takes place, it has less characteristics of a trial than have Matthew and Mark's night session of the council: there are no witnesses, no formal accusation and no condemnation of Jesus. The council's focus is on the status of Jesus, and Jesus replies in a way that does not fall into their trap, but instead defines his status in terms which transcend their own categories. The term 'Son of God' is significant for Luke (more so than 'Christ'), because it harks back to the angel's declaration to Mary in 1:35, and anticipates the preaching in Acts 9:20 and 13:33. With a hint of irony, Luke has the members of the council declare that they have 'heard from his mouth'. The point that Luke wants us to get is that they haven't really 'heard' at all because if they had, then Jesus would not be in the position he is at this point in the narrative.

Loving God, as we weep bitter tears with Peter, we pray for those who are tempted to deny you through fear of persecution. May your presence strengthen them.

Readings in Luke

4 The way of the cross

Notes based on the New Revised Standard Version by **Godfrey Chigumira**

Godfrey Chigumira grew up in Zimbabwe, southern Africa, and served as a priest there for five years before coming to the United Kingdom. He is currently working in Hawarden Benefice in North Wales, and researching the figure of Mary as a source of empowerment for women with HIV Aids.

Preparing for the week

It is natural that we tend to enjoy gospel commentaries that cheer us up and leave us feeling joyful. But the way of the cross, though good news, is no cheerful event. Neither is the overall condition of many Africans' lives. In writing these notes I have had to struggle between a desire to uplift my readers, on the one hand, and making an honest reading of Africans' lives from the passion narrative, on the other. My sense of honesty won the day, and I hope that what I have written will deepen readers' sense of the passion of Christ which continues in the world today. I speak not for all Africans, but out of my own particular context and experience.

For further thought

- Where do you see Christ continuing to walk the way of the cross in today's world?
- In what ways do you experience the struggle between honesty and the desire to find a word that uplifts?

A cry for justice for the poor and the weak

Luke 23:1-12

The two trials of Jesus in this passage portray a profound miscarriage of justice. Pilate finds Jesus innocent (verse 4), but will not execute justice by releasing him. Pilate is unable to stand for truth at the expense of his own reputation. He tries to avoid his responsibility of giving Jesus a fair trial by referring him to Herod (verse 7). On the other hand, Herod is only interested in being entertained by Jesus (verse 8). The chief priests make inaccurate and false accusations about Jesus, and get what they want from Pilate by threatening his position with Caesar (verse 2). The trials lack honesty and compromise justice.

The human rights records of the justice systems in Africa are often very poor. In different African countries, there is a backlog of untried cases, with the accused often locked up in detention without trial for many months. This is especially true of some political prisoners and of those who are too poor to afford legal representation. When the trials happen, justice and fairness do not always prevail. Political motivations and propaganda often outweigh a right concern for justice. At the same time, the rich and those who hold political power may get away with committing terrible crimes without being brought to trial. The justice systems themselves are often deliberately built to favour those in political power.

What does it take to transform unjust systems into ones that are just?

Lord, stand alongside those who are unjustly tried, and bring to justice those whose crimes cry out to heaven.

In the last half of the twentieth century, the word 'independence' sounded like sweet music in the ears of many Africans. After many a bloody struggle, many of them achieved freedom from colonial rule during that period. Wild celebrations ensued, and independence was understood to be pregnant with possibilities once only dreamt about. However, in more than a few cases, those dreams have now blown away and dissipated like the wind. With little or no marked difference in their plight, many Africans today still labour and toil for their day-to-day survival. 'Independence' has become little more than an empty word. After the colonialist came the dictator, the corrupt ruler, the violent leader, the self-centred president, economic mismanagement, and so on.

Jesus is tossed back and forth between Pilate and Herod. In the passion narrative, this could be his fifth or sixth trial within twelve hours. Like the other trials, this one is unjust, harrowing and full of violent images. Pilate is the foreign invader, the colonialist, and Herod the local oppressive ruler. For the ordinary Africans too, injustice, violence and corruption have remained part of life regardless of the particular ruler. They too are tossed back and forth from one oppressive system to another, and from one oppressor to the other. Their short lifespan of poverty, pain and lack of economic and political freedom continues.

Pray for those caught in the cycle of injustice, violence and corruption – and that God will raise up those who will bring real change to Africa.

The long walk to freedom

Luke 23:13-25

Readings in Luke

Godfrey Chigumira

'Daughters of Africa, weep for yourselves!'

Luke 23:26-31

Jesus turns and speaks to the women, but not to Simon who is labouring under his cross. Is this an oversight on Jesus' part? Probably not, from one African context.

Many African women love being mothers and having children. They work very hard to bring up their children and to care for the daily needs of their male partners. Concern for their own lives usually comes last. At the same time many women depend heavily on their male partners for the resources needed to run the family. However, the men do not always provide enough for the family upkeep. Many African men, like Simon, carry heavy crosses in the form of little reward for heavy industrial and manual labour, hard and long labour shifts. Many African men struggle to find any employment. This makes it difficult for women to care for the family, and they are the ones who usually feel the full weight of their men's crosses. Under their often limiting husbands' authority, many women also lack the power to change such bad situations, and the realisation of their full potential is often thwarted and suffocated.

Lord, to the daughters of Africa, you say the same: 'Cry for yourselves.' Encourage and empower these daughters to seek self-empowerment, so that, like the central pillar in a house, they can support and improve not only their lives, but those of their children and their male partners as well.

The death sentence

How about this for a fable? 'Once upon a time the creator visited his creatures, and the creatures said him, "You are so evil you deserve to die". So the creatures got hold of their creator and killed him.' It sounds like a story of satirical irony!

However, if taken more seriously, as an event that actually happened, significant and hard lessons can be drawn from this fable. Humans have badly erred and, without proper care, they continue to do so. They need to be more careful, especially where others' lives are concerned.

Luke 23:32-43

In the killing of Jesus, the mistake of pronouncing a death sentence on one who does not deserve it comes into today's spotlight. Still widely practised by most African countries, the ultimate penalty is fraught with many dangers. It presupposes our surefootedness in judging others, and it betrays our failure to realise how ill-equipped and defective our judgements can often be. It takes humility to acknowledge that we are not good enough to give others the ultimate penalty. The death-sentence mentality can also encourage violence on offenders by the offended in society. One violent act begets another, leading to a cycle of violence. Rather than a sign of respect for life, the death sentence itself can be a symptom of a widespread lack of sanctity of life.

May no created person find another unworthy of life.

Readings in Luke

Godfrey Chigumira

A watching that transforms

Luke 23:44-49

They 'stood at a distance, watching these things' (verse 49). They watched the things that transpired at Jesus' expiration. These were not pleasant things to watch: darkness, the sun's light failing, Jesus calling out his last words loudly and in pain and breathing his last. As they watched, they must have tried to decipher the meaning of what was happening. Their knowledge of him, of how he had bettered almost every situation, would have encouraged them to think about the meaning of this, and would have given them hope for a better outcome.

The death of infants due to curable disease, the preventable deaths of young parents and of people due to poverty, AIDS, tuberculosis, malaria and state-sponsored violence, the lack of medicine and medical expertise – there is so much to watch in Africa today, and what a painful experience it is to see it. Yet watching by itself does not change anything! It is when that experience is brought before Jesus' cross from which the resurrection is born that it can bear fruit. From Jesus' cross lessons can be learnt and new insights borne into our own experiences. The curtain of the old order of things can be torn in two (verse 45) to give way to the new era where these evils become things of the past.

Dear Lord, turn the darkness of our continent into the light of your resurrection.

Godfrey Chigumira

Have you ever seen a dog sitting before the grave of its master after the master's burial? Or do you remember your feelings during and soon after the burial of someone really close to you? One can experience a strange, sour feeling of weakness, vulnerability and even shallowness. One can feel as if in an unfamiliar and threatening territory. It can be difficult to resume normal life again.

Many African societies have large families, but also a short lifespan and many premature deaths. Africa is rampant with multiple untimely bereavements and long periods of mourning. It is a terrible time for those who must endure the loss of those they love. Africans' experiences of emptiness and loneliness come into my mind when I read about Jesus' burial and the women who followed from Galilee. With one's feelings in turmoil, it is not easy to find rest (verse 56) in heart and soul after such loss. It is most likely that the day of rest was for these women a time when their feelings of loss fully confronted them. However, the gaping hole left by Jesus' death and burial was soon filled, for the original women, by his resurrection. For many Africans today, that gap often remains a prolonged austere experience that fails to heal.

Lord Jesus, may your short lifespan induce in us the will and energy to improve the lives of young parents and children who die early in life.

Bereavement in Africa

Luke 23:50-56

Readings in Luke

Godfrey Chigumira

Readings in Luke

5 The risen Lord

Notes based on the New Revised Standard Version by **Paul Nicholson SJ**

Paul Nicholson is a Roman Catholic priest belonging to the Society of Jesus (the Jesuits). He is currently Director of Novices in Britain, and has worked since ordination in the fields of spirituality and social justice.

Preparing for the week

The Danish philosopher Kierkegaard wrote: 'Life can only be understood backwards; but … it must be lived forwards'. The first part of this proposition is well illustrated by the readings this week. For although the accounts of the risen Lord stand at the end of the gospels, it is only in the light of the resurrection that the disciples of Jesus were able to begin to understand what the life of Jesus, and what the good news that he brought, truly meant.

In the Acts of the Apostles, which we will consider at the end of this week, Luke writes of forty days after his Passion during which Jesus continued to appear to his friends. Luke's gospel, by contrast, presents a series of appearances squeezed into a single action-packed day. The day starts with a group of mourning women, terrified when they cannot find Christ's body; and ends with the disciples gathered, full of joy and praising God.

In your prayer this week you are invited to join that group of disciples as they begin to come to terms with all that the resurrection of their Lord means to them. Their awareness dawns slowly, and develops gradually. Let your own appreciation of the implications of the events recorded here similarly unfold throughout the coming days.

For further thought

- How does the light of the resurrection illuminate your own life?
- How can you share something of that illumination with others?

The women at the beginning of this passage know exactly where they are going, and what they have to do. They have a duty to honour the dead Jesus by tending to his corpse. Even without this duty, their love for him would have led them to this task. It remains, though, a desperately sad job to have to carry out, and furthermore one without hope.

Why look for the living among the dead?

Luke 24:1–12

The message of the two men they meet in the tomb changes all of that. Although the women are terrified by the men's appearance, the news that Christ is risen still gets through to them, and serves to remind them of all that Jesus has said. So there is no longer any need to stay among the graves and corpses. Filled now with hope, they set out again, this time as witnesses of what Christ means in their own lives.

Is there anything in your own experience that echoes the change in these women? Can you remember times when dutiful service kept you shackled to ways of living and patterns of behaviour which were anything but life-filled? Or when a new way of looking at things led you on into a greater freedom? Maybe that is a gift you might want to ask for today, for yourself or someone close to you.

Lord, help me to look for you among the living. Release me from anything that ties me to whatever is dead in my life.

Paul Nicholson

We had hoped . . .

Luke 24:13-27

I once lived in a house called Emmaus, in an industrial city in northern England, an area of high unemployment, poor housing, broken families and little explicit Christian faith. Since I was already a priest, the local church assumed I had come to convert my neighbours, bring them to Jesus and fill the parish pews.

Although from the outset I suspected that there was more to it than that, for a few months I wasn't sure what I was doing. But, as I got to know people and their situations better, it became obvious that I didn't have to bring anyone to Jesus, or him to them. Jesus was already with the people of our neighbourhood, as they struggled to bring up their families and care for each other in situations where the cards were stacked against them. If I had a role at all, it was to help them see the Christ who was already walking alongside them, unrecognised.

Here Luke shows great insight into how that might best be done. The risen Lord encourages the two discouraged disciples to speak of their hopes. It is on that foundation that he can build his explanations, and so rekindle the fires that had once burnt within them. With those fires of hope rekindled, all the rest follows.

What hopes did you have when you first became a disciple? Ask the Spirit, who is both wind and flame, to fan those hopes into a stronger life today.

One question might act as a focus for your prayer with this second part of the Emmaus story. What would it feel like to be one of these two disciples as they hurry back to Jerusalem? They have had an extraordinary day, a real roller-coaster. Leaving Jerusalem frightened and discouraged; meeting a stranger who draws out of them the hopes they had once had; finding those hopes rekindled as he explains the scriptures; and recognising Jesus as he breaks bread with them. Now they cannot wait to spread the news of all they have experienced.

What is true of them is true of you, too. As a disciple of Christ, your own hopes in life only make sense, ultimately, in the light of his life, death and resurrection, as recorded in scripture. It is because you have experienced the gospel as good news that you might feel drawn to share your faith with anyone who will listen, anyone who might benefit from the hope you have. You might not want to run seven miles late in the evening to bring the message. But if you never feel inclined to mention what Jesus means to you to any other person, perhaps something is missing in your religious outlook.

List today the people you know who could use a little more hope in their lives. Is there anything that you might do to bring them good news?

Lord, make me a channel of your peace.

Prayer of Francis of Assisi

Sowing hope

Luke 24:28-35

Where will you meet Christ today?

Luke 24:36-43

The British artist Stanley Spencer created a series of remarkable paintings of the resurrection of the dead at the end of time. Set in places he knew well, those who rise first reach down to help the latecomers clamber up from their graves. Families reassemble and bask in the spring sunshine. People read the epitaphs inscribed on their gravestones, or leave on pleasure-cruisers to visit other parts of heaven. God and his angels wander through many of these paintings, lending a hand wherever it is needed. The scenes manage to be, at one and the same time, full of joy and yet entirely ordinary.

Spencer captures well the kind of atmosphere that the end of this passage describes. The startling spectre who disrupts the disciples' discussions turns out to be Jesus, their friend and teacher. Although they saw him die, now he can be touched, he can eat, he is anything but a phantom. There is an ordinariness about him that fills them with joy.

Most often, we too are invited to recognise Christ in the ordinariness of everyday life. Mystical moments and peak experiences are necessarily few and far between. But enjoying spring sunshine, relaxing with relatives, or lending a hand to a neighbour in need are experiences available every day. And for those with eyes to see, they can be chances to encounter the risen Christ.

Lord, give me the joy of encountering you in the ordinary events of this day.

It's a staple of whodunits, and of TV crime investigations. After much searching, a witness to the crime is found, and their testimony alone is enough to convict the criminal. Even an unreliable witness is to be preferred to someone relying on hearsay; because there is always the chance, with enough support and prompting, that the witness will be able to recall some crucial incident that makes all the difference. Hearsay can only be repeated, and at best passed on unchanged.

At the heart of this passage, just before he withdraws from them for the last time, Jesus reminds his disciples that 'You are witnesses of these things'. The message they bring is not to be some elaborately worked-out theology, or a novel and intricate philosophy. Rather they are to tell others what it was they experienced as they travelled with the wandering preacher, Jesus of Nazareth. That alone, the risen Lord seems confident, will be enough to bring others to faith.

We, too, are called to be witnesses in the same way. Fundamentally we share with others not what we have read, or been taught. Rather we offer them a report of what we have experienced in our own following of Christ, confident that God can use that perhaps faltering report to plant and develop faith in others.

Help me, Lord, to recognise more clearly your work in my own life; so that I, too, may go out as your witness, clothed with power from on high.

Witness statement

Luke 24:44-53

Paul Nicholson

An everyday Jesus

Acts 1:1-14

I wonder what Theophilus, addressed in the first line of this passage and the supposed recipient of the books known to us as Luke and Acts, made of them – the story of how the teaching of a wandering rabbi from an obscure province on the edge of the empire made its way to the heart of things in Rome; and the extraordinary claim, on which the two books hinge, that this rabbi was not only executed but came back from the dead and empowered his followers to continue his work.

It is difficult for those of us who have known these stories from our earliest days, and for whom they are central to our cultural heritage, to approach them with fresh eyes as Theophilus would have done. But one of the gifts that the Spirit, promised here by Jesus, brings, is precisely this ability to recognise Christ afresh. The disciples are gently chided for continuing to stare into heaven, as if to catch some further glimpse of him. Instead, they are sent back to the city, to the busy-ness of everyday life, and told that from now on they must expect to encounter him there. And just as every day brings new experiences and new challenges, so it brings new opportunities to appreciate what it is that Christ continues to do in our world.

Spirit of God, give me the gift of fresh sight; that I may see Christ more clearly in the events of each day.

Resting places and sacred spaces

1 The divine imperative to rest

Notes based on the New Revised Standard Version by
Aruna Gnanadason

Dr Aruna Gnanadason is a member of the Church of South India and Executive Director for Planning and Integration in the General Secretariat of the World Council of Churches in Geneva, Switzerland. She has travelled extensively all over the world as a speaker, Bible study leader and a promoter of the power of the churches and the ecumenical movement in the context of a broken and hurting world.

Preparing for the week

I chose to write on this theme at a time when I was on holiday! I realised just how precious days of rest are – time we can take for ourselves when we are not running around busily, but relaxing, reading, taking long walks, giving quality time to family and friends. Our bodies and souls need rest and spiritual refreshment periodically – time to be still and commune with God, with each other and with nature around us. The sabbath rest is an ancient Jewish tradition which we ought to cherish – in biblical understanding this was every seven days and every seven years.

Resting in God is about celebrating the love and justice that Jesus came to give to the world. It ought to encompass our lives, our communities and all of creation.

For further thought

- When and where do you make or find time for rest and recreation? Is this a struggle for you? If so, why?
- What does 'resting in God' mean for you?

God rested on the sabbath – why don't we?

Exodus 31:12-17

God took a well-earned break after all that splendid activity of creation! We are commanded to rest because God rested. The sabbath rest is symbolic of the covenant God made with humanity, and the law requires the celebration of this day with worship, special sacrifices and sharing the bread of the presence. Breaking the sabbath was a punishable offence! The Bible records six instances when Jesus himself broke the sabbath law, but in my understanding he was not challenging the need for rest, he was only pointing to the right use of the day.

This ancient Jewish tradition has deep relevance in our hectic lives when rest, worship and building community seem to be put on the back burner. Not protecting the opportunities to take rest and neglecting our communal and personal communion with God, is perhaps akin to breaking the covenant in our own times. This neglect can manifest itself as burn-out and exhaustion and in an inability to relate to each other. How often do we fail to appreciate God's desire for us to take time to calm our souls and to immerse ourselves in communion with each other, through worship and prayer with God?

How can we instil in ourselves and in others the understanding that rest and times of worship and prayer are not an option we can dispense with, but integral to our relationships with each other and with God?

Dear God, teach us to respect and honour the ancient wisdom that makes us pause and rest our weary bodies and souls in your comforting presence.

Aruna Gnanadason

Resting places and sacred spaces

The sabbath rest: God's unbroken promise

Hebrews 4:4-11

Do we fail to recognise that the rest that God offers is something that has to be entered into? Is it an act of disobedience if we turn away from the comforting rest we could find in God's love? Have we failed to recognise the opportunity God offers us to spread God's love among all people? By our engagement with those around us we help them enter the rest offered by God. The sabbath rest is a promise for all the people of God, not just for me alone.

If we listen to the call from God and not harden our hearts we can find rest and spread that message to those who have not heard it. We recognise the presence of God in someone who comforts us – do we not often say: 'God has heard my cries and has sent you'? This is what it means to live God's love in our harsh world – to be comforted and be ready to comfort others.

The covenant that God makes stands firm – God will not let us down. We will be held in the palm of God's hand – the sabbath rest is there as a promise we can look forward to.

What does sharing the promise of the sabbath rest mean in the context where we live with people of other faiths and of no faith at all? Think how you could reach out collectively to some person, or a family or a community who are filled with a sense of despair, with the message of rest in Christ.

Give us the grace to abide in the assurance that the sabbath rest is a promise that lies ahead of us, a message of love we are called to share.

Resting places and sacred spaces   Aruna Gnanadason

Even the land rested for God!

Leviticus 25:1-7

Leaving the land fallow on the seventh year is the gift that the land gives to God! Even the land needs rest after six years of human exploitation. Today, many farmers do not cultivate parts of their land all the time. However, the biblical demand is of a more radical nature – it calls for allowing *all* the land to lie fallow for a year. It comes as a challenge to the over-use of the earth for profit and greed, an abuse which destroys its very future.

The sabbath is about recognising that the earth belongs to God and that all those who live on the land have rights, not just the landowners or the wealthy. In tribal societies in many parts of the world, land used to be owned and cared for by the whole community. Traditions of prudent care ensured strict rules against exploitation. But these have been lost due to industrialisation, even of agriculture, in recent times.

The ancient wisdom of the sabbath calls for periodic rest in God, for the land and for humanity. This is not just a law but a spiritual discipline, and it is the only way in which we can sustain life with each other, with the earth and with God.

Many of us live in cities where access to land and to open spaces is a luxury. How can we relate to the struggles of farming communities which struggle to protect the earth and make a livelihood for us all?

Teach us to care for the land with prudence and wisdom – remind us that the land too, like us, needs sabbath rest in God.

Finding strength through trusting in God

Isaiah 30:15-18

Trust in God and not in earthly power! As I am writing this, the world faces a major financial crisis. We always seem to live with some form of crisis. Unfortunately, it is at these moments that the powerful assume that they can deal with the problems finding temporary, technical solutions. The rest that Isaiah offers is the strength we could derive if we would only trust in God. Isaiah urges rulers to enter into quiet communion with God and from there to draw their strength and not to turn to earthly power to redeem them. Too often leaders believe in the power of their systems, their financial and military power as the source of their strength – they do not turn to God. They thus provoke each other to violence and war. Religion too is misused for political ends, leading to tensions and misunderstandings. Most often the wellbeing of millions of common people is overlooked.

Isaiah's call to the rulers of his time suggests a different way. Those who wait on God, who trust in God and are willing to rest in God, will be blessed. This is the rewarding message for us too today!

Think of one action you can take personally, or in a group around you, to challenge elected leaders when they too quickly resort to violence rather than seek ways of dialogue for resolving conflicts.

Teach us, dear God of mercy and justice, to wait on you, to trust in you and to turn to you for our strength.

Rest that only God can give us!

Matthew 11:28-30

Doubtless, all of us at some moments of our lives have turned to this comforting text in the Bible. When we are carrying a burden that we cannot bear on our own – we turn to God!

Recently a 28-year-old young man, the son of a colleague, who had been suffering from depression, took his own life. A bright young man with a future filled with possibilities decided he could not take it any more. I was filled with sorrow that none of us had been able to help him – and that he was unable, because of his illness, to turn to God, put down his heavy yoke and find rest.

We are offered an invitation to put down our heavy loads and to take up the yoke Christ offers, the yoke of loving ourselves and our neighbours. This yoke is light indeed. Jesus is identified here with the figure of Wisdom, confirming Jesus as God's unique representative. Jesus' promise of love goes beyond the individual to the whole community. Jesus, the gentle servant and representative of God, is an image that Matthew leaves us with – a Saviour we can bravely surrender to when life threatens to destroy us. (Read also Matthew 12:17-21.)

Take time to assist someone you know who feels overburdened with worry and anxiety and is unable to recognise the love of Christ and the promise it offers.

Remind us every single day, O God, that we can put down our heavy burden and take up the yoke that is light: the yoke you promise to us as we love ourselves and our neighbours.

Aruna Gnanadason

Resting places and sacred spaces

Jesus promises his disciples his presence with them. Faithfulness to his teachings on love is the guarantor that God will dwell in them as they dwell in him. Just like the disciples, we are called to a commitment to witness to the world what Christ's love can offer.

How do we witness to the love of Christ in our community today? How do we respond to those experiencing exclusion, disappointment or loneliness? Witnessing to the love of Christ in our world today takes many forms. To have Christ abide in us comes with a challenge to give up all odious distinctions of gender, race, class, caste and religion and all other forms of division. God dwells in everyone, even in those whom we do not really like or who are different from us! In Asian traditions we either bow to each other or fold our hands together in greeting, a symbolic reminder of the recognition of the presence of the divine in the other.

If we dwell in the love of Christ, anything we want will be done for us! Jesus is speaking to us today, encouraging us in our ministry to the community around us. We are blessed with the promise of Christ dwelling in us.

Abide in me as I abide in you

John 15:4-10

Dear Jesus, dwell in me and teach me how to dwell in you. Teach me to recognise that my faithfulness to your love in the world is a promise of your faithfulness to me.

Resting places and sacred spaces   Aruna Gnanadason

Resting places and sacred spaces

2   Resting places in the Old Testament

Notes based on the Greek and Hebrew texts, and a variety of translations, by **Brenda Lealman**

Brenda Lealman has been an RE adviser and school inspector, with a special interest in the place of spirituality in education. She is also a published poet and a former chair of the Creative Arts Retreat Movement (CARM). She has travelled widely including staying in ashrams in India and as guest lecturer at a theological college in the Canadian Arctic. She is retired and lives on the North York Moors.

Preparing for the week

The undersong of our spiritual journeying is in the rests, the pauses. It was June and I was, unusually, solitary on an island in the Outer Hebrides, Scotland. Sunshine, luminous light, the turquoise, blues, greens of the sea. I emptied myself of thoughts and goals (more or less!). I simply wandered and every so often would throw myself down for extensive periods of lying or sitting in the hot, honey-fragrant heather, on the dunes, or amongst the wild flowers. This was a real rest time, a pause in my life. But rest, pause, is not always such an idyll, nor the idyll of the Song of Songs. For those of us who live in a rapacious consumer culture, achieving rest, quietly living a life of trust in God, can be very hard. So it was for many people in the Old Testament! And there are times, when, as with Jacob, rest doesn't seem very productive. For some people, too, it is only when pausing takes them into rock-bottom (stomach-bottom in the case of Jonah) darkness and hopelessness that the journeying can restart in a creative way.

For further thought

Positively, we can hope and long for rest that brings refreshment, restoration to life-giving creativity; a space where, in the silence, we can realise and yield to the mystery and presence we call God, where we might catch a glimpse of the glory in us and in the world, a glimpse of God, and of who we are intended to be. But rest also means that we have to return to our journeying – in the expectation that jewel-like treasures await us in at least some of our resting places.

Shabbat

Shh . . . hus . . . shb . . . The moment of hush when the note of the cello ceases; when the blackbird's singing is done; when the sound of the saw stops and the woodworker gazes at what he has shaped; when the artist knows that one more touch of paint would ruin his painting and he knows that what he has created is complete; when the Creator of the universe, filled with the joy and delight of creating, says that it is finished. Then is the moment of hush, of rest, of *shbt*/*shabbat* (Hebrew) or sabbath. It is the time of going back into the primal void, into the dark mystery – a time to pause, to take stock, to remember and be refreshed. It's the time when we are still and surrender to deep silence, and we realise that that is what we long for. But rest, shabbat, is only a pause, not an eternal passivity. And so, we rest, but the cessation is also another genesis; refreshed, we move on to yet more creativity.

Genesis 2:1-3

Sit in a relaxed but attentive position, spine erect but not strained. For a few minutes concentrate on your breathing. Remain in total silence for ten minutes at least.

Resting places and sacred spaces   Brenda Lealman

Only one foot in Eden

Genesis 28:10-22

We were crossing the Sinai desert on camels. One day at about noon we stopped to rest. Pink, red, black rocks flaring with heat; sun blazing down; silence so thick you could cut it; we found what little shade we could. One of the Bedouin selected a rectangular-shaped rock about thirty centimetres high, lay down on the stony desert floor, put his head on the rock, and fell asleep. Jacob! Perhaps the 'ladder' that came to Jacob in his dream wasn't the gossamer ladder I'd imagined it to be, but much more like the rough, battered stone staircases (we'd climbed one or two) hewn up the side of huge rocks in the desert. Such a rough-hewn staircase becomes for Jacob an opening on to heaven; a place not of fluffy angels, but of communication with God, a place of terror, of awe.

One midrash (comment) on the text says that the angels were disappointed to find Jacob asleep: they'd expected more of him! But perhaps that's the point: by night, in solitude, in dream, Jacob glimpses a grander picture. But by day, his dream makes little difference to him; he remains a mediocre, rough-hewn man. He's still afraid, easily led by others, deceitful, cunning, self-pitying, so often seeing himself as the victim. Once awake, his vision of heaven evaporates, turns into petty bargaining. And yet, he's a man with a difference: he carries inside him the remnants of a strange and precious dream. Is there just some hope that his messy life can contribute to the fulfilling of God's purposes?

Recognise the messy areas of your own life; perhaps even give thanks for them because that's the stuff God works with.

Brenda Lealman

Resting places and sacred spaces

'O why do you walk through the fields in gloves,/ Missing so much and so much?' As a child, that poem puzzled me. Who would dream of going into the fields in gloves and miss the joys of tree climbing and dipping into streams? The Hebrew refugees from Egypt have left the palm trees and flowing water of Elim and moved into the desert of Sin on the west of the Sinai peninsula, on their way to Sinai. They are missing the first surprise of freedom; the climate is becoming like that so prevalent in Britain today: resentment, cynicism, complaining, blaming, greed. And the Hebrews fail to see the damaging implications of their behaviour: it amounts to complaining about God, assails the very source of life; it was God, not Moses and Aaron who brought them out of slavery.

To possess and keep on wanting more and more is, in the end, to lose. It is when they say 'Enough' that God is generous: when they stop stockpiling that they are given enough manna for immediate needs – with the exception of the sabbath for which they may take extra food. (In May and June the desert tamarisk tree lets out a sweet substance which local people even today eat and, apparently, call 'man'.) It is when they say 'Enough' to constant busy-ness, anxiety, and instead let go and take rest that God provides.

The Hebrews have begun living with their gloves on; they're setting their sights on a comfort zone. And so they are missing the glory, right there, permeating the everyday. They are missing 'the dazzling light of the Lord', 'the glory of the Lord' (verse 7).

Missing so much and so much

Exodus 15:27 – 16:26

Glory in the everyday? In what ways is that your experience?

Resting places and sacred spaces

Brenda Lealman

Radical change

Jonah 1:15 – 2:10

There are Jonahs around today, and in the Christian churches: the exclusivists who defend the fortress, keep it free from contamination by change or outsiders; they are judgemental, possessors of the truth, resenting instead of affirming newcomers and those who might be a threat to the status quo. Jonah is one of these; he's narrow-minded. Amongst the Jews who returned home after the exile in Babylonia there grew up an increasing exclusivism. Others reacted differently, and the author of the Book of Jonah is one of those people. In the tradition of the prophet Second Isaiah, they began to think of God as a universal God, concerned about all people, offering love and forgiveness to all who repent, to pagan sailors, to foreigners. And they realised that there were outsiders, foreigners, more willing to respond to God's love than were many of those who called themselves 'chosen'.

The kindliness of the pagan sailors, the horror of his descent into the darkness of the whale's belly, his gratitude at being delivered from the belly of the whale – these are all experiences that broaden Jonah's views. God's election does not only bring privileges, but the obligation to make known God's love and offer of new life to all humankind.

It's disturbing to have one's point of view changed. Change brings discomfort; but this time Jonah does not try to escape God's clutches but dares to go the way his deep-down inner voice directs him: to give the news of God's saving power to foreigners.

Do you know any Jonahs? Are you one in any of your attitudes?

God who liberates, free us from all small mindedness.

The Song of Songs is a collection of love poems, of delicious, erotic fragments that, perhaps, derive from even older love poetry from Sumeria, Ancient Egypt and Greek Alexandria. There's no real story line; images and metaphors are fleeting, dialogue moves to and fro.

In today's passage, the setting is outdoors in the dazzle of spring. The lovers' trysting place is a wild, idyllic spot, a sun-filled woodland glade. Picture the fresh green grass, aromatic cedars and cypresses, pine scents on the warm air; wild flowers: crocuses or narcissi, lilies; luxuriant vines. It's as though the trees make a canopy over them, a sacred space where the radiance in them and in the world is revealed. The natural world gives the lovers a language for their love, for sensuous delight. The blossoming of nature in springtime is matched by the blossoming of human beings.

The woman (verses 3-7) is enraptured by the man and his physical beauty: You're like a fruit tree (heavy at this time with fragrant blossom). Your shade protects me; I can rest secure in your love, delight in your kisses (verse 3). Your intention of love is so open, so obvious, that it stands over us like a banner. You've brought me to a feast of love (verse 5): feed me on raisins, that is, on wine (kisses), on the fruit of yourself. Secure in love, the woman desires to give herself totally to her beloved (verse 6). We leave the lovers in rapturous embrace. The strange plea to 'the women of Jerusalem' (who function almost like a chorus) not to interrupt the lovemaking is perhaps a plea for privacy, for respect for the natural course of love; or it could be a refrain technique to mark the end of the first poem.

How extraordinary – the ordinary touched by radiance

Song of Songs 2:1-7

In imagination, spend time in the woodland glade described, or create your own glade; linger there, savour the senses – smell, touch, sight, hearing, taste – there. Thank God for your experiences of love in whatever forms love has taken.

Resting places and sacred spaces

Brenda Lealman

Shalom

Psalms 127: 1-2; 131

Hush becomes rush. Rest becomes busyness. Work becomes the drive for possessions, competition that leads to retaliation, manipulation. Constant rush, busyness, symptoms of the commodity values so powerfully underlying many 'developed' consumer societies . . . It's all futile, says the psalmist; you're losing your souls, the deepest parts of yourselves. Builders, plumbers, policemen, all of us, can only be at rest, ex-perience wellbeing (that is, rest in the sense of Hebrew *shalom*, peace), when we yield ourselves to God and our work becomes God's work. It's like a Navajo woman weaving a rug: she puts into her work her dreams, her whole self, her very life, so much so that she 'must run the pattern out in a little break at the end/so that her soul can come out, back to her' (D H Lawrence, 'Whatever Man Makes', *The Complete Poems*, Penguin 1977, p.448). Our work becomes a source of life.

Psalm 131 is a beautiful reflection on our yielding to God. Unfortunately, some versions miss the full import of the image in verse 2. The soul is pictured as a child recently weaned from breast-feeding who is struggling and crying in frustration, but is at last quietened in his mother's arms. Quietness of soul, rest, do not always come readily but often only after distress and protest; after the hard work of letting go of pride, arrogance, self-preoccupation. Only then can we yield to the fertile silence of God's presence in us. In that resting place we can start to become the persons we're meant to be.

Pray for the gift of shalom or wellbeing in your life.

Brenda Lealman

Resting places and sacred spaces

Resting places and sacred spaces

3   Resting places in the New Testament

Notes based on the Greek and Hebrew texts, and a variety of translations, by
Brenda Lealman

For Brenda's biography, see p.108.

Preparing for the week

There was a poet/priest who took drastic measures to make space for himself: he would climb into a tree with branches reaching out over a frozen lake, suspend himself upside down above the surface of the water, and simply gaze at the astonishing patterns in the ice. Out of this person's resting places came some of the finest poetry to be written in English – it was Gerard Manley Hopkins at St Bueno's.

The importance of making space for re-creation is at the heart of this week's readings. Rather than making space, a strong impulse for those of us who live in Western Europe and North America is to *fill space* (the entertainment industry, commerce and marketing all lend a helping hand). To *make space* tends to be much more difficult for us.

Sometimes the spaces we make for ourselves simply involve resting – absorbing, gazing, day-dreaming, sleeping; they might lead to our becoming peacefully alert and attentive as when the space becomes prayer. Making space can involve initial, physical effort.

Our spaces are full of hidden possibilities. Some of these can be disturbing: demons of guilt, anxiety or anger can become active and we might need to seek friendly advice or expert help. But spaces are also where what-is-not-yet can happen; where creation, new being, rebirth happen; where the mystery we call God happens; where intense joy is sometimes given: glimpses of glory and other surprises. In the spaces we make, all comes as gift . . . and we 'know not how'(Mark 4:27).

For further thought

- Do you fill space rather than make space?
- Reflect on times of enforced or chosen space in your life. What have been some of the fruits?

Monday 26 April

Resting places are about gifts

Mark 4:26-29

This passage is metaphorical narrative, story, parable, riddle. And parables by their very nature can't be reduced to a single meaning; they have to be worked on in the light of one's own experience; they lead to fresh ways of seeing. Jesus never tells what the kingdom *is*; but what it is *like*. We are offered fragments, glimpses of the kingdom's mystery and potential. The man plants the seed, but then human activity ceases; the man goes to bed, lets go, sleeps, hands over to God. This is when the hidden growth takes place. 'The earth produces of itself' (verse 28). The kingdom is sheer gift and, if accepted as that, the glory of its fruiting is assured.

The kingdom is about adventure into an alternative way of being. As R S Thomas puts it in his poem, 'The Kingdom', it is where 'quite different things are going on': poor people are treated like kings, the sick are healed; all we need to do is to present ourselves with our need, and the 'simple offering' of faith 'green as a leaf'.

If you do not already have a physical retreat space, try making one in some corner with a mat or chair and, perhaps, a candle. If you live in a country warmer and drier than my own, a hidden place outdoors could be even more delightful. Retreat regularly to your space.

Give thanks for the gift and the mystery of life, of your own life.

Brenda Lealman

Mark 1:9-13

There is a poem entitled 'The Journey' by the American poet, Mary Oliver, about recognition that brings a turning point in life: 'One day you finally knew / what you had to do'. But the way to living out that recognition is 'terrible': friends and family tug at your ankles, try to hold you back; and when you start on the way, it is late and a wild night, and the road is 'full of fallen branches and stones'.

Whatever Jesus' baptism meant to him, it is a turning point in his life, an affirmation of identity. Heaven opens: by a gradual or sudden process of transformation, spiritual energies take over the centre of his life. He knows what is right for him.

But he needs to absorb this knowledge, to be led towards its implications; to let it enter his heart, his guts, to let it permeate his whole being. For this he needs solitude, resting space, retreat. But find the cell you longed for, and that's when the struggle begins: torment, the voices calling you back, face to face encounters with evil . . . retreat into ourselves can take us into our darkest places.

Ask yourself questions such as the following: What am I doing with my life? Do I know what is right for me? Am I following that way, or am I held back from doing so? What am I putting at the centre of my life?

Resting places and sacred spaces   Brenda Lealman

. . . Glimpses into glory

Mark 4:35-41

Many challenging questions are asked in the Bible. For many of us the question asked here resonates with our own questioning: 'Who is this man?' And we probably go on to ask: what sort of material is this? Is it miracle, or as some commentators have suggested, parable? Whatever its nature, I suggest that the truths it conveys are the same.

The Jews were traditionally afraid of the sea, which was to them a place of chaos, of lurking monsters, a pre-creation space. When the storm comes up, the disciples are terrified and call on the sleeping Jesus (they were rowing him across the Sea of Galilee for rest and retreat), reprimanding him for not caring about their safety. They are even more terrified when Jesus rebukes (using a strong Greek word) the sea as though it is a demonic spirit, and the sea is stilled.

But control of the sea is the work of God: the voice in the storm tells Job that God is he who 'closed the gates to hold back the sea', who told the oceans: 'So far and no farther. Here your powerful waves must stop' (Job 38:11). This desperately tired, vulnerable man sleeping on a pillow can hold back the primal chaos. Hence the terror, the awe, the lack of insight. The disciples can go no further than a question: 'Who is this man?'

Creator God, mysterious, wild source of life: of stars, galaxies, of the elements, volcanoes, of my cat's playful mischief, of the colour of my hair [add your own phrases here]: help me not to reduce you to a small god who can be kept in a cupboard and brought out on special occasions.

. . . Our deepest hungers

Mark 6:30-44

Once again Jesus seeks rest in a place remote from the crowds: he and the disciples can't even find time to eat. The crowds realise what is happening and are the first to reach the lonely place where Jesus planned to rest. Despite what was probably desperate tiredness and hunger, Jesus feels pity for the people. He teaches them. He is concerned about their material needs and discomfort, and tells the disciples to feed them.

The Exodus story of the Hebrew Bible shadows this narrative. Jesus provides food, just as God fed the Israelites with manna in the wilderness (yet the disciples still fail to see who Jesus is). Exactly what happened, how the crowds were fed, is impossible to say. The point is that Jesus feeds our deepest hungers, and despite the circumstances. A wider context is evoked; a new Exodus is happening; Jesus leads to freedom, to a new land, a new life.

There is more rich imagery here. Jesus takes on the role of the missing shepherd, the one who would fulfil the role of Messiah (see Ezekiel 34:15, 23). More powerful is the imagery of the Christian eucharist. It is thought that Mark's gospel was written in the 60s CE, or as is currently more often suggested, sometime soon after 70 CE. Perhaps we have in this passage an extension of the feeding into a eucharistic meditation used by the early Christian communities.

Give thanks for occasions in your life when your needs have been provided for in astonishing ways.

Resting places and sacred spaces   Brenda Lealman

. . . Life

John 14:1-6

A key word in this passage is *monai*: dwelling places, rooms. The Greek verb *menein* means to dwell, to remain, to continue being there, to be present. The focus is not on diversity or numbers of rooms in heaven, but on the spaciousness of divine presence. It is not a place to go to physically but the here and now of life in God, in the I AM God-presence revealed in Christ.

Hodos is the Greek word for way, road, or place of passage – through a door, for instance. The emphasis seems to be on 'passage' and on the uncovering, disclosure aspects of passage into new surroundings, into a fresh situation. Relationship with Jesus, the person who embodies real life and truth, is the passage to new life and ways of being.

What follows has become the proof-text of Christian exclusivity. But is it? It is worth noting that Jesus does not claim that he is the only way to God. Rather, he is saying that for his followers life within God ('in-dwelling', a key notion in John's gospel) is to experience God as Father. It is a relationship of mutuality, in contrast, for instance, to a slave–master relationship. The idea of dying to an old way of life into a new way of being is certainly not found only in Christianity but is present throughout world religions.

Give thoughtful attention to other passages in John's gospel where dwelling/in-dwelling appears in one of its forms: John 14:10; 16, 17; 23 and 25. The climax of these passages is John 15:1-17.

Brenda Lealman

120

Resting places and sacred spaces

. . . Mystery

We descend into the deep earth; into its dank, dark spaces hollowed out of primordial rock; spaces of apparent inertia, passivity. Jesus' body lies, rests, in such a space.

John 19:38-42

Could it be that in this strange, dark space mysterious energies are at work; that the life-breath of creation is stirring? Perhaps another genesis, a new creation is waiting in the deep earth, in the dark depths of the human psyche, in the darkness between the stars. But it is not given to us to witness nor to understand what happens in the darkness. However God works, the work is secret, hidden. We are left with unfathomable mystery.

Does this descent to the bedrock of creation and of being indicate the limitless extent of God's compassion and grace? If, out of this darkness, there is to be any freeing of radiance, emergence of new being, it will be the radiance of the whole cosmos, not just that of individuals, of humankind, that is set free, redeemed.

'We are left with unfathomable mystery.' Meditate on that.

Resting places and sacred spaces   Brenda Lealman

The Jesus way

1 Seeing, touching and tasting/eating

Notes based on the New International Version by

Sibyl Ruth

Sibyl Ruth is a Quaker, though her family background is part Jewish and part Baptist. She writes poetry and helps other writers to make their work publishable. She's interested in the stories we create, and how we use words to make others believe in them.

Preparing for the week

These passages from John's gospel are about the five senses: seeing, tasting, touching and hearing. (The sense of smell is involved too, even though it's not specifically mentioned.) The stories they tell us about the life – and afterlife – of Christ are very much rooted in the everyday world. Yet these texts are also concerned with supernatural, miraculous happenings.

For the majority of each day I'm a rationalist and a sceptic. If I listen to a politician on the radio, or watch an advertisement inviting me to buy some life-changing product, I am thinking, 'Is this right. Can this be true?' This could be why I enjoy poetry and fiction so much because I can switch off the doubting part of my brain, and let myself believe the most fantastic things.

Quaker meeting houses – like other nonconformist places of worship – are plain places. There's no music, stained glass, incense, no breaking of bread or communion wine. In the UK, Quakers don't have programmed services involving sermons and prayers. Worship takes place without the physicality of singing or moving about. Yet this plainness and stillness can allow us to perceive with heightened clarity. Here the believing and doubting sides of our nature can come together.

For further thought

- Are you a sceptic and a rationalist when it comes to the miraculous? If so, why? If not, why not?
- What part do the senses play in your own prayer and tradition of worship?

Ways of seeing

John 1:43-51

As mature adults we're supposed to take time over making decisions, and to avoid altering our plans in a hurry. On his first appearance Nathanael seems to conform to this ideal. When Philip rushes up to him full of excitement, he responds with a cynical 'Nazareth! Can anything good come from there?' (verse 26). But a few lines later he's proclaiming Jesus as 'the son of God . . . the King of Israel' (verse 49).

A number of different kinds of seeing account for this change of heart. Firstly Nathanael, despite his reservations, agrees to go along to see Jesus, because that's what his friend wants him to do. Then Jesus praises Nathanael as a true Israelite, saying it's not the first time he's seen him.

It's an enormously powerful experience when someone whom we don't know well shows insight into who we are, believes in us. There's a spiralling positivity here. Jesus shows faith in Nathanael, who promptly displays readiness to recognise Christ. Nathanael is then promised 'you shall see heaven open' (verse 51).

Often we miss out on opportunities, because we're unwilling to go along and see something new, too blinkered to realise that life-changing experiences may arise in unlikely places. We need to be more ready to look for goodness in our fellow beings.

George Fox, who founded the Quaker move-ment, advised his ministers to 'walk cheerfully over the world, answering that of God in every one'.

The Jesus way   Sybil Ruth

Reach out your hand

John 20:19-31

Some Quakers are very knowledgeable about the scriptures. Others are less reliant on the Bible as a source of inspiration. At times the letter kills: we need to remain open to personal experience of the living Spirit working in the world today. George Fox asked, 'Christ saith this, and the apostle says this; but what canst thou say?' Maybe one of the advantages of *not* studying the gospels regularly is that when we return to an almost-forgotten passage, it strikes us with renewed force. This happened to me when I came back to the figure of doubting Thomas, who wants proof that the crucified Christ is – somehow – still alive. Jesus' invitation, 'Reach out your hand and put it into my side' reminds me that it is through touch that we are reassured, through physical contact that we cement our strongest relationships.

Thomas prays

I was thirsty. The tap water
that you brought me tasted like wine.
Another day, one more party.
I didn't look on it as a sign.

I saw you later in a corner
with some unwashed refugee,
the type that exaggerates. He said,
'Thanks to you, I can see.'

You demanded the impossible,
turning hunger to plenty.
But death into life? They insist
your tomb was found empty.

I will not believe this. At night
in my dreams you reach out.
My hand strays to your side.
Please let me continue to doubt.

Sybil Ruth

The Jesus way

Helping hands

John 9:1-17

For some years I had a disabling illness. I couldn't earn my living and I was dependent on others to look after me practically and emotionally. I felt on the margins of 'normal' existence, and there were times when the way I was treated by former friends and by health professionals (who should have known better) made me feel stigmatised. My life was like that of the people – the outcasts and the oppressed – with whom Christ worked.

But I suspect that for many of us, stories in which the sick are miraculously cured make difficult reading today. These days there's something uncomfortable about the notion that disability and ill health exist 'so that the work of God may be displayed' (verse 3). Nevertheless, to me there is something of enduring interest in this account of a man gaining his sight, because he is healed with a paste made from earth and spit.

I used to get asked how I'd got well again. People expected me to say it was because of some weird diet or therapy. In fact I believe it was the loving care I received from a close community that helped me recover. Often it's not some wonder drug or some exotic treatment that makes us better. It can help hugely when people do everyday things like changing sheets and putting laundry into the machine.

Sometimes we forget that the stuff of miracles is beneath our feet. And within ourselves.

The Jesus way   Sybil Ruth

Life is sweet

John 2:1-11

After a Quaker dies, a memorial Meeting for Worship will take place. Though funerals are thought of as sad events, a memorial meeting can be a joyous occasion, at which an individual's life is celebrated.

For many Christians, the narratives of the crucifixion and the resurrection will constitute the whole point of the story of Jesus. But I find it easier to feel inspired by what we are told about the *life* of Jesus.

Maybe I am drawn to the story of the wedding feast at Cana because my experience of Christianity is within the nonconformist tradition, which was closely linked with the Temperance movement. Today's Quakers are sagely advised to consider limiting their use of alcohol, even to abstain altogether. But perhaps in the pre-industrialised world of the gospels (where there were no alcopops or happy hour promotions, no problems about drink driving) everyone could simply rejoice in the appearance of quantities of fine wine – just when supplies had been running dangerously low.

Christ's miracles are extraordinarily practical. What an asset he would have been at a party! How many invitations he must have received! He may have needed to be egged on by his mother sometimes, but the man could certainly deliver … And I am reminded of Ecclesiastes 8:15:

So I commend the enjoyment of life, because nothing is better for a man under the sun than to eat and drink and be glad.

This passage resembles some Hollywood action movie. It's a crowd scene. Suddenly the main character enters and uses his strength to do something wholly unexpected. Yet in films and novels I'm nearly always bored by narratives in which one man (and it does always seem to be a male) is right, while everybody else is wrong or bad. I'm much more interested in dramas where different kinds of rightness are brought into conflict. These situations are rather closer to real life, where the choices that face us are rarely clear cut.

The people selling sacrificial animals and changing money provided what were regarded as necessary services. Like so many of us they were just doing their job, trying to making an honest living. Jesus's zeal in defence of his 'Father's house' must have been highly unwelcome. It would have seemed like fanaticism.

I think this scenario is one that keeps being re-enacted – though hopefully without so much physical damage! – in all sorts of communities. Old customs do sometimes need to be dispensed with, in order for a group to be renewed and revitalised.

But when differences of opinion occur in the temples of today, perhaps we should remember Proverbs 19:2 'It is not good to have zeal without knowledge, nor to be hasty and miss the way.'

Reflect and pray on the proverb above.

Zealous house-keeping

John 2:13-22

The Jesus way

Sybil Ruth

Glorious food

John 6:1-15

As a young woman I worked in catering for a while and I've also spent years as the person who mostly shops and cooks for the family. Money's been tight at times, and then cooking a good meal for even a couple of visitors required careful thought. My instinctive reaction to this story would be, 'Oh come on, you can't expect me to believe that!'

One of my most painful memories involves my stepson at age 11. He was nothing like the boy who offered his loaves and fishes. A typical growing child, he had no intention of sharing what was on his plate. Instead, he wolfed it down, then demanded more pasta with tomato sauce. At that moment I'd have loved to possess Christ-like powers so the empty pots could be made full again. But there was nothing left over. When he kept refusing to take no for an answer, I snapped and hurled my own helping across the room.

I can only understand this text as a metaphor for the way we somehow manage to continue loving. Feeding and giving love are intimately linked. Part of caring for my stepchildren now they are young adults involves 'stretching' meals when they – and their friends – turn up unexpectedly. I also think back to when I was pregnant. My mother was sceptical when I told her I'd be breastfeeding. 'You might not have enough milk,' she said. But miraculously, despite my baby's astonishing hunger, I did.

Pray for the grace to keep loving when your resources are depleted.

The Jesus way

2 Showing, walking and praying

Preparing for the week

This week's selection of readings appears to be very random. If I see a unity at all, it has to do with Jesus' recipe for living. This includes positive ideas such as the importance for the Christian of spiritual journeying. While on the journey we must take in what we see on the way. Then there is the state of mind we carry within us. Are we aiding or blocking Jesus' intention to share his happiness with us? We have to avoid showing off or being hooked on our possessions. We must not be power obsessed.

Each reading has several strands of thought. In every case I select one strand. If you want to select another strand and take a different path, feel free to make your own discoveries.

For further thought

- What encourages you on your Christian journey?
- Can you think of another passage in scripture or a hymn that expresses the ideas in this study?
- Try contemplation as a form of prayer. Look at a flower, a leaf, a stone, a piece of wood, for an extended period of time, keeping still and silent within.

Sunday 9 May

Notes based on the *Good As New* version by

John Henson

John Henson is a writer, conference speaker and 'Inclusive Church' promoter. He is best known for *Good As New* (O Books 2005), his radical retelling of the Christian scriptures.

Showing off or showing sense?

Matthew 23:1-12

This is what Jesus had to say about the Strict Set:

The experts in the old books and guardians of public morals who make up the Strict Set think themselves, each one, a little Moses! If you want to please them, you have to do whatever they tell you, to the letter. But I don't recommend you imitate them. . . They tie up heavy parcels which they persuade other people to stagger along with, but they wouldn't dream of carrying such weights themselves . . . They like to parade in their special clothes . . . They love to have a place among the distinguished guests on social occasions . . . It makes them feel good when people in the high street nod to them politely and say, 'Good morning, Reverend.'

Any of this ring a bell?

The author of the gospel of Matthew is more critical of the 'Strict Set' (Pharisees) than the other gospel writers. *Good As New* translates 'contextually', each statement understood in relationship with the whole passage, to catch the writer's intention. There is much irony and humour in Hebrew and Aramaic thought and expression. These words of Jesus, introducing some biting criticisms of the way the super-religious behave, is an example. Jesus ridicules those who fancy themselves law-givers like Moses, thinking themselves infallible. The rule that guides their own lives is 'Don't do as I do; do as I tell you'.

Jesus, may we spot the important person by looking among the nobodies.

John Henson

The Jesus way

'Repair the road for God; straighten out the bends!'

(verse 3)

On the way with God

We are getting used to the idea that the Christian's life is a journey. Much in the scriptures shows it is not a new idea. The idea that God likes to travel is still new to many of us. The roads have to be in good repair for God to walk on! That's not just poetry but theology! Sometimes we meet God going in our direction, sometimes in the opposite direction. But we only bump into God if we travel, not if we refuse to budge.

Mark 1:1-8

John had a simple lifestyle, wearing only a camel skin with a leather belt and eating carob nuts and tree sap.

(verse 6)

Travel is easier if we travel light. Easier to run for a bus when we have lost some weight. John kept to a meagre diet. Jesus enjoyed his food, but walked it off. Christians walk better without too many dogmas strapped to their backs and without too many platefuls of piety!

'I've dipped you in the water, but he will drench you with God's Spirit'.

(verse 8)

When people travel together, they exchange experiences. God in Jesus learns what it feels like to get wet. We find out what it means to be drenched with God's Spirit. The way to God's New World is a road we and God travel together. God gives us ideas. God hopes to get ideas from us.

Keep me travelling along with you.

The Jesus way

John Henson

Looking at the flowers

Matthew 6:25-33

Jesus was a contemplative. Like the Hebrew prophets he looked at the world about him. From what he saw he captured messages from God. Many Christians today are rediscovering the value of contemplation as part of their two-way conversation with God. The religious have a way of using stuffy language to make things difficult, so they call the wonderful experience of talking with God 'prayer'. Immediately the would-be believer is put off. Jesus never did this. He used the most ordinary, homely language to make it possible even for those who say 'I'm not religious' to have a relationship with the loving God.

Be like the wild flowers. They don't earn their living, yet they're better dressed than Solomon with all his beads and bangles! . . . It's time to stop vexing yourselves with questions like, 'Where shall we eat tonight?' Or 'Have we ordered the right wine to go with the meal?' or 'Is this dress suitable for the occasion?' . . . God loves you and knows what's best for you.

(verses 28-32)

Jesus says to us in this noisy and busy world, 'Look around you. What do you see?' An artist in the Tate Modern asks us to look at a stack of bricks. He wants us to learn to look at everything as if there is more to see than we expect. God is the supreme artist. We should visit God's picture gallery more often.

God, help us to spot something today we've never noticed before.

John Henson

The Jesus way

The ascension of Jesus is historically the point at which Jesus' friends saw him for the last time. 'Good News from Sources Close to Jesus' (John's gospel) has a different date for the receiving of the Spirit from Luke's. 'Sources' also describes the experience of parting at a different point.

A different way

John 17:6-19

'The time of parting has come. I'm coming to you, but they're staying behind'

(verse 11)

'Goodbye' to our loved ones involves a physical parting and an emotional parting, often at different times. One friend of Jesus could have experienced the sense of loss at a different point from another.

The church has dressed Ascension Day in the language of songs that accompanied the ascent up Jerusalem hill after a victory in battle. The event is decked in glory and triumph, whereas it must have been more like today's reading. Would Jesus have appreciated the power and glory reflected in so many of today's worship songs? Jesus says to God,

'I've shown what you are like to those you've entrusted to me here'

(verse 6).

The God revealed in Jesus does not like show. Jesus told his friends not to copy the worldly way of power.

'They're different, just as I'm different'

(verse 14).

'Holy' means 'different'. Perhaps one of the ways we are to be different is to avoid spiritual bullying!

Jesus, help us not to seek the defeat of our enemies, but the spread of your peace and love.

The Jesus way

John Henson

133

Help me see the way

Mark 8:27-38

Some people think Jesus was like those authoritarian 'Christian' leaders who believe they are always right. That would make the desert experience and the Gethsemane experience a farce. Jesus appreciated a group of men and women companions not as a rubber stamp to enforce his authority, but as a think tank to help him see the way forward.

When Jesus asked, 'Who do you say I am?' it was not a trick question to see who got the right answer. Jesus was looking for guidance from those who knew him best, who had seen him as a human being, not just a prophet. According to Mark, Jesus did not congratulate Rocky (Peter) for his answer; just told him to keep quiet. Rocky was not quite right. Although he said, 'You're God's Chosen' (Messiah), what he meant by that was so out of step with Jesus' thinking, he was in fact wrong and Jesus told him so: 'Get away from me! You're a bad influence' (verse 33). All the signs of this account are that Jesus' ideas were emerging gradually, bit by bit. Throughout his ministry Jesus avoided the Messianic title, 'Son of God', preferring the cryptic title 'The Complete Person' (Son of Man). For us, as for Jesus, the pathway to God goes via the perplexities of our human mind!

Help us, God, to think our way forward and to check our ideas with a lively think tank.

'I've spoken to you like this because I want to share my happiness with you'

(verse 11)

The way of happiness

John 15:9-17

At the age of 45 I had a conversion experience. It was not the classic experience some religious people urge upon us. I woke up one morning with the sunshine shining through my bedroom window. A strong voice addressed my inner ear. 'Your job as a Christian is to make other people happy. You cannot do that unless you are happy yourself. Therefore you will be a happy person.' For 40 years I had been a miserable person, capable of putting on a cheerful appearance. For the rest of my life I was to be a happy person, who would still have ups and downs, but the centre had shifted.

Making other people happy was Jesus' priority. Not convicting them of sin, or keeping them on the straight and narrow; not giving them heavy tasks that would crush them; not calling them to be depressed by every ill that blights our world or to panic over the decreasing numbers attending church.

I wonder what difference it would make if God's people were to adopt Jesus' priority? The sexuality debate would be very different.

Join me in a prayer by Ken Dodd, who sang it on stage and on television, with a feather duster in his hand:

Happiness, happiness,
The greatest gift that I possess;
I thank the Lord that I've been blessed
With more than my share of happiness.

The Jesus way   John Henson

The Jesus way

3 Living and loving

Notes based on the *Good As New* version by

John Henson

For John's biography, see p.129.

Preparing for the week

We pick up where we left off last week – with Jesus' concern for our happiness. Sometimes the Beatitudes are understood as his guidebook to the happy life. Put these sayings into practice and you will be happy. Not hilariously happy perhaps, but with some kind of mysterious inner contentment. Without being able to put our finger on it, we are instinctively unsure about this. What is happy about being poor, or persecuted or sorrow-stricken? Pie in the sky doesn't work either. How do you tell someone not to mind being in deepest distress, because it is going to be all right one day, at rainbow's end? In any case Jesus seems to be talking about *now*.

Jesus does not provide a happy drug that will take the pain and sorrow away. He is rather our companion and workmate, a source of strength and encouragement, sharing the load and the sorrows we have to bear. He gives us the vision and know-how to change the world into the place where happiness becomes an attainable goal for everyone, including ourselves. We don't do it on our own. We are part of a team, with Jesus as team leader.

For further thought

- Can you think of anything for which you can reasonably expect Jesus' 'Well done!' some day?
- Which of Jesus' first friends do you most closely identify yourself with?
- How did Jesus deal with that friend?

It is difficult to translate the word usually rendered 'blessed' or 'happy' in most translations. The Hebrew equivalent is like a hearty and sincerely meant pat on the back. I express this in *Good As New* as 'splendid are . . . ' Nicholas King, a contemporary Oxford scholar, takes the same line with 'Congratulations to . . . ' in his new translation, particularly valuable for students, published by Kevin Mayhew. We didn't collude! The Spirit makes doubly sure she gets her points across!

With apologies to those who already have their copy, I present the *Good As New* Beatitudes in full. They provide an important alternative way of understanding Jesus' intention.

Splendid!

Matthew 5:1-12

Splendid are those who take sides with the poor:
They are citizens of The Bright New World.
Splendid are those who grieve deeply over misfortunes:
The more deeply they grieve, the stronger they become.
Splendid are the gentle:
The world will be safe in their hands.
Splendid are those who have a passion for justice:
They will get things done.
Splendid are those who make allowances for others:
Allowances will be made for them.
Splendid are those who seek the best for others and not themselves:
They will have God for company.
Splendid are those who help enemies to be friends:
They will be recognized as God's true children.
Splendid are those who have a rough time of it because they stand up for what is right:
They too are citizens of The Bright New World.

Thank you Jesus, for giving us your 'Well done!' just for trying.

The Jesus way   John Henson

Priorities

Luke 14:25-33

Good translations do not translate word for word. They bridge cultures. Different cultures have different means of expression. The Hebrews enjoyed hyperbole (ridiculous exaggeration). They compared by means of contrast. For 'I prefer cake to bread' they said 'I love cake; I hate bread'. If Jesus were speaking 21st-century English he would say something like this:

'Anyone who joins my band of followers and doesn't put me before the needs of family or personal needs, isn't up to the job'

(verse 26)

It doesn't mean we abandon our families. When loyal to Jesus, the needs of our families will be seen as different. We will not give relations expensive presents instead of love, time and care. We will not bring our children up in a life of extravagance they may not be able to sustain. We will not pamper ourselves with endless things we do not need while millions are in desperate straits. In asking us to 'take up our cross' (hyperbole for most people), Jesus calls us to behave responsibly.

The words of Jesus about going to war do not mean he was advocating an arms drive so that we are adequately ready for war. Every war proves more costly than anticipated in money and lives. High towers are asking for it, as every parent with a young child and building bricks knows. They will fall down or get knocked down sooner or later. Jesus wants us to stop being so stupid!

Jesus, help us to get our priorities right.

'Teacher, we saw someone healing people by using your name, and we tried to stop him because he's not a member of our team.'

(verse 38)

Abuse

'Lightning' (John), true to his nickname, was all too keen to come down on others! Jesus is all for a variety of approach and a spreading of the load, but when one sort of Christian wants others off the pitch, Jesus is not pleased.

Mark 9:38-50

'You'd be better off being thrown into the sea with a big stone round your neck!'

(verse 42).

Lightning was behaving like the 'Strict Set' who didn't believe it should be easy for people to relate to God. For some it is not enough to be a friend of Jesus. Your theology and morals must be 'sound'. Jesus, half smiling, half angry, says,

'If you think it's a good thing for others to make their way in the faith weighted with obstacles, why don't you go for a swim with a brick round your neck and see what it feels like?!'

Hebrew humour! The Strict Set told people not to touch this, go there, or look at that. Jesus paints a hilarious picture! All those 'sound' people limping into God's New World, with one eye, one hand and one foot. We are meant to laugh and cry at the same time!

The words of Jesus do not just apply to sexual abuse. There are people today in psychiatric units as a result of abuse from other Christians.

Jesus, teach us your gentleness.

The Jesus way   John Henson

Moving on

Mark 1:29-39

I have been there many times – the visiting preacher to a warm and friendly church. Getting through the service to the satisfaction of most, I then looked forward to the food prepared by my hosts for the day. It happens less often nowadays. I hope Christians of the twenty-first century will rediscover the joy of hospitality central to the first Christians. Rocky's house was not a poor fisherman's cottage – he and Andrew owned a thriving business. It was one storey, but large enough to serve as a meeting place. The hostess, Rocky's mother-in-law, had a one-day 'flu. Thanks to Jesus she was able to rise to the occasion.

The townsfolk, afraid to approach for healing on the sabbath, waited until sundown. Then, by torchlight, Jesus healed the sick, one by one. All in all a tiring but satisfying day. What lovely folk the locals were!

In the morning Jesus was missing. He was talking with God down on the beach or up in the hills. The friends could not understand. Jesus was neglecting his fans. He had been a hit. Nahum town was the place to set up his seat. People would come for miles around to hear Jesus the Prophet. But Jesus insisted on moving on. Nahum town was too easy. He aimed to reach a wider world.

Where is our place of comfort? Where are we afraid to go? Jesus calls his friends to move on!

Jesus, save me from ever becoming a comfortable Christian.

This is one of the most misunderstood passages of scripture, largely because memorable snatches are quoted out of context. Taking the words 'You must be born again' out of context has led some Christians to insist on a prescribed path to salvation for everyone – their path! The words in context were spoken to Nick and his co-religionists, the 'Strict Set' (Pharisees) (verse 1). Nowhere in scripture are the words prescribed for anyone else, though Paul, also a Pharisee, went through the process on the Damascus Road.

The Strict Set's problem was that they were so narrow-minded and bigotted that nothing short of a totally new way of looking at things would do. Jesus always geared his advice to the person, not to textbook theology. One of the new things Nick would have to learn as a follower of Jesus was how to treat people as people, not as potential clones of himself.

Jesus says,

'Like the wind, the Spirit blows where she chooses, and like the wind, you hear the sound she makes, but you don't know where she's coming from or where she's going'

(verse 8).

The Spirit brings an air of freedom. If you do not become a follower of Jesus in freedom, and if you do not feel more free as a Christian than you did before, then there is something wrong. A complete revolution may not be necessary in your case. But you may need to consider a change of direction.

Jesus, set me free.

Start again?

John 3:4-21

The Jesus way   John Henson

Body language

Acts 2:37-47

The first followers of Jesus expressed their new faith through body language, in two ways that were to become part of the life of Christians for all time. Some had been friends of John the Dipper; Jesus had been dipped in the Jordan. It seemed a good way to ask people to sign on. Dipping was a good leveller. Not all could give a testimony. All could queue for a quick wash. Later Christians were to get negative thoughts about their bodies, influenced by the Gnostic heresy that said the body was evil, the spirit good. Christians became ashamed of their sexual feelings. Two thousand years of negativity is taking a long and painful process to overcome. We must find healing from our hang-ups if we are to learn the ways of love.

Jesus was a touchy-feely person. He also loved his food. The times Jesus and his male and female friends sat round a table were the high points of their friendship. So also in the Christian community after Pentecost.

The Church has formalised these times of communion and made them deeply serious. How many would say after a service of Holy Communion, 'I enjoyed the food!'? We have restricted the body language and restricted the experience. Something else to put right in the twenty-first century! (See John Henson's book *Other Communions of Jesus*, O Books 2006).

Thank you, God, for my body. Help me use it to express your love.

Romans 1–8

1 Good news for sinners

Notes based on the New Revised Standard Version by **Chris Budden**

Preparing for the week

We are going to consider Romans for four weeks. It is one of the most influential pieces of writing in the Bible. Paul is writing to a Christian community that he did not found and had not, at the time of writing, had a chance to visit. Paul writes to the community – which was most likely made up of Jews and gentiles – to introduce himself. He wants to allay any fears they may have that he is too radical, a bit unorthodox, or may cause strife among them. Remember, this is a community that has already had a lot of trouble with the political authorities.

Much of the letter is written as if he is in dialogue with a fellow Jew. In this dialogue he debates the benefits of the Jewish faith and the privileges that pertain to God's chosen people. In the face of the impending judgement of God, Paul has a clear message: all have sinned and all who are saved will be saved by the grace of God received through faith. Law, good works or circumcision will not do: only faith in response to grace.

Chris Budden is a parish minister of the Uniting Church in Australia. He is married to Wendy. Chris has a particular interest in exploring the question of why God actually matters, how it is that Jesus brings real *life*, and what it means for Australian Christians to acknowledge that they live on indigenous land.

For further thought

- Do you begin the reading of Romans with excitement or trepidation?
- Consider the impact of this epistle upon your own church tradition – how has it shaped the theology and practice of your church?
- Pray for new insights and challenges as you embark upon this challenging text.

Credentials established and beliefs shared

Romans 1:1-7

Paul begins by establishing his credentials – a servant of Christ, called to be an apostle, set apart for the gospel, and given particular responsibility among the gentiles (verse 5). This gospel that has been entrusted to him was promised in advance through prophets in scripture. It is about Jesus, who as a human being is descendent from Abraham, and was declared Son of God according to the Spirit through the resurrection (verse 4).

A key part of the letter is the way it more clearly defines the place of the gentiles in God's plan. This is a crucial issue. Would there be first- and second-class Christians in the church? Would some have greater privileges? Would gentiles have to stop being gentiles? Fortunately for us, the answer is 'no'.

In this letter Paul builds on the beliefs he shares with the Romans, and expounds the gospel in that framework. They shared a monotheistic belief, a view of Israel as a chosen people, the authority of scripture, promises made to the ancestors, and a sense of the world that is marked by opposing forces (God and Satan), distinctive ages, and an immanent act of judgement and salvation. They shared a belief in Christ's atoning death, the power of the Spirit, the need for a life lived 'in Christ' and conformed to Christ, and the role of the apostles. The central issue is impending judgement and how they could achieve righteousness.

How would you introduce yourself if you were writing to a church to share the gospel?

Pray for those who care for and nurture local churches.

Paul feels constrained to explain why he has not visited Rome. He is now intending to go to Rome, but it will be on the way to somewhere else (Spain). He doesn't want the people in Rome to get the news of his visit and say 'Oh, we are not that important to Paul. He is just stopping off here on the way to somewhere more important'. He wants them to know that this visit really is the fulfilment of a long held desire and intention to visit (verses 9-10), and that he has not visited before because something has always prevented him (verse 13). And he wants them to know that he has good reasons for coming to see them (verses 11-17).

Verses 16 and 17 are, of course, a summary or statement of the theme of the entire letter: the gospel, the good news of Jesus Christ, is the power of God leading to salvation (verse 16), which is claimed by those who have faith, whether they be Jews or gentiles. The gospel is open to all people because it is claimed not by law but by faith. Paul provides a great example for us to really love and care for the people of the church, and to pray for other churches and other Christian communities and not just our own.

If you wanted to share the gospel with another person, how would you summarise it in a sentence or two?

Pray for the worldwide church that it continue to learn that it lives by grace and not its own achievements.

Visiting to share the gospel

Romans 1:8-17

No excuses for ignorance

Romans 1:18-27

How and where is God to be known? The traditional answers are: in the scriptures, in the life and teaching of the church, in the lives of the least, and in the Holy Spirit. In this passage Paul is concerned with impending judgement, and with the claim that such judgement is unfair because people have not had a chance to know God. Paul says that this is not so, for God has made himself known through the world which God has created. God reveals herself in the creation.

Paul is not suggesting that God is known in nature, but in the created world, in God's handiwork. We know from our own experience that, even though there is a chance for misunderstanding, words are a reliable way of understanding another person. Actions are a less clear revelation, because they are more ambiguous and unclear than words. Paul says that while knowledge obtained from the created world may not be perfect, and certainly is not knowledge leading to salvation, it does leave people without excuse. The logic of Paul's argument is that people ignored what they should have known, refused to acknowledge God, and decided in their pride to make idols which had none of the glory of the invisible God (verse 22). Because they worshipped the creature they lost their real life (which can only be found in God).

What do you learn about God from the created world? How does that fit with the knowledge you have through the person of Jesus?

Pray for those who have tried to banish God from the world, that God's light might still break in.

Paul continues with the point that people could know God but they have turned aside. And because they exchanged God for idols they exchanged their real human nature for a false one. Paul means more than that they refused to acknowledge God's existence or attributes. He means that they had tried God out, found the experience less than helpful, and decided they did not need a deep relationship with God. They refused that which made them human in the first place.

People fall into delusion and foolishness when they refuse to know and relate to God. Paul doesn't believe in the sincere atheist, but follows the psalmist who claimed that the fool says there is no God (Psalm 14:1). The passage seems to suggest that it is God who leads them into depraved behaviour. I think it is more that God allows them to follow their own choices until the right time.

It is easy to claim we know God, at least to the extent that we acknowledge God, but not to live by that belief. We can confess the name of Jesus and yet still act as if our lives are not shaped by that relationship. That is one of the reasons we need Christian friends and the church: to speak to us of self-delusion, foolishness of mind, pride and all that takes us from God.

In what area of your life are you most tempted to say the right words, and make the right confessions, but to act wrongly?

Pray that you will have good friends who will honestly keep you on the path of discipleship.

Whose image do we really reflect?

Romans 1:28-32

Faith is also about good deeds

Romans 2:1-11

In the previous verses at the end of chapter one, we have a list of the wickedness of those who deny God. How easy it is when we hear of the wickedness of others to take pride in our own righteousness, and to make easy judgement of their lives! In the first three chapters Paul has a singular concern – to exclude the possibility that people will claim righteousness apart from the righteousness of God claimed through faith. His message is simple: the law that you cling to will not make you righteous, and nor will being God's chosen people. God is always impartial and judgement is always according to each person's deeds.

This seems a little contradictory, doesn't it? First Paul says we are made righteous by God, a righteousness we claim by faith. Then he says all people are judged according to their deeds. The contradiction is more apparent than real. We tend to drive a wedge between faith and works that actually does not exist. Faith for Paul is primarily an act of discipleship. The passage reminds us that because we are God's special people, because we can name the name of Jesus, does not mean that we automatically get God's favourable treatment and can poke fun at others. This is not about confessing Jesus as Lord with our lips, but doing the will of the Father (Matthew 7:21).

What do you mean when you talk about your 'faith'? When you invite people to faith in Jesus are you asking them to confess certain truths or to adopt a particular, discipleship-forming lifestyle?

Pray that God will help you deal with any tendency to self-righteousness.

In verse 12 Paul says that possession or non-possession of the law is irrelevant to God's impending judgement. All that matters is whether people have been doers of God's desire. Paul says that the sole criterion of God's judgement is our performance. He seems to be saying that in principle it is possible for some people to be so good that they will be accepted by God. While he believes that it is in principle possible, he does not believe that in fact it is possible. No one can live well enough. The only performance that can earn approval from God is that of Jesus Christ, claimed by us through faith.

Verses 14-15 are what a modern writer might put in a footnote, and the real flow is from verse 13 'doers of the law will be justified' to verse 16 'on the day of judgment'. In this footnote Paul says that the gentiles will know what to do because it is written in their hearts, and their consciences witness to what they should do. Paul clearly does not mean all gentiles, or even that the few who act well obey all the law. His point is simply that the righteous behaviour of a few gentiles stands as a criticism of the claim that the law is the sole moral grounds for right behaviour.

In what ways is your daily life a reflection of your wish to be a 'doer of God's desire'?

Pray that the people in your local church will not only confess faith in Jesus but actually act as disciples.

In principle we can earn our righteousness

Romans 2:12-16

Romans 1–8

2 All have sinned and are now justified

Notes based on the New Revised Standard Version by

Chris Budden

For Chris's biography, see p.143.

Preparing for the week

In this week's readings Paul continues to build on his central theme – we cannot earn our righteousness before God. The law will not save, nor will external signs of a good life. In reality all are under the power of sin, but sin does not have the last word. God is faithful to all people, who are saved by God as they respond in faith (trust and obedience) to what God has done in Christ. God reveals God's righteousness not by punishment and judgement as one might expect, but by salvation offered to all people. This inclusive message is the good news we have for the world. This is a deeply challenging message for the church which is always tempted to overlay the gift of God's love and grace with another set of requirements. We dole out the good news as if it were something we owned, when we are called to share it with the same joy and surprise with which we received it.

For further thought

- In what ways has your church denomination or tradition been tempted to overlay the inclusive gospel with its own set of demands or requirements?

- Who are the people in your own context most in need of hearing the amazing gospel of God's inclusive grace?

- How can you share this good news with others?

Claiming false privileges

Romans 2:17-24

This passage is arranged in three sections, each of which names the dangers of relying on the law. Verses 17-18 name the privileges that are claimed by those who are Jews. We need to be careful in the light of the church's history with the Jewish community that we don't misunderstand Paul at this point. Paul is not criticising people because of their race or religious affiliation. He himself is a Jew. His concern, as will become clearer in later verses, is with those who rest their confidence in the law and refuse the gift of God's grace in Christ. The privileges Paul names are being a Jew (i.e. belonging to God's covenant people), having the law, knowing God's will, and knowing what is essential in life. Verses 19-20 list the roles that people take on because of their privileges – guide, light, instructor, teacher and possessor of the truth of the law. Verses 21-23 list the things that the people tell others not to do, yet which they do themselves. The passage finishes with a quote from scripture (Isaiah 52:5) that makes the harsh judgement that such behaviour is one of the reasons why God's name is held in such disrespect among the gentiles.

As Christians we claim to know the key to life. The danger is always that what we actually do leads people to despise Christ.

In what areas of your church's life are you in danger of allowing people an excuse to despise Christ, and what can you do about that?

Pray that the church in your area will act in ways that attract people to Christ.

Chris Budden

External signs are of no value

Romans 2:25 – 3:8

Paul continues his affirmation that everything rests on the demand that we act faithfully and, failing that, need the grace of God for salvation. In this passage he makes the point in regard to circumcision. External signs are of no value apart from right action. This is a difficult passage. At first sight verses 28-29 seem viciously anti-Jewish, and appear to destroy Jewish identity. He appears to destroy the relationship between the mark of circumcision and community identity, and to insist that the 'real Jew' is actually a Christian. It is important that we understand that Paul writes as if he had a dialogue partner in the Jewish community. So, Paul is not making an accusation about Jewish people, but is having an in-house conversation between himself and a fellow-member of that community.

The problem of Jewish identity is an acute one for Paul. He agonises over the question of what will happen to the bulk of Israel that has not recognised Jesus. He will return to this issue in chapters 9–11. The real issue in our present passage is God's faithfulness and righteousness. The faithlessness of the few does not nullify God's faithfulness. Indeed, in the light of our injustice and our falsehood, God's justice and truthfulness are seen the more clearly, though we should not use this as an excuse to sin.

Write a prayer in which you acknowledge God's faithfulness and righteousness in your life.

Pray that the church will be careful in its relationship with the Jewish community in the country where you live.

Chris Budden

Romans 1–8

The reality of sin and evil

Romans 3:9-20

Can anyone claim to be better off than others? Not at all, for all are under the power of sin. In verses 10-18 Paul provides a quite unparalleled and lengthy set of quotations from scripture to support his point. It is a dire account of human infidelity and unrighteousness. There is real evil in the world, and those who know the scriptures should not be surprised about that. People sometimes say that there is enough difficulty in life without stressing evil. That is why Christians begin with grace and forgiveness. Evil is real but does not have the last word.

In verses 19-20 Paul continues his insistence that all people are unrighteous. No person will be able to provide excuse for their behaviour. Sometimes Christians say that the purpose of the law must be to remind us of our sin. Verse 20 seems to support this claim, but there are two things that need to be said. First, the purpose of the law is to enable people to be obedient to God. It becomes a reminder of sin when we fail to obey it. Second the 'knowledge of sin' referred to in verse 20 is not simply information about what is wrong. Rather, the law reminds people that wrong acts are not simply moral transgressions but are contrary to the desire and will of God. They are sin.

What does your church do to name evil in your community, without being self-righteous and acting as if you have no sin?

Pray that the church will not co-operate with evil either by action or silence.

Romans 1–8   Chris Budden

The righteousness that saves

Romans 3:21-31

Paul has been building a picture of human failure and of God's impending judgement that could, one might think, lead to despair. The question before Paul is: if all are sinful, how can God's saving promises to Israel be realised and God still be righteous? Must God simply punish and destroy? No! Wrath is not God's final word.

There is a wonderful shift here in the way the reader is to understand the righteousness of God. Before Christ it was assumed that the only way the righteousness of God could be protected would be by God's righteous judgement of the world. In Christ, though, God displays God's righteousness in a way that saves. God's righteousness is found in God's faithfulness to a sinful world, and in the way in which Christ deals with sin.

All have sinned, and all deserve judgement. The great news about God's salvation is that it applies equally to all people, for it is based on faith. Human life depends on a relationship with God, and God has taken the steps to restore the relationship, not simply by forgiving our sin but by dealing with it in Christ. What an extraordinarily liberating message, one that takes away any pretence of righteousness on our behalf, or any ability to look down on others! We can only be grateful for God's grace, and seek to share the news with others.

Think of a person you do not like, who may even be your enemy. Write a prayer that asks for their salvation, for new life in Christ and for God's blessing.

Pray that your local congregation will grow increasingly open to welcome every single person into its life and into God's salvation.

Chris Budden

In this chapter Paul continues with his imaginary dialogue and allows his gentile audience to overhear an important conversation about Abraham. Paul has made the point that the law does not save, and that Jew and gentile are treated the same by God. But some would object: 'What about our ancestor Abraham? Surely as his descendants we can claim privilege?' It is important to remember how central Abraham was (and still is) to Jewish identity and hope for the future. His response to God, the choices he made, and the promises he received determined the shape of the nation. He is not only an ancestor, but one whose choices have determined people's present lives as his descendants.

In Paul's day a great deal of emphasis was placed on Abraham as an example of obedience. What he did was considered to be an act that won blessing for him and the nation. Paul, though, seeks to show that scripture actually portrays Abraham as a person of faith. And it was this faith which put him right with God and provided the foundation for God's promises. As a great person of faith, and not works, Abraham is not just the father of Israel but of all believers. Paul wants his readers to know that Abraham is an example of the pattern of people declared righteous through faith which is found throughout the scriptures.

Who are the people in your local congregation who are examples of faith? What can you do to honour them?

Give thanks for all the ancestors of our faith who provided us with great examples of faithful and courageous living.

Abraham is the father of all who believe

Romans 4:1-12

Anguish and challenge and wonderful grace

Romans 4:13-25

Paul's letter must have caused deep anguish and extraordinary joy. One can only imagine the struggle of the Jewish Christians as they sought to understand their new identity in Christ, and what Paul was saying to them about righteousness through faith. Where is the security when there is no law, and how do you change generations of understanding? This is the struggle of the present church as we face an enormously different world and try to witness faithfully in new situations. Imagine, also, the joy of the gentiles who heard Paul speak of their place in the purposes of God, equal children of Abraham through faith. This, too, is a challenge for us. Too often we forget that we belong to the church because of the grace of God expressed through the death and resurrection of Christ. We turn faith into a good work, rather than seeing faith as what God gracefully draws forth from us. The act of faith is always somehow surprising, and we should with humility praise God for God's grace. Abraham's faith remains for us a great example. In human terms the promise of God that he will be the father of nations (verse 17) is ridiculous, but Abraham trusts God. Surely this is what faith is about: not just words but real trust and acting on what we claim to be true.

How does your life as a disciple of Jesus continue to challenge your national identity and place in the wider community?

Pray that God will strengthen your faith, and give you the ability to trust as Abraham and Sarah did.

Introduce a friend to

Light for our path 2010 *or* *Words* for today ■■■■2010

For this year's books, send us just £3.00 per book (including postage), together with your friend's name and address, and we will do the rest.

(This offer is only available in the UK, after 1 June 2010. Subject to availability.)

 **IBRA**
International Bible Reading Association

Order through your IBRA representative, or from the UK address below.

Do you know someone who has difficulty reading *Words for Today*?

Light for our Path and *Words for Today* are both available to UK readers on cassette.

For the same price as the print edition, you can subscribe and receive the notes on cassette each month, through Galloways Trust for the Blind.

Please contact the IBRA office for more details:

International Bible Reading Association
1020 Bristol Road, Selly Oak, Birmingham B29 6LB

0121 472 4242

sales@christianeducation.org.uk

IBRA International Appeal

Imagine the only book you have to help you read the Bible is in French (or if you're a French speaker, try Tagalog!). Maybe you can understand bits of it, but imagine your joy when you discover someone has translated it into English for you!

Hundreds of thousands of people around the world experience similar joy when they discover the IBRA books and readings lists have been translated into their language. And this is all through the generosity of IBRA readers.

Each year, the IBRA International Fund provides funds for local groups to translate, print and distribute IBRA Bible notes and reading lists. Last year more than 68 000 people in eleven different countries received copies of the IBRA books which had been translated, printed and distributed by IBRA partners. The reading list was also translated into French, Spanish, Telugu (India), Tokelau (Samoa) and several Congolese languages, enabling 250 000 people to receive them in a language useful to them.

The funds are given exclusively by IBRA readers like you, who give generously towards the fund, raising over £20 000 each year. With your gift, more people will be able to experience the joy of reading the Bible using notes or a list of readings in a familiar language.

Please consider either giving for the first time, or increasing your donation this year. You can donate using the envelope which is part of the leaflet insert that came with this book, or add your donation to your order for next year's books.

Thank you!

International Bible Reading Association
1020 Bristol Road
Selly Oak
Birmingham
B29 6LB
Tel. 0121 472 4242

Romans 1–8

3 We have peace with God

Notes based on the New Revised Standard Version by **Helen Stanton**

Preparing for the week

Chapter 7 of Romans is not easy. The rhetorical style that Paul adopts to press his argument can prove awkward and seem overly repetitive to a modern audience. The context for which Paul was writing has many resonances with our own age, however. Writing shortly before the time of Nero's persecution, Christians had already made themselves *persona non grata*, for in becoming members of the church they had put themselves outside the hierarchical code of honour that ruled Roman society. It is believed that very many Christians were to be found in two of the most unpleasant slums of Rome. In this situation Paul makes it clear that all honour comes from God, that the worth of a human being is established through God's love, and not by any other means.

This chapter also sets out some of Paul's richest doctrinal thinking. In it he states clearly that the life and death of Christ Jesus has radically altered the status of the world. Life has triumphed over death, and although this triumph is not yet wholly achieved, everything has changed. The same is true of the life of Christians. They too are free from the hegemony of sin, and though they continue to commit sins, they too will in due course enter wholly into the life of God.

An Anglican laywoman, Helen has worked for Christian Aid; in university chaplaincy; and in promoting social justice and responsibility. In recent years her work has focused on training people for ordained and lay ministries. She currently lives with the only Anglican Poor Clares in the world, in Oxfordshire.

For further thought

- What difference does it make to your understanding of Romans to imagine that the readers lived in the slums?

- What does it mean to you to be free from the hegemony of sin?

Self-confidence in God

Romans 5:1-11

In what do we ground our dignity, our sense of worth, our value? Though it has sometimes seemed that the church has tried to undermine any confidence we may have, Paul's response is clear. However much Christians are oppressed and devalued, there is the fundamental certainty of God's love. Through the life and death of Jesus Christ we are made one with God, and so not only have we no grounds for asserting our superiority, but we also have no need to bolster ourselves by reference to false gods – money, success, social standing, even virtue. By the grace of God we can all stand up straight and take pride in ourselves, for whatever else we are, we are loved extravagantly by God.

Yet these verses are problematic. Can Paul really be suggesting that suffering is good for us? Suffering often undermines faith and virtue rather than strengthening them. What Paul seems to have in mind here is the suffering of the martyrs and the type of suffering at the heart of the Trinity, freely chosen for love of humankind. This witness against materialism and violence may give us hope.

What sense can we make of the phrase 'the wrath of God' in the light of what we know of God in Jesus Christ?

Pray for those who suffer from the violence and evil of this world and for those whose faithfulness to the gospel is the source of their suffering.

In these verses Eve doesn't get a mention. Paul's typology, that parallels one man (Adam) with one man (Jesus Christ), leaves out entirely any suggestion that it was the first woman who caused the first man to sin. The blaming of Eve for the fall, which some later theologians developed into a belief that women were especially culpable for leading men astray, finds no place in Romans!

The age of grace is here to stay

Romans 5:12-23

It is not sin, however, that is the main focus of these verses. Rather, Paul uses the Adam/ Christ typology to emphasise the radical in-breaking of God's reign of grace. If the time of the first Adam is characterised by sin, disobedience, judgement and condemnation, the second Adam (Jesus Christ) overthrows the power of that time. Instead he ushers in a time of abundant life, righteousness, justification. And all this as free gift! The age of sin has ended, the life and death of Jesus Christ moves humanity to the age of grace. This is the kingdom of God (or heaven) of the synoptic gospels. This second Adam affects life for all, and for all time.

Where in the life of your community or society do you see signs of the age of grace?

God, our Creator and Redeemer, you have set us free from the power of sin and death. Fill us with your Spirit, that we may be agents of your new age of grace in your world today.

Yet we go on sinning . . .

Romans 6:1-14

A rabbi welcomed into his study a member of his congregation: 'The Messiah has come!' said the man, excitedly. The rabbi looked out of his window and saw a cat chasing a bird. 'No', said the Rabbi, 'When the Messiah comes, there will be peace in all creation.'

The new age of God's rule of grace has indeed come. We have passed from death to life. The trouble is that we do not live as if we are under the aegis of grace. As individuals we sometimes act unlovingly, the church itself has been guilty of great violence in its history, and when we look at the world, peace and harmony do not seem to reign.

Paul begins to answer these difficult questions. First, he dismisses those who suggest they should sin more so that God's forgiveness can be shown in all its graciousness. He then strongly asserts that through baptism we participate in the new age, we are set free from sin, but our formation is not yet complete. God's grace continues in us, transforming our lives so that they are more and more congruent with the life of God's reign.

How can I co-operate with God as God seeks to transform me, and the society in which I live?

God, whose reign is known in peace and justice, forgive us and renew us, that we may share in your work of transformation, and embody your steadfast love.

Alison Swinfen says, of the Iona Community Rule: 'It is not so much that I keep the rule, it is rather that the rule keeps me.'

Again Paul seems to be arguing with an adversary: this time making it clear that sin continues to matter under the rule of grace, no one should pretend otherwise. But although sin continues, something very real has happened at the heart of things. Objectively, ontologically, the dominion of death is over and that of life is begun. We may sin, the church may be overcome by the values of the world sometimes, the world may be in a violent mess, but the life and death of Jesus Christ means there is no going back. It is in this context that Paul writes of slavery. What Christ has done for us is ineradicable; we have become 'trapped' in the age of freedom and love. We have crossed the border from one realm to another, and in this crossing we are so changed that we cannot return. We have become alien beings in relation to that old realm: we can no longer breathe its air.

How far is Alison Swinfen right that the 'rules' of the kingdom of God keep us? Can you see that process in your own life and that of your community?

God of life, Companion on our journey, help us to embrace the realm to which you bring us, and to endure until its life is made complete.

Enslaved in freedom

Romans 6:15-23

What purpose the law?

Romans 7:1-12

Paul's relationship with the law is often seen as ambiguous, and throughout the centuries the relationship between the Hebrew scriptures and the Christian faith has been contentious. The second-century heretic Marcion even claimed that the God of the Hebrew scriptures was not the same as the Christian God. But orthodox Christianity has never allowed such a distinction, and Paul makes his position quite clear too. The function of the law for Paul is to make transparent the nature of sin, and make human beings conscious of it. Self-deception about the very real evils of our world, and the sins of our individual lives, is exposed through the lens of the law.

Christians today are often bewildered by books of the law like Leviticus. What is contained in such books may be culturally and historically conditioned, and no longer prescriptive for those who inhabit the age of grace. Yet there may be something helpful in recognising that God is interested in the minutiae of our lives – what we eat and drink – to say nothing of how societies are organised to care for poor people. Perhaps we are called to pay attention to whether our food is fairly traded and whether the animals we eat are kept and slaughtered in a humane way.

In what other areas of the minutiae of our lives might God be interested?

Pray for respect between the faiths, especially those which share tradition: Judaism, Christianity and Islam.

Flesh versus spirit?

Romans 7:13-20

Bible study usually asks, 'what do these verses mean?' In these particular verses commentators also ask questions about the authority of what seems to be said. Is Paul setting up a dichotomy between flesh and spirit here? And if so, is the church bound by it? Certainly Paul does not always use 'flesh' (*sarx* in Greek) in a negative way, but here flesh and spirit do seem to be set up in opposition to one another, the former associated with sin, the latter with grace. This kind of opposition was common in the Greek world of the New Testament and is still prevalent today.

Indeed, dualisms have been used to oppress individuals and peoples for centuries. The powerful have associated themselves with all that is spirit, light, white, good. And the same powerful people have named those they oppress as flesh, dark, black, bad. Not least women were associated with flesh because of menstruation and childbirth, and were devalued and excluded for centuries as a result. Yet Psalm 139 says 'The darkness and the light are both alike to you', and surely the incarnation, which unites the fully human and fully divine, calls dualism into question?

How should we deal with Bible verses that seem to support the dominion of sin rather than that of grace?

Creator God, who declared the whole creation good, give us grace to worship you with body, mind and spirit, that our service may reflect your unity in Trinity.

Romans 1–8   Helen Stanton

Romans 1–8

4 Life in the Spirit

Sunday 13 June

Notes based on the New Revised Standard Version by **Helen Stanton**

For Helen's biography, see p.159.

Preparing for the week

Chapter 8 of Romans focuses on the work of the Holy Spirit in effecting the process of the transformation of the whole of creation from death to life. What seemed impossible in chapter 7 – the reality of freedom from sin – is made possible as human beings orientate themselves to the Spirit. As they do this the Spirit acts to bring about a level of intimacy with God that is comparable to the relationships of the Trinity – though Paul doesn't put it quite like that. And this work of the Spirit is not just for humanity – the whole of God's creation is to be redeemed though the Spirit's work. Finally Paul abandons all sense of waiting for the fulfilment of the new age, and asserts the overwhelmingly extravagant nature of God's love from which nothing can separate us – here and now.

For further thought

- Reflect on the fact that we are invited into intimacy with God – the same intimacy as that enjoyed by the Trinity!

- How can we translate into action the good news of redemption for the whole creation? In what ways are you or your community involved in working out this redemption?

No plaster saints!

Romans 7:21-25

The final verses of chapter 7, though still undergirded by the influences of dualism, perhaps show Paul at his most human. Biblical commentators disagree as to whether Paul has been referring to his own experience before he met the risen Christ in this chapter when he writes of 'I'. Generally it seems to be agreed now that Paul uses 'I' to refer to all of us: humanity in general. But verse 24 does seem to point to something very personal, and perhaps offers us a glimpse of Paul's own anguish and impatience with the divided state of humanity in which he shares. And though he asserts that Christ has indeed rescued him, his somewhat less emotional assessment in verse 25b suggests that Paul goes on living with a tension that is not likely to be resolved in this life. Paul has not become someone he is not: the caricature of a saint, peaceful and even-tempered. Paul's passion and sometimes anger – with himself and others – is something that emerges in all his letters, and that God uses for the promotion of the new life in Christ Jesus.

What aspects of your personality cause you anguish and frustration? Can you glimpse ways in which God can and does use these characteristics creatively?

God of tenderness and compassion, look with mercy on the exasperating aspects of our lives and world. Give us patience with ourselves and others, and courage to be open to your transforming love.

Romans 1–8   Helen Stanton

The Spirit gives us life

Romans 8:1-11

Chapter 8 begins with one of Paul's great statements of confidence in God – all that is redolent of death is overcome and we are brought to life through God's Spirit. The Spirit of God enables us to grasp the life that Christ has achieved for all the world, and it is the presence of the Spirit that makes it clear that we belong to Christ and his kingdom. That presence means that we do not have to make superhuman efforts (and fail!) to be good enough Christians, or strive to achieve social status. All we need is to take the step of being open to the work of God's transforming Spirit in us; to set our minds, as Paul writes, on all that expresses the life-giving Spirit.

One of the most joyous celebrations of the eucharist I have ever attended was in El Salvador during the civil war there. Surrounded by soldiers pointing weapons at the congregation, and buzzed by helicopters, the people celebrated their rebuilding of a village that had been destroyed by bombing some years earlier. Despite the continuing harassment they experienced, these people were able to express with great joy the new life God was giving them.

How might it be possible to turn our minds to all that is life-giving while praying in solidarity with those who endure what is of death?

Pray for communities who are most in need of God's life.

Paul begins these verses with a warning not to be complacent. We have to keep alive to the Spirit of life, and act accordingly, in order to enter into the fulfilment of God's life. Although Christ has changed everything irrevocably, we must continue to appropriate his new life in our lives. When we do so, however, we become powerfully identified with Christ: adopted sons and daughters alongside the one who was Son from the beginning.

A warning and a promise

Romans 8:12-17

This is an insight that the theologians of the Eastern Churches have taken especially seriously, developing an understanding of the work of Christ in which he takes on our humanity in order that we might take on the life of God. Gregory of Nazianzus wrote, 'What is not assumed is not healed (saved)', suggesting that by entering into (assuming) our life, Christ enabled us to be healed (saved). Paul in these verses describes the action of the Spirit in this process, enabling us to address God as Jesus did – as our 'Abba' – and entering as it were into Christ's sufferings with the promise of his resurrection life.

Jesus addressed the first person of the Trinity with enormous intimacy, as well as with great reverence. How might we enable God to develop this intimate relationship with and in us?

Christ our brother, you lead us on the path to freedom.
Inspire us with your Spirit that we may accept the disciplines of your way, and come to share your glory.

The labour pains of all creation

Romans 8:18-25

The theme of waiting is significant again in these verses, but the metaphor Paul uses is not at all passive. The birth of a child, visceral in the extreme, and often involving extraordinary pain and the bloody rupture of a mother's body, provides an image of waiting that is shocking in its demands – for in order to give life, the mother must risk her own life. Yet this, writes Paul, is the sort of waiting to which all Christians are called. And not just Christians – for here Paul recognises that it is the whole of creation that participates in the sufferings of Christ that lead to resurrection.

These verses perhaps refer to Genesis 1, and they can also be seen as echoing God's covenant with all living things in Genesis 9 where it is not just to humanity that God promises to withhold death, but the whole of creation. As the abuse of our planet, often through human greed, becomes more and more apparent today, these verses are especially important.

Sallie McFague (in *Models of God*, SCM 1987) and Grace Jantzen (in *Becoming Divine*, Manchester University Press 1998) are two recent theologians who have both explored the metaphor of the earth as God's body. They suggest that although the incarnation uniquely embodied God's love, that love is also seen in all God's creation.

If we took this metaphor (the earth as God's body) seriously, how might it affect our relationship with the earth?

Give thanks for the ways in which you perceive God's love embodied in creation.

'The interrogation of silence'

Romans 8:26-30

The phrase I have chosen for today's title, from George Mackay Brown, seem apt here. In so much of our praying words fail us: perhaps when we are overwhelmed by God's love and grace, and perhaps when the sufferings of the world just don't make sense. Like the psalmists, we cry out to God in anger and incomprehension, and we may literally groan, unable to say any more or take any more. The interrogation of silence may work in two ways – perhaps we call God to account; or perhaps the silence interrogates *us*, calls us to account for our actions or our failure to act. Either way Paul does not suggest that the Spirit provides us with words that do not fail or with answers to our most intractable questions. Rather Paul presents us with the Spirit as an ally in our inarticulacy, helping us to keep on addressing God even when it seems most impossible.

There are times when only silence or a heartfelt groan will do. Paul presents prayer as God's work. Again it is not a matter of our effort – all we need to do is to make ourselves open to the action of the Spirit in us.

How is it possible to go on living in relationship with God when evil seems to triumph in the world?

Try being in silence as part of your prayer time. It may at times be painfully difficult, but it can represent a radical openness to the Spirit.

Nothing can divide us from God's love

Romans 8:31-39

Here is a great hymn of assurance to the Christians of Rome who, Paul implies, have been cast out of the social hierarchy. But it is by the standards of God's love that worth will be judged. Our status as disciples can be called into question today also. There are those who ask whether people can be committed to Christ if their lives go wrong, if they suffer, or suddenly become ill or poor. The whole of Romans 8 provides a reply to that kind of thinking. Christians *will* suffer, for they are identified with Christ's suffering, and in our suffering God identifies with us. Archbishop Romero said that there would be something wrong with the church if priests and religious were not killed during the time of great violence in El Salvador that caused his own martyrdom. None the less, according to Paul, nothing at all can separate us from God's love and nothing can prevent the triumph of the age of God's love.

What do you think Oscar Romero meant by the statement above? How do his words resonate with what you see in the communities with which you are concerned?

Holy God, you are the creator of the universe. We give you thanks that through Jesus Christ you bring us from death to life. Give us the grace of your Spirit that we may have confidence in your overwhelming love, and know that your reign of justice and peace will come on earth.

Peter the apostle

1 Peter and Jesus

Notes based on the
New Jerusalem Bible by
Joseph G Donders

Joseph Donders, a Dutch
Roman Catholic priest of the
Society of Missionaries of
Africa, is Emeritus Professor
of Mission and Cross-Cultural
Studies at the Washington
Theological Union. He was
formerly Head of the Depart-
ment of Philosophy and Reli-
gious Studies and Chaplain to
the Catholic Students at the
State University of Nairobi,
Kenya.

Preparing for the week

Peter is a key person in the New Testament. He
is mentioned 102 times in the gospels and in
the Acts of the Apostles some 55 times! Being
the most frequently mentioned disciple of Jesus
is not the only reason that he is interesting or
important. It is not even the role he had that is
significant. The most interesting aspect of Simon
Peter's life is the fact that he can stand as a
type and a model for us in the way we relate
to Jesus. Like Peter, we are both believing and
sometimes doubting, faithful but capable of
being treacherous, above all longing to be totally
loyal. Peter is someone we might use as a mirror
of ourselves.

For further thought

- How would you describe the apostle Peter?
- Do you like him as a character? Identify
  with him?
- In what ways do you see yourself as similar
  to Peter, in what ways different?

How it all began

Luke 4:38-39, 5:1-11

Peter's story begins in a simple way. He is a fisherman, which in his time and setting was the occupation of a rather well-to-do person. This fisherman called Simon (it is only later in Luke's gospel that Jesus calls him Peter – see 6:14) attends a sabbath service in his hometown Capernaum. He hears Jesus speak in a way he has never heard anyone else speak before – with 'authority', with a power that makes people listen and not only listen but become acutely aware of themselves. Jesus speaks in a way that makes people grow and change.

Simon Peter witnesses Jesus help and heal an obsessed man. He is so awed by this event that he invites Jesus to his home. There they find Simon's mother-in-law in the grip of a high fever. Simon and the others ask Jesus to do something about her suffering. Jesus responds immediately, standing over her, rebuking the fever – and the illness leaves her instantaneously.

In this story, Simon asks Jesus to be his guest and yet, rather than render to Jesus a service as the host would typically do, the host pleads with the guest to give him something – which Jesus is glad and prompt to do. It is the unnamed woman who, having been healed, gets up and begins to serve. Although her name is not mentioned and we know nothing more about her, she is the first person in Jesus' ministry who follows his example of service and kindness and acts accordingly.

Reflect on the example Simon Peter's mother-in-law presents to you. Pray for all who, while nameless, offer service upon which others depend.

Jesus' disciples appear reluctant to go to the other side of the lake – Jesus has to 'make' them go (verse 22). They preferred their side, perhaps wanting to go home, rather than strike out into new territory. Or perhaps Peter and the other experienced fishermen had read the signs and knew there was going to be a headwind and maybe even a storm.

Lord, save me!

Matthew 14:22-33

When the wind gets stronger and the waves higher they become afraid, but when they see someone walking over the water towards them, their fear takes new proportions and becomes terror. They think it is a ghost until they hear Jesus' voice saying: 'Courage! It's me. Don't be afraid!' (verse 27). This is the voice of the one they had left behind, the one who is changing their lives radically.

Have you ever had the feeling that you would like Jesus to leave you alone? That you are afraid to change your life? That the cross you are supposed to bear is too heavy?

Peter, impulsively, wants to excise that fear once and for all. He shouts: 'Tell me to come to you across the water.' When Jesus says: 'Come!' Peter gets out of the boat, but he doesn't get very far! Jesus saves him from sinking, adding: 'Why did you doubt?' Peter's astonished response is one of faith: 'Truly, you are the Son of God.' But, as we shall see, his faith has further to grow.

If it is you, tell me to come to you across the water.

Peter the apostle

Joseph Donders

Peter's faith

Matthew 16:13-23

When Jesus asks his friends, 'Who do people say the Son of Man is?' he is not asking them a rhetorical question. It is a real question. He wants their answer. First they all try to dodge the issue. Jesus repeats his question. It is finally Simon who gives the answer: 'You are the Christ, the Son of the living God.' Jesus replies, 'Simon, son of Jonah, you are a blessed man, because it was no human agency that revealed this to you, but my Father in heaven.' It is the moment in Matthew's gospel that Jesus gives him a new name: 'I now say to you, you are Peter and on this rock I will build my community.'

Peter did not only discover the real identity of Jesus that day. Jesus helped him to discover his own identity, too. Simon the fisherman discovered something in himself that made him Peter. That something was the reality of God's presence in himself. Peter is not the only one who carries God's presence, but he is the first one who discovers it through Jesus. He is the first one to understand and to feel what all this will lead to. He remains a first among equals.

Peter's conviction is shared by others. It is shared by you and by me. It is that faith that taps into the same divine presence, the voice of the Father in all of us.

Meditate on Peter's new name. What new name does Christ give you?

Peter the apostle

Peter's misapprehension

Mark 9:2-10

Once on top of the mountain, Peter, James and John liked what they saw. At last! This is what they been had been waiting for – Jesus revealed in his full glory, in the company of Elijah and Moses: Elijah, the great prophetic restorer of his people, and Moses, its liberator. They were overwhelmed, reflecting themselves the brightness that shone from him. This was what they had hoped and longed for. They were seeing it now with their own eyes. 'Glory, glory, alleluia!'

Hadn't they made the right choice following Jesus? No wonder that Peter thought: 'This is what it is all about. Let us keep it like this, let me build three shelters for you, for Elijah and for Moses.' As Mark rather grimly notes, 'He (Peter) did not know what to say.'

Then there was that voice from the heavenly cloud that overshadowed them, telling them: 'This is my Son, the Beloved. Listen to him.' While coming down from the mountain Jesus warned them not to speak to anyone about their experience until after his death and resurrection. They did not tell the others but, discussing among themselves what he told them, they did speculate about his resurrection, the glory part. However, just as Peter had done earlier (Mark 8:32), they remained in denial about the cost of such glory. They did not talk about his death.

Let us not only meditate on the glory promised, but also on the price he paid.

Peter the apostle

Joseph Donders

Was it only Peter's betrayal?

Mark 14: 26-31, 66-72

The story of Peter's betrayal of Jesus is a heart-rending one. When the cock crowed early that morning Peter remembered Jesus' words that he would betray him three times before the cock crowed a second time. He had been so sure of himself when he had told Jesus, 'Even if all fall away, I will not' (verse 29). He had indeed fallen away. Peter was a good man, but unforeseen human interaction, his fear and his cowardice had made him fail. So he breaks down and weeps as he realises his failure.

Retelling this story might make us see Peter as an exception in his unfaithfulness to Jesus. He was not. Judas betrayed him, but also all those others we do not hear about, because they had already deserted him and fled that night. We mentioned at the beginning of these meditations on Peter that we might see him as a mirror of ourselves. Of course, we never betrayed Jesus as Peter did. Or have we . . . ? Our failure in our relation to Jesus was never as personal as in Peter's case. Or was it . . . ?

Do you remember Jesus' verdict in Matthew's description of the Last Judgement, when he says that whatever is done by us to even the least one among us is considered by him *as done to him*? (Matthew 25:40).

'Lord, when did we see you hungry or thirsty, a stranger or lacking clothes, sick or in prison, and did not come to your help?'

Matthew 25:44

Peter the apostle

Peter's trust

John 20:1-10

It had not been Peter's intention to disown Jesus. He was not a coward. Peter had tried to defend Jesus during his arrest. He had drawn his sword and cut off the ear of one of the soldiers that came to arrest him. He escaped and remained to follow Jesus. He even managed to enter the compound of the palace of the High Priest where they had brought Jesus. Recognised by the doorkeeper as one of the followers of Jesus, he told her that he did not even know Jesus – a denial he repeated when a relative of the soldier whose ear he had cut off also recognised him. At that second denial a rooster crowed, and Peter burst into tears.

Yet on the Easter morning of John's text, Peter did not hesitate to run to the empty tomb. He realised at that moment that the Jesus story was not over. Not only that! He must also have realised that – knowing Jesus – he could risk meeting him notwithstanding his betrayals! He had left Jesus, but Jesus in his mercy would not leave him. His running to the tomb was the sign of his trust in Jesus.

Peter stands here again as a model for all those who fall short in their relation to Jesus; for all for whom Jesus stood, died and rose.

'Simon, son of John, do you love me?'

John 21:15

Peter the apostle

Joseph Donders

Peter the apostle

2 Peter, a leader

Notes based on the New Jerusalem Bible by **Joseph G Donders**

For Joseph's biography, see p.173.

Preparing for the week

It was Simon who answered Jesus' question, 'Who do people say the Son of man is?' His answer was: 'You are the Christ, the Son of the living God' (Matthew 16:17). It was his answer that made Jesus call Simon 'Peter' or 'Rock'. All of us who share Peter's belief are built on that same persuasion, that foundational 'Rock'. Jesus himself spoke to all of us in the same regard: 'Everyone who listens to these words of mine and acts on them will be like a sensible man, who built his house on rock' (Matthew 7:24-25). Notwithstanding his betrayal and failings, Peter's conviction was not shaken. It should remain ours.

For further thought

• Think about your daily tasks in the light of Peter's encounter at the last breakfast he had with Jesus at the lakeside (John 21). What new perspective does that open up for you?

• Does the gift of the Spirit Peter preached about in the first days of the church tell you something about yourself in your day?

• Peter came to realise that there is no favouritism with God (Acts 10:34). How do you understand that truth in the world in which you live and work?

Every Christian knows what the Last Supper is about. It is an unforgettable meal, one that is commemorated in most Christian communities in one way or another. However, we rarely hear about that last breakfast Jesus had with his disciples after his resurrection.

Evening meals are often pleasant. The day is over, the work done. Breakfast is a different issue. It is at the beginning of the day. Work has to be begun, organised and assigned. Some breakfasts are truly working breakfasts. That is what happened that day. Peter and some others had gone out fishing. They hadn't caught anything. When they approached the lake shore they saw a man who asked them for some fish. When they told him that they had not caught anything, he suggested throwing their nets out once more. They did, and caught 153 big fish.

By that time, of course, they had recognised Jesus, and were surprised to be invited to breakfast. Jesus had already baked the bread and some fish. It was after the breakfast that he asked Peter, 'Do you love me?' Peter (and the others) got to hear what loving him really means: going out to the whole world and taking care of his sheep and his lambs. Peter's task and role were assigned at that breakfast.

Lord, you know everything; you know I love you!

John 21:17

Jesus' last breakfast

John 21:1-17

Peter the apostle

Joseph Donders

Peter's inaugural message

Acts 2:14, 22-39

When Peter began his mission as leader of the apostolic body on the day of Pentecost, he started his speech with a quote from the prophet Joel: 'In the last days I shall pour my Spirit on all humanity' (Joel 3:1). And later on in the same inaugural address, announcing the newness brought into this world by Jesus Christ, he stressed this reality by adding: 'You must repent, and every one of you must be baptised in the name of Jesus Christ for the forgiveness of your sins, and you will receive the gift of the Holy Spirit' (verse 38).

Until recently, Western theologians would often remark that this being gifted with the Holy Spirit had almost become the Church's best-kept secret. German theologians even had a word for this situation: 'Geistvergessenheit', which in translation means, 'Spirit-oblivion'. Times have changed, however, and Peter's message is resounding louder and louder throughout the world. The interest in the Holy Spirit, the third person of the Blessed Trinity, has been growing over recent years, as is evident in the growth of Pentecostal and Charismatic movements worldwide.

More traditional communities sometimes have difficulties in understanding this current move of the Spirit. But all over the world where Peter's message is heard for the first time, the realisation of the presence of the Holy Spirit is often enthusiastically received with accompanying signs and wonders. Did Jesus not promise that he would send us the Holy Spirit, the Paraclete? (John 16:7)

'As the Father sent me, so I am sending you!'

John 20:21

Joseph Donders

Peter the apostle

Equipped with their new risen life, Peter and John met a cripple who asked them for some money. They did not have any. They healed him instead. Peter said: 'I will give you what I have; in the name of Jesus Christ, walk!' A miracle! Peter's first one.

I knew that almost every talk I gave to newly baptised Christians, especially when they were young, would end with the same question: 'Why can't we work those miracles? Why aren't there any miracles any more in the church?' But what was the miracle in the case of Peter and the lame man? His healing, of course. But that was not all. It was not even the main thing that happened. It was a wonder that Peter and John paid attention to the lame man at the gate and stopped to help him. Without their new life from Jesus neither Peter nor John might even have noticed the lame man at the gate. At the instant they did, they gave a sign of being equipped with Jesus' spirit. The healing followed from that. They paid attention to the man as Jesus would have done. Jesus lived in them.

This kind of moral miracle has never disappeared from the Christian community. Every time we reach out to someone in the name of Jesus, his spirit is at work in us. Miracles are still happening, day after day.

'They were astonished at what had happened' (verse 10). What cause have you for astonishment and wonder at the acts of God in your life?

Peter's first miracle

Acts 3:1-16

Peter the apostle

Joseph Donders

Peter's growth in global awareness

Acts 11:1-18

Jealousy is a terrible thing. It harmed the relationship among the disciples while Jesus was with them. They would fight over who had the first place, whom he liked most. They could not stand the idea that 'outsiders' used Jesus' name to heal. In the first Christian communities, too, some people seemed to be jealous and possessive of the Spirit they had received. Peter himself had a hard time understanding that foreigners – even Romans – were favoured in the same way he was. He needed several divine interventions before he admitted that God gave them the same gift that he himself had received.

Possessiveness and exclusivity are temptations faced by every group that forms itself around Jesus – temptations that must be overcome. If they are not, they divide the church into competing and self-praising cliques such as Paul fought in the early church. In our contemporary church they have led to polarisations that harm our wholeness.

The different gifts we receive from the one Holy Spirit should complement each other and support the wholeness of all. It is no help to place yourself or your group apart from others. A 'holier than you' attitude shows the arrogance Peter finally overcame when he said: 'I realised then that God was giving them the identical gift he gave to us when we believed in the Lord Jesus Christ; and who was I to stand in God's way?' (verse 17).

'Who am I to stand in God's way?'

Notwithstanding Peter's conversion and his re-alisation that there is no favouritism with God, he did not apply that principle consistently in his own life. When visiting Antioch he was willing to stick to it and to eat with non-circumcised gentile Christian converts only up to the moment of the arrival of some circumcised Jewish Christians. Afraid of what the latter would say when they saw him eating with the gentiles, he withdrew from his principles and started eating only with the circumcised Christians. Acting like this he caused a scandal. He was double-minded and insincere. Or to define it more correctly, he was a hypocrite.

It was an insincerity Paul could not tolerate. It sinned against all Jesus stood for, the bringing together at the banquet table of all whom Jesus came to call. This is what Paul told Peter. He reminded him that he himself was no longer living according to his older Judaic tradition, so why was he obliging gentiles to do so? He told Peter without any further ado that he was manifestly in the wrong and that his behaviour was not true to the gospel. In other words, Paul insisted that the one who was the head of the apostolic community must live up to what he himself had once understood – that the time had come in which the Spirit of God, the Spirit of Jesus Christ, was to be all in all.

'There is no favouritism with God!'

Peter the apostle

Joseph Donders

Peter's witness

2 Peter 1:16-18

Peter writes this letter just before he prepares to 'lay aside' the 'tent of this body' (verse 13). He wants to remind his readers of two realities before leaving them: 'the power and the coming of our Lord Jesus Christ'. He reminds his readers that they should increasingly 'share the divine nature! (verse 4), and also of their eschatological hope. In other words, he reminds his readers, including us, of the Second Coming of Jesus, when Jesus' kingdom will be visibly inaugurated. He stresses that these truths about Jesus' power and coming are not just 'cleverly invented myths' (verse 16). They are the truth.

Peter strengthens his testimony by not only referring to himself – one witness would hardly count – rather, he uses the word 'we'. Peter was not the only witness of Jesus' majesty and glory on Mount Thabor. 'We saw his majesty with our own eyes; we heard the voice of God the Father saying: This is my Son, the Beloved, he enjoys my favour with our own ears. We were there with him on the Holy Mountain' (my paraphrase).

In the rest of this short letter Peter insists also on the reality of Jesus' return at the coming of 'the new heavens and the new earth' (3:13). But no further information about time or date is given. It will come 'like a thief' (3:10). There is only a warning that 'uneducated and unbalanced people' (3:16) might distort the issue. 'Instead', Peter finishes his letter, 'continue to grow in grace' (3:18).

'Continue to grow in the grace and the knowledge of our Lord!'

Joseph Donders

Peter the apostle

Moods and emotions

1 From sorrow to joy

Notes based on
the Russian Orthodox
Bible by
Lucreţia Vasilescu

Lucreţia Vasilescu is a professor at the Faculty of Orthodox Theology, Bucharest University. She has degrees in French language and Orthodox theology, and a PhD in philology, and is the author of books and articles on French grammar and on religious life and culture.

Preparing for the week

The biblical writings reflect many different moods and contain every kind of emotion, expressed with great honesty. Indeed, this honesty is often too much for us, because the feelings expressed are not pious or holy at all! But the holiness lies in this very honesty, in the fact that here are people being utterly real before God; willing to recognise the truth of themselves and see that truth in the light of God's truth, mercy, grace and love.

Pain is the starting-point of many prayers. When we are saddened and perplexed by events, we can lose sight of God to the point of wondering whether God even knows, let alone cares, about what is happening. At such times we are invited to trust that God does see what is going on, and takes responsibility for doing something about it. God takes the situation 'in hand' and facilitates a process of change. The workings of this process may be so slight and subtle that for a long time we cannot be certain that things are improving: it is up to us to trust that God's saving power is at work now as it has worked in the past – and to act as if this is true.

For further thought

- How do you understand the relationship between holiness and honesty?
- How has God spoken to you through your own moods and emotions?
- In what ways do you bring your pain and sorrow into your prayer?

God sees and takes action

Psalm 10:12-18

God, dwelling in Zion, is the Most High One, the world's righteous judge and eternal King. God is the hope and deliverance of the pure and humble in heart. It is to this God, the Saviour of the world, that the church addresses thanksgivings, rejoicing in the salvation which is the free gift of its Saviour. Even when we think God is absent from situations of distress and need, the Almighty sees and notes our trouble and grief (verse 14).

'God's hand is the creating power, that is the only begotten one by whom everything was created, who is both the goal of those running and the path being run', according to St Gregory of Nyssa. God's providential care for his people is manifest especially in his compassion for the poor and needy, and in those who believe in God truly and deeply, and carry out his commandments without hesitation. God notes the distress of the poor and reaches out to help them. Thus, 'the Lord is a stronghold for the oppressed, a stronghold in times of trouble' (Psalm 9:9). Merciful and gentle to the oppressed, the Lord has given them power to prevail against their sufferings, and has also given them the holy cross as their weapon. They are the ones who will see God (Matthew 5:3, 8). This same God is, however, harsh on his 'enemies', that is, all the strongholds of Satan, because they have distorted the holy scriptures and led people into deception and error, and ultimately into death.

Thine own, of Thine own, we offer unto Thee, in all, and for all.

The Holy Liturgy of Saint John Chrysostom

Moods and emotions

A hymn to laud the Almighty, Hannah's song of praise symbolises the church's chants of triumph over adversity and fecundity out of barrenness. Faith and prayer are the source of human strength. Hannah's faith and steadfast prayer, with tears and longing, led to her conception of a son. Out of God's action in her life, she now speaks freely, with new emotion and strength – with joy rather than with anguish, in triumph rather than despair.

In her humbleness, Hannah prays insistently, and, what is more, she prays in the presence of God. We all pray, says John Chrysostom, but not all of us truly pray in the presence of the Lord: 'in the presence of God prays the one who attains perfect detachment from everything earthly, the one whose mind is entirely in heaven, and has completely left behind any worldly concern'.

God especially hearkens to the voice coming from the depth of the soul. Where the prayer of supplication and praise to the Lord prevails, the grace of the Holy Spirit will descend and all adverse powers will be defeated (verse 9).

Turning the world upside down

1 Samuel 2:1-10

Allow me, Lord, to become holy by praising you and to be purified by remembering you. Renew my life . . . guide my thought and make me forget my lame behaviour through renewal of thought . . . Let my will be in accord with your will, for you give prayer to those who pray.

St Isaac the Syrian

Moods and emotions

Lucreţia Vasilescu

God can do it again

Psalm 126

The term *bondage* has various meanings in the scriptures. There is bondage in a positive sense, that of obedience to Christ, as well as a negative sense of captivity of soul and that of the body weighed down with sins or, as in the experience of exile that lies behind this psalm, the bondage imposed by conquering enemies.

The psalm celebrates God's deliverance of the exiled Jews from bondage. This rescue is the source of their joy. The repetition of the phrase in several variations – 'our mouth was filled with laughter, our tongue with shouts of joy' (verse 3) – illustrates the loftiness of divine action and evokes powerfully its effects upon the soul.

The psalm evokes more than the tranquillity and relief of bliss, however. There is also the picture of the one who sows with tears. The nurturance of virtues within our lives is like the work of sowing, a work that requires much strain, tears and sweat. The prospect of an abundant harvest, though, encourages the sower not to yield to hardships and to keep on with his or her labour. 'Life's events are many, but they all have a common purpose . . . Let us withstand trials with a heroic, resolute soul, and thank God, praising him in order to be worthy of the eternal things' (St John Chrysostom).

Lord Jesus Christ, . . . accept my tears. By your passions heal mine, by your wounds cure my wounds . . . Though I have left you, do not leave me; though I have strayed from you, seek me out . . . Your glory is the comfort and rest of those who have endured hardships and afflictions for your sake.

St Isaac the Syrian

Lucreţia Vasilescu

Moods and emotions

Rejoice in God's saving power

Isaiah 25:1-9

This hymn is both prophecy and vision, which Christians have read as a foretelling of Christ's victory over death and the Messianic banquet which will be enjoyed at the end of time.

In ineffable wisdom, God fulfils everything he had planned in eternity. God the Lord is the hope and salvation of the one who has withstood trials, of the one pure in heart and steadfast in faith. The faith of the one thirsting for the heavenly Zion is often put to the test, yet everything worldly is transient, the earthly Jerusalem will be destroyed and we are but pilgrims on this earth, journeying towards our eternal destination.

Jesus our Saviour is the one who has 'destroyed death forever' (verse 8); he is the one who will guide humanity on the path to deification, since he is himself 'the way, the truth and the life' (John 14:6). By knowing and following Christ, tears and shame are replaced with hope and the joy of resurrection to eternal life. 'This is the fruit of perseverance: endless joy and contentedness. These are the fruits I have gathered on the mountain, that is the result of devotion' (Theodoretus of Cyprus).

Note, too, the universalism in this prophecy – all peoples are called to climb the mountain, to partake of the mystery of divinity (verse 6). The fruits gathered on the mountain at this great banquet are not only for Christians, but for all humankind.

Gracious God whose will is for all to enjoy the delights at your banquet, show us how to share our knowledge of you with the others we meet.

Moods and emotions

Lucreţia Vasilescu

Gladness for sorrow

Jeremiah 31:10-14

All peoples will hear the word of God, and the church of Christ the Cornerstone will spread to the ends of the earth. The new Israel will be rebuilt in and through Christ, and 'each will be rewarded according to their own labour' (1 Corinthians 3:8). There will be rejoicing, singing and dancing, and both young and old, women and men, will join in the spiritual feast of the Lamb.

This is the vision of the restored Israel, which Christians see as a prophecy of the church, the Bride of Christ, offered in today's passage. How far this can seem from the reality of the churches we know! Struggling, ageing perhaps, overburdened by huge buildings often unfit for purpose, ravaged by political and theological divisions – supply the characteristics of your own local Christian community!

Yet it is these same all-too-human communities – fragile and frail as they are – which are called to be the vibrant, renewed and jubilant gatherings such as Jeremiah's prophecy describes. 'This is a great mystery', says Paul in Ephesians 5:31, speaking of the church as the Bride of Christ. It is indeed mystery and paradox, that the human institutions of church can become the Messianic banquet. When we are tempted to despair of the church, we do well to remind ourselves of our heavenly calling.

Christ, you call your church to be your Bride, your community of love and joy. Show us how to dance and sing, in the midst of struggle and trials.

Lucreția Vasilescu

Moods and emotions

Blessed are those who acknowledge both their inner and outer wounds and come to God, the great doctor, praying for healing. This is a constant theme of the psalms, which offer us both the cries of anguish of those who long for healing and, as in this psalm of thanksgiving for recovery, the joy of those who have discovered healing.

Our prayer should be uttered strongly and confidently, with a pure, humble heart which bears spiritual fruit. God grants joy to the one who laments their sin sincerely and humbly. Sackcloth, symbol of contrition and humility, is the clothing of the penitent. God removes the rags of penitence and replaces them with the garments of joy and the robe of salvation (verse 11).

Thankfulness is an expression of the penitent's knowledge of forgiveness. 'The glory of the righteous one is the spirit within him. Therefore, the one who sings in spirit shall say: "O Lord, my God, I will praise Thee for ever more"' (Saint Basil the Great). Because the sins of the one who has erred are forgiven, there is a renewal of life and of joy and of glory, an overflowing of praise.

Mourning into dancing

Psalm 30

Forgive my trespasses and grant me justification. You know the multitude of my evil deeds, you know my abscesses and see my wounds, but you also know my faith, see my good will, and hear my sighs . . . See my humbleness, see my striving, and forgive all my sins, O God Almighty.

St Simeon the New Theologian

Moods and emotions

Lucreţia Vasilescu

Moods and emotions

2 From despondency to hope

Notes based on the New International Version by

Eun Sim Joung

Eun Sim Joung is a lecturer in Women's Studies at Dongduk Women's University in Seoul and author of *Religious Attachment*. Her interest is in the affective and relational dimensions of faith development, and how this can be applied to pastoral care and education, particularly for women.

Preparing for the week

As long as we live in this world, we cannot escape some degree of unhappiness. However, sometimes the feelings of despair and helplessness are too great to overcome and reach the point where we may feel hopeless and guilty. This despondency was not unknown to the great figures in the Bible, such as Job and Elijah, presenting them with some of the same challenges that contemporary Christians face. We sometimes feel much anxiety and anguish because we think that God does not care about our suffering. The stories we will consider this week, however, do not end in despondency but move towards a resolution, thereby offering comfort to those who are in despair. Reflecting on the readings can give us courage to be honest before God, whatever our wounds are and however deep and painful they may be. The texts also encourage us to appreciate God's gentle care for us which will carry us through every step of our journey of suffering, discovery and renewal.

For further thought

- Go out for a walk, and observe the natural world, appreciate its beauty and how God cares for it in the right time and the right way.
- Look for people around you who are despondent. Pray for them, write an encouraging letter to them or have a meal with them.

In Christian tradition, expressing negative feelings in prayer, such as doubt, despair and depression, has generally been neither praised nor encouraged. It was and is regarded rather as an act of unfaithfulness or evidence of weakness in faith. This approach, however, discourages those who are suffering in the present. Sometimes we feel miserable not because of the suffering itself but because we can't understand its causes or the reasons for it. We are also afraid of being rejected by others and being consumed by our own suffering. We may feel angry or anxious that God does not seem to care for us in such moments. Above all, guilt can be the biggest obstruction of all in our suffering. Blaming the self, or our closest ones, exacerbates our pain. At such times, prayer may not seem possible because we consider that prayer should not include wondering or grumbling.

The psalmist, however, cries from the depths in the midst of despair and despondency. The psalmist's cry, which comes from the grave, the very lowest pit, the darkest night, expresses the deepest and most honest emotions that it is possible to feel. This encourages us to disclose our human emotions to God – even if they seem to us negative feelings. In fact, faith *is* to be honest to God.

O Lord, listen to our cries in the darkest night! Let our crying, weeping and sighing come before you.

A cry from the depths

Psalm 88

Moods and emotions

Eun Sim Joung

Symptoms of despondency

Job 3:11-26

Recently Korean society was shocked by the suicide of a famous actress, following severe depression. Christians and Christian leaders were doubly shocked by the fact that the actress was a Christian.

'Why was I ever born?' Job's cry of despair is quite similar in form to that of the psalmist in Psalm 88, which we considered yesterday, and also echoes the feelings of the recent incident in Korea. Job even lamented his very birth and existence. He felt hopeless. The comfort of his closest friends couldn't help him but merely added to his burden.

No one has pleased God with their faith as much as Job did. No one in the world, from the past to the present, has been blessed as much as Job was. Yet even these great blessings could not sustain him in his situation of total loss and long-term trial. There was no joy; hope had vanished; only physical and psychological pain remained. We probably all experience such feelings at crisis points in our lives. Of course, it is easy to believe in God when everything is going well. It is only when things go wrong and begin to fall apart, that our faith is really tested. Perhaps Satan seizes an opportunity at that very moment – the very moment of agony between choosing life and being tempted by death. At such times, we can only call on God to rescue us.

Lord, help us to come to you with our most dreadful feelings, especially when they seem to overwhelm us. Help us to endure the trials in the midst of life, and keep us in your loving care when we are tempted by death.

Moods and emotions

'Get up and eat'

1 Kings 19:1-8

Elijah was disappointed and dejected after the great exploit on Mount Carmel when he had showed God's power to the people – and yet still they had not turned from their evil ways. He lost confidence and cried out to God, 'I have had enough, take my life.' Perhaps in his disappointment he wanted to run away from his heavy responsibilities as a prophet and just be alone. Perhaps in his despair he lost his appetite and his sleep patterns were disrupted – as happens frequently to those who suffer from depression, making the sufferer even more weary and fatigued, exacerbating the problem. At such a time, leaving home and going out to meet people can seem like an impossible mountain to climb. Those who suffer from depression will recognise only too well how such feelings of melancholy spiral into a downward cycle.

Sometimes what is needed is neither profound thought nor 'useful' counselling but simply a good meal and a good rest. A gentle, loving human presence, being alongside the sufferer and providing for their basic needs, may be the best way that a friend or carer can express their concern. So we see the divine care for Elijah. After leaving him to lie down and fall asleep in his depressive grumbling, God rouses him with a gentle touch, providing him with a cake of bread and a jar of water so that he may regain his strength. What a gentle and wonderful carer God is!

Lord, reach out your gentle hand to those who are suffering, and show me how to extend a hand of gentle service to those who need to know your love in practical ways.

Moods and emotions   Eun Sim Joung

Listening to a gentle whisper

1 Kings 19:9-18

After he had regained his physical strength, Elijah was ready to resume his journey and face his mission again. But not before facing further obstacles. Although he wanted to hear God's wisdom, all he could hear was 'a great and powerful wind' tearing the mountains apart and shattering the rocks, and all he could see was a mighty earthquake and a fire.

It is common for those who are depressed to think that everybody and everything around them are against them. They feel that they are set upon by obstacles on all sides. They know that they need to do something to cope with it but they are not sure what to do, where or how to start. Nothing is easy for them. Focusing only on the lowering mountain in front of them, they cannot see the details of each tree that is there to offer shelter. Focusing only on the sound of rage and fury, they cannot hear the sounds of birds singing within the tumult.

When he was finally ready to listen, Elijah was given a detailed plan of action. The huge mountain was broken down into small manageable pieces, he was told where to go, what to do and how to do it.

Sometimes when the task facing us seems overwhelming, it may help to distance ourselves somewhat from the immediate pressures and break down what seems overwhelming into manageable bite sizes. More importantly, if we want to receive God's good guidance, it will help to turn aside from the task itself for a while in order to find a quiet place (internally, if not externally) where we may seek to listen to a gentle whisper from God.

Lord, let us not to be overwhelmed by our worries and sense of despair. Show us how to be wise and listen to your gentle guidance.

Eun Sim Joung

Moods and emotions

How on earth can we have hope and recover our joy when the sky is falling down on us and the darkness overwhelms the light? According to Habakkuk, we can, because the Sovereign Lord is our strength, *even though* there is nothing to hope for and no cause for joy.

Today's verses remind me of a story of a Korean couple who were taking care of a small church and lost one of their children on the railway crossing when the child was ten years old. The child was bright and talented. The father spoke of how she was good at everything – studying, singing, playing the piano and painting, and she was also popular in school. When the couple found the dead body of their daughter, they held it and thanked God in prayer for giving abundant joy through her and their relationship with her for the past ten years. Of course, they were also in deep anguish, wondering what they had done wrong or what God wanted them to learn from this terrible incident. Afterwards, however, their ministry became more life-centred. A subway has been built under the crossing as a result of their campaign. The minister confessed, 'God who comforted us in the midst of pain gave us valuable things to learn'. He also said, 'thanking is the fruit of healing'.

'Though-there-are-no . . . ' faith, as Habakkuk sings and prays, is what we need when we are in despair. This is possible only when we believe in the sovereign God. This leads us to a healing process and enables us to thank, *even though there are no causes for thanks*.

'Though-there-are-no . . . ' faith

Habakkuk 3:17-19

Sovereign Lord, let the wounded be healed. Let their sorrows be turned into joys and their cries be transformed into thanks. Let them find hope in you.

Moods and emotions   Eun Sim Joung

New every morning

Lamentations 3:19-23

Depression is not just the occasional blue feeling but a prolonged period of suffering which affects every aspect of an individual's life. Libby, who was one of the interviewees for my doctoral study, was a very bright and well-educated woman. She has suffered from depression all her life. In her university days, the campus was surrounded with tear gas and smoke. Political demonstrations against the military government were common and many students, including her, were arrested. In fact, she confessed that she became involved with the protest movement not because of her political convictions but because she was lonely. Around that time, she realised that her parents' love was conditional, and her depression reached its peak. Then, she realised that only God's love was unconditional and everlasting, and so she was led to accept Jesus as her saviour.

Throughout this week we have seen how even the great heroes of the Bible suffered from a similar depression. As we end the week, it is time to learn that God is not only the sovereign Lord but also everlasting love. The traditional hymn, 'Great is thy faithfulness', is based on today's reading, and expresses well the sense of hope in God's daily renewed mercies that we read about. Certainly we need to remember that God gives strength for today and bright hope for tomorrow. God's love is great and his compassions never fail; they are new *every* morning.

Lord, help us to trust in you who are everlasting love and bring new possibilities each day.

Moods and emotions

Moods and emotions

3 From anger to creative action

Notes based on the
New Revised
Standard Version by
Tony McCaffry

Tony McCaffry is a theologian with a particular interest in adult religious learning. A family man, he lives in active retirement in Surrey, UK.

Preparing for the week

This week we will be looking at our capacity, as human persons, to hit the heights and to plumb the depths. We can often times be ugly in our relationships – with God, with others, with ourselves – by being fearful and untrusting, but at other times we can be remarkably noble, open and honest, generous and confident. What makes the difference?

Anger can be a hindrance or a help. The strong feeling of antagonism towards self, or another, or others, is common enough. Sometimes it is merited, other times not. We can run with it or set it aside. Either way it is upsetting because our steady centre is disturbed.

I am no expert. I know only too well what it is like to be angry – with God (who, frankly, does not seem fit for purpose sometimes), with others (not just the maniac driver who carves me up on the road but even my nearest and dearest who do not always seem to be fully aware of just how much effort I am putting into my thoughtful regard for them) and with myself (whom I know all too infuriatingly well and whose 'warts and all' can be most unappealing).

For further thought

- With whom or what am I currently angry? What is the root cause of my anger?
- How can I change my negative anger into positive love?

For God's sake, listen!

Psalm 4

This is a psalm of supplication, an exasperated cry against the unfairness of everything. There is no peace of mind, seemingly no grounds for hope.

Those of us who have met depression, in ourselves or others, know that there is no cheering the depressed person up, it is impossible to snap them out of their misery. Anger does something similar: there's a fire burning inside us for which we make everything into extra fuel, stoking the flames. The anger boils all the more wildly!

What should we do? Anger clouds our sight and stops our ears; we are obsessed with our own feelings, we ignore the bigger picture, the quiet word of sweet reason. It's time to lie down in a dark room for a moment, really or figuratively. It is time to give the still small voice inside us a chance, rather than to rave on to ourselves endlessly. Don't let the anger fester; make it a gift to God, a sacrificial offering: it is us as we are, sadly, but there is no point in pretending. Perhaps a sheepish smile, at ourselves and for our God, will ease our embarrassment and show the sincerity of our intent?

Risk a smile three times today.

Lord God,
I offer you this anger
and the confusion it causes.
Transform it and me with your love
and help me smile again.
In Jesus' name I pray.

Human existence can be a complicated business. We can get ourselves into a real muddle in tense situations, looking to hoard our cake and yet eat it too! It's like pulling both ways in the tug-of-war, as we find ourselves caught between what we know, long term, we should be doing and what we fancy doing at the time.

When we are hopping mad about something, the rage can get in the way. Paul offers a check-list: is this anger from the Spirit (sane and sensible, clear-sighted for good) or from 'the flesh' (bitter, twisted and perverted)? Of the fifteen 'works of the flesh' named, count how many have traces of anger in them. How many of the nine 'fruits of the Spirit' named can be seen as useful antidotes to anger? Mull on!

If I am really serious about being on Jesus' side, I will 'crucify' the negative in order to 'rise' with the positive. It's not a game, it's for real. If, with God's help, we get it right, we will see it in our loving relations with others, not doing them down or scoring points at their expense: we'll be living the life of love.

Action point: memorise those gifts of the Spirit.

Lord God,
help me to love you,
my neighbour and myself
in the way you want me to.
Keep me from getting muddled
about whose side I am on.
In Jesus' name I pray.

Whose side am I on?

Galatians 5:16-26

Moods and emotions

Tony McCaffry

The bigger picture

James 1:12-21

'Lead us not into temptation', we say in the Lord's Prayer – and with good reason! It is all too easy to be bamboozled by the seemingly attractive particulars – and so miss the bigger picture. This is the reality of God's kingdom, the ruling of God's will, on earth as in heaven. In this God-view, all is gift, all are important, everything and everyone is connected in godly purpose.

It is a struggle to avoid the confusion of chasing what I want rather than looking for what God wants, not just for me but for everyone else too. Life is a miracle. It is for relishing. Looking outwards is godly: being tied up in self-centred introversion is deadly.

Anger festers. If we let it take over, it will stifle everything else. It acts like rank weeds in a garden: you have to pull the weeds out to allow the flowers of righteousness to flourish! Don't be bamboozled: God is indeed friendly. Being hopping mad with God, with others or with yourself is not going to help at all. Take the rage as a clarion call to conversion, a change of heart!

Action point: pull out at least one deadly 'weed' today.

Lord God,
lead me not into temptation;
deliver me from evil.
Help me to learn to be godly,
appreciating the bigger picture
and what really matters,
not being choked by selfish anger.
In Jesus' name I pray.

Moods and emotions

Wise up!

Proverbs 22:17-25

The Book of Proverbs has given our language a great number of wise sayings, distilled from lives carefully lived. Today's extract presents wisdom like a person passing on wise teachings, designed to help readers live their lives well.

It is a call for consistency: if we are following the God of love, then we must be loving too, loving God, neighbour and self. Wisdom tells us to set our compass in the true direction, irrespective of whatever others get up to. Know who your real and true friends are and do not get caught by the seeming glamour of errant ways.

Be careful not to pick on the already vulnerable in order to take it out on them and so escape having to face up to the frailties closer to home! If we are truly wise, we shall calm down, look beyond ourselves to the bigger picture and see that God is full of respect for, and very much on the side of, the poor, the marginalised and the oppressed. That is where we belong, too, standing up for them and being intolerant of anything less.

Who has given me wise insights? Have I said 'Thank you'?

Lord God,
teach me to be wise.
Help me to keep to your ways
with loving respect for the seeming weak
and saving my anger for the bullies.
In Jesus' name I pray.

Moods and emotions

Tony McCaffry

God bless you!

Ephesians 4:25-32

Paul gives a call for consistency here, seeing how the grace of God is freely given to us – and is for giving, in turn, by us. The members of the one body of Christ are necessarily well-knit together: being at odds with each other is clearly a recipe for disaster. Anger, the passionate feeling, is not in itself wayward, but the brooding and brewing we allow to fester from it certainly is. Our commitment to Christ, stamped with the seal of God's Spirit, sits uneasily with bad-mouthing others: either say good things or say nothing at all.

Destructive prejudices and chips on shoulders have no place in the perspective of the loving God. So, is it possible for me to live in this godly way, treating all as gift, being gracious to others, no matter how irritating I may find them to be? Does my feeling of anger prompt me to complain about and curse the other – or to smile at myself and say a prayer for them?

Catch yourself out thinking badly of someone today – and pray for them instead.

Lord God,
give me your Spirit of love
so that I can be big-hearted in your service
and not a selfish misery.
Help me to smile today
and to love those whom I find it hard to like.
In Jesus' name I pray.

Moods and emotions

The crunch comes at the end of this week on what to do with our anger: how, in heaven's name, can I love my enemies (whom, by very definition, I hate)?

Firstly, calm down! It is not the feelings which make the difference, but what I do with them. Do I use them to lash out at the other, giving as good as I get, scoring points at least even if I cannot quite supply the knock-out punch? Can I take people as they are, leaving judgements for God to make? To be obsessed with others' faults and failings is to miss the point: God loves them and so ought I.

So, how can I see the infuriating other in a positive light? Instead of being in their face, seeing nothing of the bigger picture, why not get alongside them, seeing life from their perspective? Am I a good advertisement for the Jesus value system? There is more than enough hatred in the world already: let's contribute some peace instead, unfashionable though that might be.

Make an effort to be friendly at church this weekend.

Is tit for tat the best we can do?

Romans 12:14-21

Lord God,
help me to love you,
help me to love my 'enemy' [name him/her/them]
help me to love myself,
especially when I don't feel like it.
Teach me to live your love to all
and mean it!
In Jesus' name I pray.

Moods and emotions

Tony McCaffry

Moods and emotions

4 From jealousy to contentment

Notes based on the New Revised Standard Version by **Doff Ward**

Doff Ward is an Anglican Reader working and learning in a parish and in spirituality.

Preparing for the week

How often negative thinking robs us of peace of mind! It could be supposed, for example, that those of us who have a sufficiency of what we need would not find envy and jealousy pressing temptations, but they can gain admittance to our thinking in subtle ways. We can be like the psalmist who wrote, 'I was envious of the arrogant; I saw the prosperity of the wicked' (Psalm 73:3). We too can quietly envy those who have skills we lack, or who have become what we would like to be. Fearful of loss, we can cling on jealously to what we regard as ours, and feel resentful towards those who threaten to take it, or sometimes simply want to share it. This can be true of individuals on their own account or as members of a group or organisation. We can be envious of those who find the easy road to success by comparison with our own struggle.

In the readings for the coming week we are privileged to meet and learn from characters who recognised the value of a positive and quiet mind as something unattainable by those who allowed themselves to be enslaved by the negativity of envy and possessiveness.

For further thought

• Use and reflect on the following prayer:

Caring God, whose will is always for our deep inner peace, may the coming week make clear which paths to follow as we journey in your company.

At the beginning of today's passage things are going according to plan – God's plan. Moses was finding running the affairs of the frequently complaining Israelites stressful. He had been told to assemble seventy elders to support him in organising the food supplies, which God had promised would be plentiful. In view of the size of the community, Moses questioned whether, in practical terms, the promise could be kept, hence God's response to his doubts, 'Is the Lord's power limited?' (verse 23).

Sharing the load

Numbers 11:23-30

Reassured, Moses gathered the seventy and, just as they were to share responsibility with him, he accepted that they would share the power needed for the job. This was too much for Joshua, his second in command. Perhaps in support of Moses and with an eye to his own future, he questioned whether others should share the leadership role on an equal footing. To him the power of leadership once gained should not be shared but jealously guarded. Was it Moses or Joshua who had greater peace of mind?

Many leaders in different fields today would concur with Joshua's viewpoint that power and control once gained should be held fast. Looking instead to the teaching of Jesus, whom Moses foreshadowed, we see that he bestowed the unlimited power of the Holy Spirit upon all prepared to work with him in revealing the kingdom of God.

Gracious God, bestow your Spirit upon us afresh that we may work with you in revealing your kingdom on earth.

Moods and emotions   Doff Ward

Letting go

1 Samuel 18:5-16

Although Saul and David shared the desire for Israel to be a successful nation, jealousy led Saul to lose sight of that goal and perceive David as his enemy. He found a threat to his status and power more damaging than setbacks encountered when leading his army. Even the songs of the women rejoicing over his successes as well as David's were not music to his ears, but mockery. Saul had shifted his focus from God's objective of establishing peace and a settled lifestyle for his people to his own jealously guarded evaluation of his role as leader, and the shift had brought him nothing but wretchedness. Truly, he was a man at a loss.

That same loss can be felt today by people who have enjoyed status and power in political positions, in the world of business and in academia, and have reached the point of needing to relinquish it and hand over to successors. It can happen when positions have been held in voluntary and leisure organisations; it can happen in a family; it can happen in a church.

What we encounter in such situations may entail loss but we must face the need to adjust to a change of role throughout life. In God's sight we have an ongoing appointed part to play towards the fulfilment of his vision of our world as a place where love of neighbour is commonplace.

Guiding Spirit, help us to recognise the role you would have us fill.

Moods and emotions

Given the opportunity, as he was, it must have been a sore temptation for David to kill Saul. He had the backing of his men, and Saul had earlier made an attempt on his life. It would have been an act many would have seen as perfectly justifiable, but David held back. Had he not done so the outcome would have been very different. Saul's life would have come to a sudden and untimely end, which might well have aroused bitter resentment in his supporters. It would have meant David taking the kingship by a coup rather than succeeding Saul according to God's timing. It would have been an action that would have meant David having to live with the king's murder on his conscience for the rest of his life.

Instead David followed the lead of the mercy that was aroused in him when he saw the defenceless Saul. His restrained action surely helped to build his reputation as a man of courage and leadership, but also a man of wisdom and compassion. Rather than a death, he achieved some degree of reconciliation between Saul and himself, as evidenced by Saul's tears. And his inner peace remained intact.

Does today's reading not give us an insight into the richer outcome of acting according to the promptings of the Holy Spirit rather than the dictates of our narrower thinking?

When we are faced with difficult decisions, Holy Spirit, give us pause and be our guide.

Which path?

1 Samuel 24:1-17

Moods and emotions   Doff Ward

Directions for city-dwellers

Philippians 4:2-9

In the readings during the past three days, we have been in company with some of the principal figures of the Old Testament, great 'actors' on the biblical stage – and we have had the privilege of being 'audience' to what has been happening. Today's reading draws us closer into the action.

Paul was addressing Christians living in a city where Roman culture and customs had a high profile. His letter offered them guidance for living a Christian life in the midst of it by fostering an attitude of joy in their faith, following a pattern of prayer and directing their thoughts into positive and creative channels.

No doubt the citizens of Philippi would have heard scandal, accounts of anti-social behaviour and reports of sad and shockingly bad news, as we do today through even more channels. As a result perhaps they were tempted, as we can be, to see the world negatively as unfair, unjust and beyond hope.

Sometimes we need to search them out, but it is still possible to find people and actions that are true and honourable, just and pure, pleasing, commendable and excellent. If we think on these things too, as Paul recommends, our prayers can not only be constantly provided with people and causes that call for our intercessory prayers, but also with people and causes that arouse in us worthy praise, thanksgiving and inner peace.

Holy Spirit, give us vision that is clear and true.

What is needed?

Philippians 4:10-20

How confidently Paul wrote to the co-operative church in Philippi: 'God will fully satisfy every need of yours according to the riches of his glory in Christ Jesus' (verse 19)! Are the needs of those around us today substantially different from the needs of those early Christians?

Paul recognised Jesus as a man of discernment, someone who saw situations for what they were and who saw people for who they were and discerned in both evidence of human need – the need for change; for good relationships with others and with God; for prayer; for teaching; for healing and for an appreciation of true values. Throughout his earthly ministry Jesus answered those needs for people of his day and he laid the foundation of a church to which he gave the instruction, 'Follow me!' Can we co-operate with that direction?

Do we see the need for change in our world and if so, can we make a contribution to it? Can we build and sustain good relationships with people and with God? Can we pray? Can we teach directly and by example? Can we contribute to healing by caring for the sick in body, mind and spirit? Can we base our values upon Jesus' values? As his followers we are limited, but through his grace and the gift of the Holy Spirit we can rejoice in having a role in today's sharing church.

Jesus, my inspiration and friend, I accept your invitation to follow you.

Moods and emotions   Doff Ward

Rejoice and move on!

1 Timothy 6:1-12

Can we feel comfortable with Paul's apparent easy acceptance of slavery? When this letter to Timothy was written there were hundreds of thousands of slaves in the Roman empire. Had those who joined the early church been encouraged to regard themselves as free, and acted accordingly, they would have endangered their lives and given good reason for the Roman authorities to annihilate the church membership. For slavery to be abolished then was probably an unimaginable dream. Some problems human beings set up for themselves take time to be resolved.

For slaves to live and rejoice in their faith, within their boundaries, and so act as Christian witnesses, was possible, and that was the course they were urged to follow. The writer was concerned to address the situation as it was and sadly, for some, still is in this twenty-first century. There is slavery in our world today that needs to be addressed. Human beings, and women particularly, are forced into slavery by their culture, by tradition, by trafficking in the sex trade, as well as hundreds of thousands of people worldwide enslaved by poverty and addiction. The need is as urgent as it was when the letter to Timothy was written to address positively the plight of the enslaved, rejoicing in what has already been achieved and avoiding the temptation to consider the end of all slavery as an unachievable dream.

May freedom for all people be our ongoing vision and our aim.

Moods and emotions

Order now for 2011!

It may seem early, but the copies of *Words for Today 2011* and *Light for our Path 2011* are now available to order.

Order now:

- with your local IBRA Rep*
- in all good Christian bookshops
- direct from IBRA

online: http://shop.christianeducation.org.uk/

email: sales@christianeducation.org.uk

phone: 0121 472 4242

post: using the order form at the back of this book

If ordering direct, postage is free of charge.

*If you purchase 6 copies or more, and you live in the UK, you can sign up as an IBRA Rep and claim the 10% IBRA Rep discount on all IBRA products. You will also receive a free poster and samples to help you share IBRA more easily with family, friends and others in your church. Contact staff at IBRA to sign up now!

A whole year's Bible reading notes for only *16p* a week!

Readings in Luke

6 Forerunners and followers

Notes based on the New Revised Standard Version by **Barbara Calvert**

Barbara Calvert is a Methodist minister in the Orpington and Chislehurst circuit in Kent. Previously, she has been an RE teacher, worked for Christian Aid and been a university chaplain in Glasgow.

Preparing for the week

God's people have always been on the move. Moses and the children of Israel, Abraham and Sarah, Joseph, Ruth, Mary and Joseph – all people on the move. God sending the Son, Paul and the apostles, missionaries throughout the ages, the Methodist movement – all are part of the ongoing, living story of God's people. What an awesome thought!

In recent years the exciting rediscovery of the God of the scriptures as a God of mission (*Missio Dei*, the mission of God) has inspired a shift from church understood as an institution to church as a movement. The church moving outside its comfort zones has led to a flowering of fresh expressions. A Fresh Expression is a form of church for our changing culture, established primarily for the benefit of people who are not members of any church (see www.freshexpressions.org.uk). In the first century there was no such thing as what we would recognise as traditional church. All was new; all was moving; and at the forefront were the forerunners and followers.

For further thought

- What does it mean for you to be 'on the move'?
- How do you understand the *Missio Dei*?
- Who or what do you think of when you imagine 'forerunners and followers'?

In recent years, many churches have come to recognise that they are set in a time warp appealing only to those who are already members. Recognising that 'something needed to be done', some have thought that the solution lay in introducing guitars, new songs or changing the furniture by removing the pews. The expectation has been that if we just tweak things, make a few minor changes, then people will come in, new wine invited into roughly the same old wineskins.

'He went out' (verse 27). A forerunner has to go out first. Jesus is out amongst the people demonstrating a radical newness about discipleship – and crowds of people are responding. Imagine a mission today. Levi responds to the call. What would our next move be? It could well be to invite him to church on Sunday morning!

But in this story Jesus' invitation to Levi is fol-lowed by Levi's invitation to Jesus to a banquet at his house. This exchange has established a relationship of mutuality and respect between the forerunner and the follower. Levi has not been humbled or humiliated. His dignity is intact, enabling him to grow and mature in faith, first as a follower and then further maturing into a forerunner himself. Jesus' willingness to go out brings about this transformation, and not only for Levi. Imagine the fun Jesus would have had at the banquet, the conversation and laughter. Life-changing encounters for all, through moving out!

What steps can I take to help my church become a church without walls?

In or out? Church walls

Luke 5:27-39

Beckoning God, transform us by your grace.

Readings in Luke

Barbara Calvert

Contemporary culture

Luke 6:12-26

Many churches today feel that they ought to tackle the widening gap that they have perceived between the majority of the population and the traditional church. They would like to become mission-shaped churches, sensing God's call to go out where people are. But they recognise that before they set out they must understand our present cultural setting, if the church is to be reshaped appropriately for its mission.

We might use terms such as 'consumerist', 'greed', 'cult of celebrities', 'big brother mentality' and 'populist' to describe our contemporary culture and think these are new phenomena. But Jesus warns his followers of just these very things! Beware, he says in the four woes, of having loads of money, being overfed, laughing at others and seeking to be popular and famous. Jesus knows that we need to understand contemporary culture in order to be shaped for mission, yet not be seduced by it. We are called to be in the world but not of the world.

The teaching of Jesus in these 'blessings' and 'woes' has hard lessons for all his followers. None of us feels up to the task any more than did the named and unnamed disciples, but we do have a choice. We can choose the way of the world or we can follow Jesus and take radical action to ensure a different future.

What steps can I take to help my church become culturally sensitive?

Reshaping God, transform us by your grace.

My childhood holidays were always spent in Cornwall. For two weeks every August, my family stayed in a rented cottage in Trebetherick and every Sunday morning we went to Polzeath Methodist Church. I remember sitting in church with the sun pouring in, listening to the distant sound of the waves and children's voices from the beach. Yet it was peaceful inside, comfortable and welcoming – a traditional but happy experience of church even for a child. Now Polzeath is so popular with holidaymakers, surfers in particular, that local people can rarely afford to live there and just a few years ago Polzeath Methodist Church was facing closure.

However, the minister of the church had the vision to develop a Fresh Expression of church specifically for the surfing community. The church was pulled back from the brink of closure and is now enjoying a whole new lease of life as the Tubestation Church with skate ramp, plasma screens and café. Mostly young people are coming together, living out a 'Love thy neighbour' attitude both locally and globally and presenting the gospel in a way which is culturally relevant. The church now has forty regulars each week with several services on a Sunday, midweek Bible study classes and, during the summer months, struggles to fit everyone in.

'But is it church?' people ask. Jesus said, 'Look at the evidence'. 'Go and tell John what you have seen and heard' (verse 22).

What steps can I take to help my church become part of the Fresh Expression movement?

Exhilarating God, transform us by your grace.

Is it church?

Luke 7:18-35

Readings in Luke

Barbara Calvert

Get into the boat

Luke 8:22-25; 9:1-11

When I have been by the Sea of Galilee, I have imagined Jesus and the disciples walking by the shore. There is always a boat! In our story, Jesus invites his followers to go with him across to the other side of the lake. And even then they do not know exactly where they are going. They know it can be dangerous on the Sea of Galilee, but still they go. They could have said, 'No'. As often, out of nowhere, a storm blows up and it is frightening. The power of the wind and the waves is terrifying, but Jesus stills the storm and there is calm.

If these followers of Jesus had not had the courage to get into the boat, they would have missed the awesome experience of God's power in Jesus as he stills the storm. Only then are the disciples, empowered by what they have witnessed, ready and equipped to be sent out on a mission in God's name and with God's power.

Going out, being on the move, is risky and challenging but the disciples take the good news and cure diseases as they are instructed. They fulfil their mission, people's lives are changed and so too are the lives of Jesus' followers.

God's people today are being called to get into the boat. And just as the twelve go out as 'disciples' but return as 'apostles', so this is the possibility for the followers of Jesus today. It is indeed the only way.

What steps can I take to help my church become a church of apostles?

Empowering God, transform us by your grace.

After much study, reflection, discussion and prayer, the people at one of the churches in Devon where I used to be minister decided to form a Fresh Expression of church. Conversations and enquiries had indicated that Saturday teatime would be a good time to start a group for young families, which we called 'The Ark'. This gave us the theme for the first gathering one Saturday in November 2007.

The transforming feast

Luke 9:18-36

The story of Noah's Ark was told; children and adults then participated enthusiastically in all sorts of messy workshops related to the story. Then we all had a cooked tea together. After tea, the children enjoyed performing a dramatised, improvised version of Noah's Ark, and then we closed with singing and a time of reflection. It had been really hard work but families had come who were not members of the church, and one mother on leaving said, 'It was just like a party.'

It was just like a party: fun, participatory, noisy and boisterous – until the end. As the children took turns in lighting a candle and saying his or her own prayer, the sound of silence was powerful and the candlelight shone, if only momentarily. Our organising team went home exhausted but joyful. As followers of Jesus, we had accepted the gospel invitation to journey together up the mountain, and the experience had been transformational, for everyone.

What steps can I take to help my church become a transforming presence in society?

Transforming God, transform us by your grace.

God goes ahead

Luke 10:1-20

What is refreshing and exciting about the Fresh Expressions movement is the willingness of people to go out. A new energy, fired by God's Spirit, is setting men and women free of church structures, prepared to take risks, willing to learn from the world, recognising that God is already ahead of us in mission. In the early church too, they were not so arrogant as to think that the traffic was only one way. Jesus had taught them to recognise the signs of the kingdom in the world around them in unexpected people and places – in the Good Samaritan, the Syro Phoenician woman, the shepherd, the sower and the widow.

These seventy followers, men and women, are to accept hospitality given, offer a greeting of peace, and be sensitive to their hosts who might indeed already 'share in peace' (verse 6). They are instructed not to move from house to house. By staying in one house, rather than looking out for better lodgings, they have the opportunity to build kingdom relationships. Belonging before believing, putting human relationships at the heart of mission, allows the possibility for glimpses of God which might otherwise be missed.

Both forerunners and followers together are called to journey out, discovering and sharing in the transformational possibilities of being servants in someone else's house.

What steps can I take to help my church become a journeying people?

Journeying God, transform us by your grace.

Readings in Luke

7 Making people whole

Notes based on the New Revised Standard Version by
Barbara Calvert

For Barbara's biography see p.216.

Preparing for the week

We all long for healing. God too longs for our healing. Jesus was moved to compassion by suffering, and anxious to relieve the misery it entails. While there is much debate on how spiritual and medical healing relate to each other, I believe there is no distinction between the healing of medical science and divine healing. They are one, for this is God's world and nothing is outside God's domain. Our whole ministry is one of healing, and the ministry of healing is as much part of the Christian life as the ministry of preaching or service.

Every act of Christian worship celebrates the grace of God who desires the wholeness of body, mind and spirit for all people. In this sense, every service is a healing service and every aspect of worship – singing, praise, prayer, silence, confession – can contribute to the healing of both individuals and groups.

For further thought

- When and how have you experienced healing in your life?
- In what ways do you find worship, at its best, a healing experience?
- Think of individuals and communities in need of healing and pray for them.

Carer and cared for

Luke 7:1-17

The healing of the centurion's slave took place in Capernaum, and the healing of the widow's son in Nain. The precise geographical location of Nain is not known but Capernaum was a small fishing town on the shores of Lake Galilee. It was destroyed in the seventh century and now lies in ruins. I was in Capernaum a few months ago staring into the foundation stones of a home that evidence strongly suggests was Peter's house – the site of another healing story, the healing of his mother-in-law. Many can testify to a healing experience of some kind by simply being in such a place. This is because we are all in need of healing, of being made whole. This is the testimony of each of the readings this week.

Today's two stories also illustrate another fundamental truth: you cannot divide those in need of healing from those who care for them, for they too have a need of healing. It is the slave and the son who experience physical healing, but the centurion, who valued his slave highly, and the widow, who loved and depended on her son, also express their own need in asking for the healing of their dependent ones. Indeed, I myself have observed in my own experience that often the need of the carer is greater than the one being cared for.

Jesus restores to these two people the ones whom they loved, responding to their own need for wholeness too.

How do we recognise the healing that we need?

Caring God, heal us through your love.

The one and the many

Luke 7:36-50

The other day, I visited an elderly member of our church who is now in a care home. In her time, she had been one of the church stalwarts. Always there when needed – at church teas, jumble sales, she helped in the Junior Church for years. She didn't like any fuss; she just got on with it: practical and dependable.

Now she is dependent on others. The care home is for those in the advanced stages of dementia. She didn't know me; she doesn't know anyone, neither family nor lifelong friends. She sits in her room all day, with the door open, making repetitive loud shrieks. Another resident stops and tells her that if she doesn't stop making that noise she will ring for her parents to take her home from school. It is surreal.

A young nurse slips into the room – gentle, kind and with a warm smile. She takes the old lady's hand and puts it against her face, gently caressing the woman's cheek with her own hand, drawing close. The old lady stops screeching; there is a response. The nurse tells me that gentle caressing, touch, is the only thing that the old lady responds to, but even this had taken time.

The nurse is infinitely patient; she pours out her love and care for this woman, as if she were the only one in the home that needed her. The lavishing of precious resources, our precious ointment, on the most vulnerable in our society is the pathway to wholeness for us all.

How do we learn how to pour out our whole self for the healing of God's world?

Vulnerable God, heal us through your love.

Readings in Luke   Barbara Calvert

Naked and clothed

Luke 8:26-39

I am often invited to take assembly in the local primary schools. My usual approach is to tell a Bible story and the children act out the story as I tell it. A sea of eager hands goes up when I ask for volunteers to take part. Most of the children love to act, to dress up, to pretend to be someone else. The dressing-up clothes are very simple: just a black shawl for a widow, or a coloured shawl for a young woman, an Arabic scarf for Jesus or a disciple, simple hats for soldiers or guards. But these simple adornments transform the children and enable them to 'become' the character. What we wear expresses so much of who we are.

The demoniac wore no clothes at all, so who was he? He wasn't himself. Jesus asked him, 'What's your name?' and the man replied, 'Legion', because he was so many people all in one, so possessed by demons he didn't know who he was, with no clothes to identify him. We never discover the man's real name but we do know that, cured of his demon possession, he becomes a disciple in his home town, made whole by Jesus, his healing symbolised by being clothed.

How do we discover what are the new clothes of the kingdom?

Naked God, heal us through your love.

Each member of our church is in a pastoral group with a specially designated person in the role of pastoral leader. Other roles held by people in the church include those of steward, property officer, worship leader and of course those who look after the money. We order our lives by dividing up our responsibilities. But, irrespective of roles, we may all pastor to one another at church and in our daily lives, simply by listening and caring. And every time we gather together in an act of Christian worship, we celebrate the grace of God who desires wholeness of body, mind and spirit for all people.

Jesus did not categorise people or his activities. His ministry of healing cannot be separated from his ministry of preaching and teaching; all of these are going on all the time to all people. The woman with the haemorrhage is physically healed but Jesus also listens to her story; in front of the whole crowd she told him everything. Imagine the effect on the crowd!

It is Jairus' daughter who is physically healed, but who else goes to bed that night changed? Not just her, but the girl's whole family, their friends and neighbours, members of the synagogue, Peter, John and James, the whole crowd – and, as we read and ponder, us too.

How do we use our own healing as a means of the healing of the whole of humanity?

Listening God, heal us through your love.

The individual and the crowd

Luke 8:40-56

Readings in Luke

Barbara Calvert

Dogs and humans

Luke 9:37-50

Every Tuesday and Thursday afternoon a woman walked past the house where I used to live with her dog, Bonny. She was taking Bonny to the cottage hospital across the road to visit the patients suffering from mental illness, the elderly and frail and those recovering from strokes. The patients were greatly helped by Bonny's visits. Bonny was gentle, trusting, loyal and friendly, and a dog helped to keep them in touch with the world outside or brought back happy memories. On another occasion on holiday in France, I saw a man out with his dog. The man's face was terribly disfigured. But dogs do not see disfigurement or disability; they do not recoil from outward appearances. These dogs were contributing, perhaps unknowingly, to the healing and wholeness of human beings.

Our whole lives are a journey towards healing and wholeness. And some things will help that process and some things will hinder, as today's collection of stories illustrates. Distorted notions such as our own inferiority or greatness or that of others, of faith-healing over and above medical-healing, will hinder. Openness to God, a willingness to learn and journey in faith will help. All that contributes to healing of mind, body and spirit is of God.

How can we be more open to all the avenues of healing in our world?

Open God, heal us through your love.

When I visit someone in hospital, it is often difficult to find them. Even if I know them well, patients lying in identical beds wearing nightclothes, without jewellery, make-up or usual hairdo can be very difficult to spot. Often they see me first – looking slightly lost. They smile, our eyes meet and contact is established. I then wonder how I could have failed to spot them immediately. My own problem in identifying someone in a hospital bed is illustrative of our tendency to compartmentalise people with an illness or disability: they become patients, or cancer sufferers or 'the disabled'.

To see or not to see

Luke 17:11-19

In today's story these ten people are identified by Luke by their illness – they are lepers. As lepers, they had to be treated differently, to be isolated. Thus they lost any individual identity of their own. We tend to assume they were all male, all Jewish – except one who was a Samaritan. But there could have been more who were Samaritans, and perhaps some of them were women. We know more about this one simply because he did not go with the crowd. He chose to set himself apart, to turn and recognise the source of his healing, to offer praise to God and be made whole, not simply cured of his leprosy.

How do we look beyond the labels to the common humanity that we all share?

Seeing God, heal us through your love.

Silence

1 Old Testament silences

Preparing for the week

Biblical scholars tell us that much of what Christians know as the Old Testament was gathered together during the exile of the leaders of the Jewish people in Babylon in the sixth century BCE. This was a time of great creativity and soul-searching as the Hebrews wrestled with the calamity of the fall of Jerusalem to the Persian army. How could God have let this happen to his chosen people? Why did God seem to be silent when they had called out in distress, and what words could be adequate for the response of the people to God's presence and seeming absence?

During the same century, two other religious traditions were defined in teachings of great beauty and profundity. In China, the sage Lao Tsu left his sayings in a book called the *Tao Te Ching*, or The Book of the Way of Virtue, the founding text of Taoism. In India a prince called Siddhartha became the monk known to posterity as the Buddha, the Awakened One. His experience of enlightenment has echoed through the centuries producing all the varied forms of Buddhism in our world today. Lao Tsu and the Buddha both valued silence highly, and the notes this week and next will be in dialogue with these two venerable religious traditions. Quotations from the *Tao Te Ching* will come from the translation by Gia-Fu Feng and Jane English (London: Wildwood House 1972).

Sunday 15 August

Notes based on the New Revised Standard Version by

Nicholas Alan Worssam SSF

Brother Nicholas Alan is a member of the Anglican religious community, the Society of Saint Francis. He has been a friar since 1995, and has lived at Glasshampton Monastery in Worcestershire, England, since 2002.

For further thought

- How and where do you experience silence?
- Do you think of silence as something positive or negative – or both?
- Which persons, texts and traditions have taught you about the spiritual value of silence?

This story about the prophet Elijah is one of the great theophanies, or revelations of God, in the Hebrew scriptures. Yet God's self-revelation is simply silence. At this Elijah hides himself, wrapping himself in his mantle.

The most secret name of God, YHWH, cannot even be spoken, with the word Adonai or 'The LORD' being substituted instead. If the name YHWH can be said to have a meaning it is something like 'I am who I am', or 'the One who Is'. God is Being Itself, on which everything else depends. God is here in the beginning, making all things to be, the father and mother of all creation. 'Ten thousand' in Chinese is the equivalent of 'countless' in English – all things begin here in the named, which itself returns to its root in that which cannot be spoken.

How quick we are to define God, and how offended when others contradict our definition! Should we even be wrapping ourselves in names that separate us from each other, identities that exclude and deny? God does not name God's intimate self, which can only be found in silence and awe.

Lord, teach me the name above every name; may I listen and be wrapped in your silence.

The sound of sheer silence

1 Kings 19:9-18

The Tao that can be told is not the eternal Tao.
The name that can be named is not the eternal name.
The nameless is the beginning of heaven and earth.
The named is the mother of ten thousand things.

Tao Te Ching, 1

Silence

Nicholas Alan Worssam

No fight, no blame

2 Kings 2:1-11

The highest good is like water.
Water gives life to the ten thousand things and does not strive.
It flows in places people reject and so is like the Tao.
In dwelling, be close to the land.
In meditation, go deep in the heart.
In dealing with others, be gentle and kind. . .

Tao Te Ching, 8

The Tao, or Way, is a path of mystery. It has no name, yet it is the foundation of all names. It makes no show of force, yet it is the strongest thing in the universe. Like water it flows close to the earth, it yields at the meeting of an obstacle, yet in time can wear away even the hardest stone. The prophets of Israel did not always show this way of non-confrontation, like Elisha striking the water to make it part. Their words are like flint, and their actions like fire. To the Chinese, this is the way of *yang*, the bright, active energy of the sun. The sage follows the way of *yin:* the soft, yielding relative darkness of the moon.

Jesus, a later prophet and sage of Israel, also came to bring fire to the earth, and both dreaded and desired its kindling (Luke 12:49), but he refused to call down fire on the Samaritan village that turned him away (Luke 9:51-56). Instead, Jesus yields to political power in his trial, and in both fire and water he is baptised into the ocean of God's love.

Holy Spirit, fire of God, brood over the waters of my soul.

Nicholas Alan Worssam

Silence

In the face of Job's sufferings, what was there to say? In the experience of pain there is very little comfort in words. Rationalisations about the will of God seem to raise more questions than they answer. And yet, himself standing alone and unchanging, Job holds on tenaciously to the righteousness of God and his own place in that righteousness. If God is the source of all things, who creates both pleasure and pain (Isaiah 45:7), then there is nothing that can separate us from God, not even the loss of all things.

Call God 'great', 'eternal', 'loving', 'just': all are approximations that fall short of a grandeur that would overwhelm us were we to be brought unprepared into that roaring silence and bursting void. Yet God is ever present, always the still point at the centre of our pain. And Christ is our preparation, the cloak of our nakedness as we approach God's throne. In Christ we are righteous, worthy of God's delight, standing before and within God, our mother and our eternal home.

Is there someone you know in pain who would benefit from your silent, loving presence?

Loving God, be my comfort, my shelter in the raging storm.

No one spoke a word

Job 2:7-13

Something mysteriously formed,
Born before heaven and earth.
In the silence and the void,
Standing alone and un-changing,
Ever present and in motion.
Perhaps it is the mother of ten thousand things.
I do not know its name.
Call it Tao.
For lack of a better word, I call it great.
Tao Te Ching, 25

Silence

Nicholas Alan Worssam

Be still, and know that I am God

Psalm 46:1-11

The softest thing in the universe
Overcomes the hardest thing in the universe.
That without substance can enter where there is no room.
Hence I know the value of non-action.
Teaching without words and work without doing
Are understood by very few.

Tao Te Ching, 43

Verse 10 from today's psalm is a charter for Jewish and Christian contemplation. Stillness and taking refuge in God bring absence of fear 'though the earth should change, though the mountains shake in the heart of the sea' (verse 2). In these days of ecological concern, when the climate of the earth is changing around us, there is an imperative for all people to act. We desperately need to change the destructive patterns of modern life. How can the sage value 'non-action'?

The sage in Taoism does in fact act, but always with and not against nature. The sage closely observes the way of all things, and acts in harmony with the natural world. Nothing is done forcefully, yet nothing is left undone.

Jesus also taught without words, his actions left no political or ecological mark. Yet the results of his non-action in the face of his accusers are sustaining us still. He was the wind, blowing where it will, flowing over and around all things, the substance that can enter even where there seems to be no room.

Holy Spirit of Jesus, steep me in stillness, teach me to know and to live God's way.

Nicholas Alan Worssam

Silence

The first two lines of today's quotation from the *Tao Te Ching* can be called the quintessence of Lao Tzu's teaching – and yet he went on to write a whole book! In Psalm 50, God keeps silence while others give their mouth 'free rein for evil' (verse 19). But God also knows when to speak, when to rebuke and to show the way of salvation.

In Genesis, we read that God created humanity from the dust of the earth, and it is to dust that we return. We emerge from silence and return to silence; would it not be better to know the value of this silence before the end? So much of our thinking and talking magnifies our problems. We create crises that need never exist. Entering purposefully into silence can be the way to true self-knowledge, the entrance to a humility that unites us with God.

Think back over the last 24 hours. When might you have helped others by speaking less? When could silence have been your gift?

Unite me, Lord, with your silence, that your brightness may shine in my life.

I have been silent

Psalm 50:16-23

Those who know do not talk.
Those who talk do not know.
Keep your mouth closed.
Guard your senses.
Temper your sharpness.
Simplify your problems.
Mask your brightness.
Be at one with the dust of the earth.
This is primal union.

Tao Te Ching, 56

Silence

Nicholas Alan Worssam

Let all the earth keep silence

Habukkuk 2:18-20

A tree as great as a man's embrace springs from a small shoot;
A journey of a thousand miles starts under one's feet. . .
Therefore the sage seeks freedom from desire,
does not collect precious things,
learns not to hold on to ideas,
brings people back to what they have lost.

Tao Te Ching, 64

The essence of idolatry is greed, says Paul to the Colossians (3:5). It is attachment to the finite in the vain hope that it will guarantee the infinite, the God who is beyond all representation, beyond all names. Knowing this, the sage does not collect precious things, even the things of religion, but allows them to be markers on the way which direct the faithful to the invisible God. This journey of dispossession begins with each step, this very moment in which we know ourselves to be still in transit, not yet arrived at our goal. Therefore each moment is precious, a stillness when we can survey the journey ahead, when we can hold the seed of faith in our hand and know that by God's grace it will become a great tree reaching even to the heavens.

God is in his holy temple, says Habakkuk, and where is that temple but within and among us here and now? Letting go we realise that we have already been given that for which we have been searching all our lives; the end of our travels is right here, in God's presence, in the rediscovery of what we have lost.

Lead me into your holy temple, Lord; open me in silence to your word.

Silence

2 New Testament silences

Notes based on the New Revised Standard Version by

Nicholas Alan Worssam SSF

For Brother Nicholas's biography see p.230.

Preparing for the week

This week we continue the theme of silence, but now in company with the teaching of the Buddha. The particular text we will follow is the Dhammapada, a concise summary of the Buddha's teachings much beloved by Buddhists of many traditions. (Quotations from *A Dhammapada for Contemplation,* translated by Ajahn Munindo, Harnham: River Publications 2000). The Buddha was a rich young man who gave up his sheltered life for that of a wandering monk: a pattern so close to that of the founder of my own tradition, St Francis of Assisi. What the Buddha discovered in the forests of India 2500 years ago was the Uncreated and Eternal, the knowledge of which brings true peace and an end to all suffering. But to know this reality, this release which he called Nirvana, it is imperative that we make friends with silence. Only when the mind is still and clear enough can we see through the deceptions of our hatred and greed, and enter the stream of the holy life.

Jesus too entered silence many times and knew it as a place of struggle and nourishment. Journeying into the deserts of Palestine, climbing mountains to escape the crowds, or engaging with the political and religious powers of his day, he searched for and found the silence that nurtured his relationship with God. In solitude and in the midst of a crowd he knew that God was always with him: the Eternal found in each breath of time.

For further thought

- What do you know of the struggle and the nourishment of silence?
- What commitment to the practice of silence might you be called to make this week?

Being amazed by his answer, they became silent

Luke 20:20-26

*Never by hatred is hatred conquered,
but by readiness to love alone.
This is eternal law.
Those who are contentious
have forgotten that we all die;
for the wise, who reflect on this fact,
there are no quarrels*

Dhammapada 5,6

When spies from the scribes and chief priests came to Jesus they were not entering into an honest debate. They were trying to trick him, trying to make him favour one side or another. Should we pay taxes, pollute ourselves by handling the image of the emperor on the Roman coins, and acquiesce with their occupation? Or should we rebel, and risk all in a fight to remove the hated oppressors? But Jesus isn't fooled. He doesn't fall into their categories of opposition. His way was not about hate, but about love, including even one's enemies. He knew that before God all stood as sinners, but that God loves us still, regardless of how far we have strayed.

The Buddha spoke often of peace: within oneself and with others. Not just the absence of war, but positive, radiating peace, based on a compassion like that of a mother for her only son. Dwelling on past wrongs helps no one, least of all ourselves. Remember your mortality, and quarrels fall into perspective. Conquer yourself not others, and know the security of true peace.

Who are your enemies? How can you love them as friends?

Teach me, Lord, the way of your love.

When Jesus looked at Peter there was a world of meaning in his eyes. He had no need of words. Peter understood perfectly, and he wept. He had denied the one he loved more than any other, the one he had followed, leaving everything behind. But Jesus wasn't angry, maybe not even sad, for he knew that all this was going to happen and that somehow God had everything in hand. This was the cup he had to drink, the suffering he had to endure, and Peter's denial was simply part of the story unfolding grimly around him.

Patience is a virtue, we sometimes glibly say, but how many of us really want the opportunity to practise it? And yet without the gift of opposition and disappointment, how can we know how patient we really are? The early Christian theologians taught that God the Father never suffers, only God the Son. Though modern theology disputes this, is it not true that deep within us all there is a pool of still water, a reservoir of strength and calm that in fact saves us in the most desperate of situations? Is this not the peace of God, fleshed out here in Jesus, looking at his friend with unutterable love?

Be peace within me, O Lord, the rock from which I spring.

The Lord turned and looked at Peter

Luke 22:54-62

There are those who discover
they can leave behind confused reactions
and become patient as the earth;
unmoved by anger,
unshaken as a pillar,
unperturbed as a clear and quiet pool.

Dhammapada, 95

Silence

Nicholas Alan Worssam

Jesus gave Herod no answer

Luke 23:6-12

Better than ruling the whole world,
better than going to heaven,
better than lordship over the universe,
is an irreversible commitment to the Way.

Dhammapada, 178

Herod plays with Jesus. He wants to see a sign, or hear words of great wisdom. He wants to be entertained. But Jesus does not answer. He has gone beyond games. He knows that this conversation could mean for him life or death, but he is unconcerned. Herod flaunts his power, orders his soldiers around, but eventually gets bored and sends Jesus back to Pilate again.

Jesus knew that he was surrounded by worldly power greater than that of his few followers, but he also knew that he could command angels and all the powers of heaven if he chose. And yet there was something more important here than a display of power. Ever since his temptation in the desert, Jesus had consistently chosen against self-promoting display. His was the way of the obedient Son, the path shown him by his Father, a way that would eventually lead him to death. In fact, to hold fast to God's will was a display of power more potent than anything Herod or Pilate could muster. Jesus continued to the end, and showed all people the Way.

What is it that you seek in your practice of religion? How can your commitment be strengthened today?

Lord, show me your way.

The suffering servant who is also a king, the lion of the tribe of Judah who appears as a lamb: these are some of the paradoxes or ironies of salvation in the scriptures. Here the weak overpower the strong, the silent are more eloquent than those who speak. This is the foolishness of God, greater than human wisdom, stronger than human strength.

Silence is often interpreted as weakness. It may indeed mask a fear of engagement, even a denial of our own voice. But with Jesus it was something else. Silence for him was communication. It spoke of his transcendence beyond the bonds of his imprisonment. He was stilled and free, regardless of whether others regarded him as a helpless captive. His was the silence of strength, having gone beyond all personal desires. His only will now was that God's will should be done, whether in death or in life. He knew the uncreated as his source, his true nature. He had gone beyond death and birth while still in this body, just as he had gone beyond enemy and friend. Nothing at all could harm him now.

Is there craving still to be discarded in your life?

Silent God, reveal to us the uncreated, that we may truly find peace.

Like a lamb silent before its shearer

Acts 8:26-40

Those who know the un-created,
who are free and stilled,
who have discarded all craving,
are the most worthy beings.

Dhammapada, 97

Silence   Nicholas Alan Worssam

The Lord's will be done

Acts 21:10-14

Cease to do evil,
cultivate that which is
good;
purify the heart.
This is the Way
of the Awakened Ones.

Dhammapada, 183

These words of the Buddha are often used as a summary of his teaching. Jesus said 'Blessed are the pure in heart, for they will see God' (Matthew 5:8). The Buddha didn't use theological language. He was wary of the endless debates that he saw going on around him: Are the soul or the world eternal? What happens to an enlightened being after death? These kinds of questions he avoided at all turns. 'All I teach,' he said, 'is suffering and the ending of suffering.' He was like a doctor curing a deadly wound without pausing to debate the ethics of its cause. But the Buddha did speak of Nirvana, a state beyond all pain, the final release from our self-centred greed, hatred and delusion. He was silent among theologians, but among the suffering ordinary people he was infinitely patient and calm – teaching by his life and actions the way to freedom from fear.

In the reading from Acts, Paul's companions do not understand his actions. He wants to return to Jerusalem at obvious risk to his own life. This, for Paul, was cultivating the good: purifying himself in the generosity that led to imprisonment and death. For a heart as open as this no words were necessary, no bonds could make him less free.

Purify my heart that I may walk in your way.

Silence in heaven

'When the Lamb opened the seventh seal, there was silence in heaven for about half an hour.' What a surprising sentence that is! How could John the seer have judged the time? The Book of Revelation seems to swirl in and out of linear consciousness, expanding and contracting the ages of humanity. Worship and terror and stunned silent awe weave a picture almost too vivid to contemplate. Finally all the pain and the tears of God's people are wiped away and God is all in all.

Revelation 7:9-17, 8:1

The Buddha also taught the end of all suffering, the further shore across a sea of distress. But to get there one has to discard all that hinders, even the raft which carries one across. Let go of past, future, even present! No more lingering in memories or dreams, not even holding onto the securities at hand. Just let go – put it all down – and the heart in its freedom is released from within. When you reach that point, nothing needs to be said, nothing needs to be added at all. Heaven and earth have passed away, and the former things are no more. See! Everything has become new!

Let go of the past.
Let go of the future.
Let go of the present.
With a heart that is free
cross over to that shore
which is beyond suffering.

Dhammapada, 148

Wipe away, Lord, every tear from our eyes. Enable us all to see.

Silence

Nicholas Alan Worssam

Rivers of the Bible

Preparing for the week

Rivers have always been crucial for the flourishing of human life and civilisations. They nurture life – human, animal and plant life – sustain economies and enable communities, languages, religions, art and science to grow by their banks. However, rivers have also been sources of intense conflicts and wars, and of death and devastation, when there is scarcity of water for human consumption and for agriculture, when floods occur and when rivers are polluted. As much as these are sources of life, they are also sites of death. No one would deny the importance of rivers and water in spite of these negative consequences, which are themselves a result of human intentions and actions.

In many religious traditions, rivers are regarded as sacred, as abodes of God, and as spiritual and physical purifiers. Ritual bathing in rivers is a sacred ritual, as it is for my Hindu friends. So is baptism for us Christians. So it was for the people of the Bible. The four major rivers that are mentioned more than others in the Bible are: the Tigris, Euphrates, Nile and Jordan. There are also other mythical as well as imaginary rivers mentioned at the beginning and the end of the Bible. We shall examine some of these during this week with a view to seeing what these stories and images tell us about what our attitudes ought to be towards this wonderful aspect of God's good creation.

Notes based on the New Revised Standard Version by

Deenabandhu Manchala

Deenabandhu Manchala, a Lutheran pastor and theologian from India, is an executive secretary of the World Council of Churches, Geneva, Switzerland.

For further thought

- How much water do you use in comparison to others around you, and those in different contexts and economic locations?
- If Jesus is the living water, how does our faith in him effect changes around us?

A threatened ruler sees the river as an instrument of violence, but the subversive power of love of a sister sees it as a means to sustain life. One wants to abuse God's gift of life to protect his own power interests, another uses it to save the life of the other. While greed kills, love and compassion affirm life. Ironically, Moses, who was thus saved, turns the same river into one of blood later (Exodus 7:14-24).

'I drew him out of water'

Exodus 1:22 – 2:10

Creation is God's gift, and its rich and varied features express God's wisdom and generosity. These can be gifts or curses to us as well as to others, depending on our intentions and approaches. Rivers are sources of life and will remain so if they are not monopolised and abused. Private ownership of land, rivers, forests and other common natural assets has always been the cause of conflict, violence and wars in many parts of the world throughout history.

Similarly with our relationships and opportunities: we can abuse them for our selfish interests or we can use them in ways that are mutually edifying and enriching. We can waste but we can also conserve; we can pollute, make business out of water, but we can also safeguard and share this limited but important source of life. While greed kills, love and compassion affirm life. Rivers proclaim this divine generosity and wisdom that constantly calls each one of us to account for the other.

Help me, God, to use your gifts of resources, time and talent to protect life, mine as well as others'.

Rivers of the Bible

Deenabandhu Manchala

'Waters flowing from above'

Joshua 3:1-17

The Lord who brought the slaves out of bondage sees them through insurmountable obstacles. He makes the sea and the river part to keep his promise of liberation (Exodus 14:21-25). Images of an omnipotent God, often aggressive and violent, who is not constrained by the laws of nature, are dominant in many major religious traditions. We find such images in some sections of the Bible too: a God who was able to part the sea, darken the sun, calm the storm, walk on water, and so on. While these stories open to us the faith-world of the people of the Bible, these images have also inspired some destructive attitudes and responses – such as the viewing of unlimited power as divine blessing, the glorification of power; an attitude towards nature as if it is an object to be controlled, exploited and dominated; and the seeking of supernatural interventions in crisis moments as proof of God's presence and the lack of it if they don't occur.

People demonstrated such attitudes when Hurricane Katrina struck the US, the tsunami devastated the Indian Ocean countries and when floods and typhoons happen all over the world killing millions, mostly the poor. Scientific research has proved that many of these natural disasters are the result of human intrusion into the complex web of life. The fact that the poor are the worst victims of these natural disasters exposes the unethical values that govern our lives and social structures.

The absence of obstacles and hardships is not a sign of divine presence. Rather, it is our ability to discern God's will that helps us to overcome all hurdles, including the sense of helplessness and hopelessness.

Open my eyes, God, to see you by my side in my struggles and crises.

Creation, preservation, healing and restoration are the attributes that we ascribe to the divinity, and rivers testify to these life-nurturing characteristics of God.

Naaman was sent by Elijah to find healing by dipping in a river. He was annoyed at being asked to bathe in the river that belonged to his subjects. He took it as an insult because he attached human characteristics to God's gifts.

It is often hard for dominant groups to accept the resources of tradition and wisdom of excluded groups. The forests flourished as long as they remained under the stewardship of indigenous or agrarian communities, but the traditions of prudence of those peoples are often obliterated by modern scientific and economic analysis and policies. In my country, India, the caste-minded Hindus look at water as a source of pollution and hence restrict any contact with the Dalits (the untouchable castes). Our arrogance of power often blinds us to the moral self-disfigurement that it causes us.

Our healing and restoration are possible only when we enter the identity of the despised and excluded. Is this not what the story of the Good Samaritan teaches? Is this not the story of the cross? In today's story, the lesson of the river is to recognise the equality of all before God.

'Wash in the Jordan seven times'

2 Kings 5:1-14

Heal me, O God, from the sin of arrogance and grant me humility to recognise your presence in all that you have created.

Rivers of the Bible

Deenabandhu Manchala

'Beside the river, the vision of God'

Psalm 137:1-4,
Ezekiel 1:1-4

In many religious traditions, water is portrayed as the locale of God's presence, grandeur and mystery. In the cries of the exiles on the banks of rivers, visions of liberation were formed, visions of God received, and the hand of God felt. The prophet Ezekiel narrates how it was in exile, beside the river, that he saw the vision of God.

God's wisdom, generosity, self-expression and purposes are found in much of what makes our natural world. But human greed and selfishness, pride and arrogance, contradict God's purposes for life and for all. The exiles in Babylon could not celebrate life as they gazed at the waters, the very waters that stood as a symbol of their identity and liberation, a symbol of God's unconditional and boundless love and the source of new life. 'Beside the river Jordan, we sat and wept as we thought of Jerusalem.' God's will for life is freedom and life in its fullest expression. God's creation, especially rivers, amply testify to this purpose and generosity, and the free nature of life itself. But these natural resources can only be a blessing when greed and aggression do not abuse and diminish life.

Enable me to feel your presence as I celebrate your creation and as I yearn for justice for all.

We are at the Jordan again, the same river that stood aside to let the captives flee to freedom, the same river in which Namaan was cured, and by the side of which Ezekiel saw the vision of God and felt the hand of God. This same river is now the place of John's confession of Jesus as the Messiah and the place in which he baptises Jesus and testifies to the Spirit's descent. This river which is so much a part of the history of Israel is also an important landmark in the history of Christian faith because of its association with Jesus' baptism.

In all this, we find the power of God being revealed – a power to liberate, to heal and to mark new beginnings. Note, however, that the riverside where all this happens is that of a small village called Bethany. This insignificant village marks the beginning of God's plan of salvation and a new creation. Many great things have small beginnings.

The custodians of religion often tend to attribute power and grandeur to faith traditions in order to make them serve the interests of the dominant sections of society. The priests and Levites were not convinced that divine revelations could take place in a village through the leader of an insignificant grassroots rebel movement. John announces the new era in simple faith but with firm hope and determination.

'In Bethany across the Jordan'

John 1:19-28

Grant me courage to embrace new beginnings and the humility to find them, even among the remote and the insignificant.

Rivers of the Bible

Deenabandhu Manchala

'Rivers of living water'

John 7:37-39

The Spirit is like water. Like a river, it flows wherever it wills, effecting new life, nurturing life, healing and restoring the sick and the dying.

Some Christians believe that spirituality is an exclusively personal and mystical relationship with God and consequently tend to ignore the need for our relationship with God to be reflected in our attitudes towards and relationships with others. Resurrection stands for the unflinching determination of the Spirit of life to triumph over all that kills – including greed and selfishness. Genuine spirituality then is not something that makes one more selfish and inward-focused but an energy that enables life to flow outwards to those around. The fruits of the Spirit are love, joy, peace, long suffering, gentleness, goodness, faith, meekness and temperance (Galatians 5:22-23). One who is endowed by the Spirit is one who enables and releases life.

How do we witness to Jesus as living water to people who are deprived of or destroyed by rivers? Rivers purify and give life, water for drinking and for agriculture, and food. But rivers are also polluted; they become graveyards for the poor, through floods and big dams. It is, therefore, unethical to spiritualise Jesus' offer of living water in a world where there is so much water scarcity and pollution as well as the commercialisation of water.

What rivers of living water flow from our hearts?

Cleanse me so that I may reflect the goodness and generosity that I have experienced of you.

Deenabandhu Manchala

Rivers of the Bible

Writing

1 Stones, letters and graffiti

Preparing for the week

The earliest forms of writing are attributed to accountants. Sumerian clay balls, marked with records showing the amounts of grain which had been stored for the winter, point to the essentially demotic nature of writing. Once something has been written down it belongs to more than one person. Writing over the centuries, in various times and places, has not only been appropriated by a learned elite, but actually forbidden to women and those of low rank. It has also been a tool for liberation and empowerment. The scriptures themselves, which tell the story of liberation and good news for the poor, have been among the instruments of the rich in maintaining their status. The passages below tell part of the story of writing. I teach adult literacy among other things, and witness daily the empowering effect that learning to read and write has on people's lives. The struggle for life of the written word, memory and storytelling continues to triumph over vested interest, corruption and oppression.

For further thought and action

- How do I use my power as a literate person?
- What do I read and what do I write? What effect do these activities have on me and those around me?
- Read something new, by a writer from a country you know nothing about.

Notes based on
the Jerusalem Bible by
Ruth Shelton

Ruth Shelton is a poet and theologian who has worked in a variety of settings including prisons, hostels, a city farm and for the Church of England. She is presently teaching in a further education college in Nottingham, based in a hostel and a supported factory for adults with learning difficulties.

Monday 6 September

Representing the word

Deuteronomy 31:9-13;
Joshua 8:30-35

The distance from Washington to Mississippi is 1948 miles. An elderly black couple from Mississippi interviewed in Washington on the day of Barack Obama's inauguration told the reporter, 'It was imperative that we were here.' As the cameras panned the crowd, we saw unprecedented numbers of the poor, black and Hispanic, their faces lifted up to hear their hopes and dreams spoken out loud, their story reflected in the ceremony.

When the people of Israel heard the words of the law, they heard their own story. Joshua seems to have understood this. Exhausted by their final occupation of the city-state of Ai, the tribes are led to Shechem in the valley between the mountains. They gather, six by one mountain, six by the other, with Joshua and the elders, and the Ark in the valley between. There Joshua reads the law, and each tribe responds to the other, the blessing and curses echoing back and forth, ringing around the valley.

Moses and Joshua knew that the words of the law had to be living words. Even when they were forgotten or distorted, there would be a recapitulation: the whole tribe, including the strangers who lived among them, gathered to hear the story of their liberation come alive for them all over again.

In the Joshua account the tribes have defeated a wall of water, the walls of Jericho, a wall of smoke, and still have to face a wall of light and hailstones. But in the middle of them was a collapsed wall, the opposite of a wall, a pile of undressed stones. This was their altar, and Joshua wrote on the stones, offering their story, their memories, and their fidelity to God, the echoing Promise who would never fail to reply.

We pray for all who embody the hope of the word,
for all who echo the word,
for all who search for the word.
God is near.

Ruth Shelton

Writing

A friend of mine recently spent a day in court with an asylum seeker making his final plea. If it fails he will be deported. Although she had known him for a few years, she hadn't heard his harrowing history until it was read out in court.

A lost book, a shared memory, an undiscovered manuscript, an eleventh commandment? In our contemporary world the truth is often fragmented, compartmentalised, hidden.

Since the time in the desert when Joshua read out the law, missing out not a single word in front of the whole tribe, and the strangers that lived among them, something has changed. Dignitaries are in a flurry. Great repairs and refurbishments are being carried out in the temple. Among the items in his report of the day's activities, Shaphan the secretary adds that a book has been found. Once again the words, lost from sight among the splendours of the temple, break open into the air. Once again, all the people, of low and high degree, hear a lost fragment of their story and remember.

'Speak the truth to one another,' says Paul, 'for we belong as parts of one body. If we forget one part then the whole is damaged'.

The life of the asylum seeker is a jagged fragment, displaced, unheard, unknown. Until the stories of the dispossessed, past and present, are known and understood, our prejudices and denials dusted off, we cannot understand or know ourselves.

Keeping the word

2 Kings 22:8-13; 23:1-3

We pray for all asylum seekers, refugees, and displaced people,
for all those who work with them and alongside them,
for the keepers of their story.
God is near.

Writing   Ruth Shelton

Wednesday 8 September

Meeting the word

Daniel 5:1-9, 13-17,
23-28

As someone who does a great deal of cooking, I hope that a 'thousand' just means 'a lot'! There is something darker, however, about this 'thousand'. It's a rent-a-crowd, a rabble, the sheer numbers designed to flatter the host, rather than to offer hospitality. You feel that if you tried to leave this party you would be met by an armed guard. Even the drinking vessels have been looted from the temple.

In Rembrandt's painting of the scene, the sense of chaos is accentuated by narrow wedge-shaped pieces having been cut from all four sides of the canvas in the past. When remounted, the canvas was twisted very slightly anticlockwise, and as a consequence, Rembrandt's turbulent effects are exaggerated by the table running uphill and the wine spilt by the woman on the right of the picture falling sideways instead of vertically.

This is a eucharist in reverse in which hospitality becomes corruption, the free-flowing wine drains uselessly from defiled cups. The shiny gods praised by the guests can only offer back their own reflections. The truth, although terrifying, is obscure, inscribed on a plastered wall or hoarding. Those present are forced to turn to flesh and blood for illumination, to a man indifferent to wealth or status, one who would dare to walk freely among his enemies. In Genesis 17:13 we read about 'the covenant in our flesh'. This kind of promise is not conditional, limited on both sides by a set of rules, but the loving attention of flesh and blood to flesh and blood, which God shares and continually celebrates with us.

We pray for all those working in dangerous places,
for smashers of idols,
for all who give life to the word.
God is near.

Ruth Shelton
254

Writing

There is a pleasing physicality about the efforts of Jeremiah and Baruch to write down what God had said and to make sure that other people read it. A written document in the ancient world generally had a very short life. Unless written on stone or maintained by unusual climatic conditions, it had to be copied in order to be preserved. Writing seems to have developed for economic reasons rather than literary ones. Writing enabled the collection of taxes, marked property and verified transactions. Literary texts were not preserved as records to be consulted, but as cultural artefacts, whose stories, philosophy, laws or prayers furnished the social reality. These texts were organic: they were copied with reasonable fidelity, but were also creatively altered by editing, or combining with other texts.

Jeremiah and Baruch's attempts to write down and read out the words of the scroll could be seen as their conversation with society, their effort to hold up the truth to a corrupt regime. Although Jeremiah is forbidden to go to the temple, his visionary determination sees through the closed doors to all the people gathered for the fast. He hears the murmurings and the gasps as the words take their effect. As the book of Jeremiah is a wide-angled view of the lives of many generations, far beyond Jeremiah's own lifetime, so his scroll – written, rewritten, transcribed, read aloud, destroyed and rewritten – speaks to us of the unfailing insistence of God's truth, against which we fear to measure ourselves, against which we bar the door, certain that his love will find us.

We pray for all those who document the signs of the times, for those who campaign against injustice.
God is near.

Insisting on the word

Jeremiah 36:1-10

Writing   Ruth Shelton

Liberating the word

Jeremiah 36:11-26

'Where they have burned books they will soon burn human beings', the German author Heinrich Heine warned in 1933. The British Muslims who, twenty years ago, burned copies of Salman Rushdie's novel, *The Satanic Verses*, in the streets of Bradford, were largely unaware of the cultural heritage left by the Nazi book-burnings. They were unprepared for the outrage their actions caused, particularly to the British Left, their natural supporters. There is a complex dialectic at work here. For the British liberal intelligentsia, the burning of a book was blasphemy, but they were unable to understand the offence against the holy that the book represented.

For us, the king's almost comical desperation to destroy the scroll is hard to understand. But the burning of the scroll was a sort of inverted reverence. The king recognised and feared the power of the scroll, so by burning it, he could destroy its power.

For centuries, governments, dictatorships and regimes have read, suppressed and destroyed documents behind closed doors. But there is always someone, a group or a community, who will risk imprisonment and death to rewrite them, and read them out loud again to the people to whom the truth belongs.

We pray for all writers, poets, journalists and artists in prison,
their families and supporters.
For those who have died in prison or been executed for their art,
for their families and supporters.
God is near.

Ruth Shelton

Writing

The scroll has been burnt; Jeremiah and Baruch are in hiding, under threat of death. Whatever their privations, we hear nothing of them. The story continues at a relentless pace. Yahweh speaks again: 'Take another scroll . . .'

Generating the word

Walter Brueggeman, challenging the idea of a variety of literary sources in Jeremiah, says 'we may think of these several distinct perspectives within the book as crucial interpretive voices in the community that insisted on a hearing and that, for whatever reason, were given a hearing in the final form of the text' (*Theology of the Book of Jeremiah*, Cambridge University Press 2007). Part of the book's dynamism is that it allows several contesting voices to stand alongside one another, without noticeable harmonisation, so that the reading of it becomes an experiential paradigm for what it describes. The traditions of Jeremiah are 'immensely generative', says Brueggeman. The 'surround sound' of the text, with a multiplicity of interpretive voices, produces more and more words and meanings.

Jeremiah 36:27-32

Contemporary commentators from within and outside the church have recognised a form of idolatry in the Christian community: we are only speaking to and for ourselves, from within locked doors. The air and the words have become stale and no one is inclined to breathe them in.

Jeremiah and Baruch, focused on the crisis outside their place of hiding and still envisioning the crowds of all the people 'of low and high degree' who would gather to hear 'every word' that God had spoken, found new words to write and new words to speak.

We pray for people on the fringes of the church,
for those seeking new models of church,
for the 'thorns in the flesh' of the corporate body.
God is near.

Writing   Ruth Shelton

Writing

2 Keeping what is important

Notes based on the *Jerusalem Bible* by **Ruth Shelton**

For Ruth's biography see p.251.

Preparing for the week

I have just finished reading Juliet Barker's *History of the Brontës* (Phoenix, 2001). It is a clear-sighted work, based rigorously on textual evidence, which told me slightly more than I wanted to know. A fascinating subtext of the work is the account of the letters and manuscripts generated by the Brontë family and their correspondents. What was kept and what was destroyed and why has a powerful impact on the story and on the delineation of the characters.

Luke and John go to some trouble in their prefaces (among the passages we will consider this week) to say why they thought it was important to write an account of Jesus' life and death. They each focus on different aspects of the story for different reasons and for different readers and listeners. They were also, part of the time, drawing on different sources. What they wrote down, what they selected and what they left out was of great significance to them and that subjectivity is more precious than a congruent historical report of what happened would be, even if such a thing were possible.

As we read, whoever and wherever we are all over the world, our subjectivity, our cultural and faith perspectives, mingle with those of the writers of scripture in a daily explosion of insight, inspiration and sustenance – continuing to keep what is important alive.

For further thought and action

• I am one of the keepers of the story of liberation and good news for the poor. What is my part in keeping that story alive?

• Become a volunteer in a local literacy project.

• Find out about projects at home or overseas which need books – organise a collection.

I was recently in the old market square in the centre of Nottingham, watching the remnants of a St Patrick's Day parade. A few older women were dancing with each other to the ersatz Irish music. The word that came to my mind was 'exile'. These were people in the midst of one culture, still yearning, however unconsciously, for another.

Since the city of Jerusalem had not been destroyed in the first Babylonian invasion in 598, many Israelites were still holding out hope for some last-minute reprieve from the destruction that Jeremiah had so long been proclaiming. The exiles, who had been taken to Babylon after the first invasion there, were agitating for rebellion. At the heart of this uncertainty and conflict lay the theological dogma of the inviolability of Zion, the idea that Jerusalem could not be destroyed because God dwelt there in the temple. 'God's own country' as people sometimes describe their home town or region.

Exile separates us from our own self-image, whether by political upheavals, bereavements, loss of mental health, redundancy or ageing. The revellers at Belshazzar's feast could only see themselves in the mirrors of their metal gods.

But God will find us wherever we go, however painful the journey, because he is already there. He has left the temple and walks with us down the ordinary shabby streets of our daily lives, the living stones of the new Jerusalem.

We pray for travellers, and all those in transit,
for those suffering loss, or bereavement,
for those facing the loss of their home or jobs,
for those facing death and those who are alongside them.
God is near.

The calligraphy of the holy

Jeremiah 29:1-11

Writing   Ruth Shelton

The calligraphy of attention

Proverbs 22:17-21

The constant exhortation throughout the book of Proverbs is to listen. These verses include the only reference to writing in the book of Proverbs, a rather daunting sounding 'thirty chapters' (verse 20) in the Jerusalem Bible translation.

The opening lines, however, seem to refer not to the reason or the intellect but to the body, the ears and the heart. It is the heart thast listens and learns, and the lips that speak.

The heart, nowadays the place of conscience and seat of the emotions, was in the Old Testament considered the seat of understanding and reason. According to Deuteronomy 29:3, for example, one has a heart in order to understand. Solomon asks God for a listening heart (1 Kings 3:9) so as to be able to distinguish between good and bad. At the same time, the heart is the place of human intentions, it contains secrets (Psalm 44:21) and affections, and it can be sad (1 Samuel 1:8) or glad, 'a delight' as in these verses (verse 18).

The Hebrew for 'thirty sayings' could be translated as 'three days ago', or possibly 'three days worth of attention' or more interestingly, 'things in threefold form'. The heart, the ears and the mind, as one organ, bent passionately upon the truth – suddenly it becomes quite possible that 'thirty chapters' could be a 'delight'!

We pray for those who pray and for those who act, for scholars and students of holy scripture in all faith communities.
God is near.

Writing

The calligraphy of the Spirit

Luke 1:1-4

'Seeing that', or as it is sometimes translated 'inasmuch as', seems a strange way to start an important piece of writing addressed to an important person. The Greek for 'inasmuch as' is *epiedeper*, normally used as part of a sentence which gives the reason for something we already know. Just as Joshua and the tribes echoed their story from mountain to mountain, just as Jeremiah and Baruch defied the rulers, facing imprisonment and death to write out the scroll again and again, your identity and mine is being defined as we read and hear the same stories, the same scriptures.

Later on in Luke, Jesus tells his hearers in the synagogue, 'Today the scripture is fulfilled in your hearing' (Luke 4:16-27). As he speaks, Jesus is the fulcrum of the past, the present and the future, a moment of perfect balance and integration. In opening the scroll, Jesus opens up our story with all its memories of pain, captivity and loss. Then he hands the scroll back to the attendant (handing our story back to us) and sits down, the very one of whom Isaiah was speaking, the embodiment of our future hope. For us, as for the first hearers of Jesus' words, the preaching of the good news to the poor, of liberty to captives and sight to the blind are the fulfilment of the story. This is who we are and who we were meant to be from the beginning.

When we read Luke's strange little 'inasmuch' he places us where we are, at the heart of a story that is past, present and future, continually remembered, continually renewed, continually calling.

We pray for all who work with prisoners,
for befrienders and listeners,
for faith communities responding to local need.
God is near.

Writing   Ruth Shelton

The calligraphy of response

John 20:30-31; 21:20-25

The theme that unifies John 20 as a whole is seeing and believing. Mary, the first witness to the empty tomb, feels that she has lost Jesus all over again, but later sees him and not only understands, but goes to bear witness to the others. John and Peter both run to the tomb. The beloved disciple sees, believes and – more significantly – realises that he has not believed fully until this moment. Peter has to check all the details and look around, before he too gives assent. Others are still hiding in the town somewhere. Thomas is resistant at first but his story ends with a passionately humble statement of faith: 'my Lord and my God' (John 20:28). All these great saints are responding to the life and death of Jesus in their own way.

The gospel which begins with the Word and ends with a name is one great question. What about you? I have recorded all these signs for you, do you believe? Not in a message but in a person, not in a history, but in a human story whose contours have shaped life and death in us. 'That you should have life through his name' (20:31) is not an ending but the beginning of a question that Jesus will ask of us, again and again, gentle but relentless, meeting every refusal with the gift of himself.

We pray for all doubters, strugglers, wrestlers with the truth,
all women of faith who are silenced,
all artists, visionaries and seers.
God is near.

The calligraphy of remembrance

Revelation 1:1-3, 9-11

A leading Catholic critic recently asked, 'Does the Vatican know about Google?' He was responding to the present scandal (as I write) in the Roman Catholic Church about Pope Benedict's lifting of excommunication on a former archbishop who is a Holocaust denier. It seems the pope and his advisers did not know what a simple Google search would have told them.

Urgency is the hallmark of the Book of Revelation. The fearful messages so graphically described in John's visions are real and impending and that is why John's response was to write everything down, a painstaking process in the ancient world. The strangeness of the text makes it easy for us to distance ourselves, but, aware of the events of the last century and our own time, many of us may well have a feeling that we are living in the last hour. It is always the last hour. If we are not judged, we are not known, except by ourselves, an arid idolatry, which can only lead us back to our crimes and failings.

For many Jewish agencies, it is a primary and urgent task to research and record the names of every single individual who perished in the Holocaust. Those of you who have been to Yad Vashem will not have forgotten the memorial to the two million children who perished. A voice reads out the names and ages of the children. There is no sound other than that single voice. 'Blessed are they who read and those who hear the words of the prophecy, and who keep the things written in it, for the time is near' (verse 3).

We pray for Jewish communities throughout the world, for people and organisations who work for Jewish–Christian relations.
God is near.

Writing   Ruth Shelton

The calligraphy of the weak

Romans 15:1-6

Every day, somewhere in the world, despairing, sick and desperate people turn to the stories written in the gospels, in anger, in scorn, in faith, maybe as a last resort. They find stories about people like themselves: the woman with a haemorrhage, the centurion, the widow at Nain, the man by the pool at Bethsaida, lepers, mad people, outcasts and beggars. These are the people who refused to give up, whose insight, courage and persistence brought peace and healing.

When Paul asks us to be strong and look after the weak, it may be time to look around and see who is looking after us. The woman I went to see in the hospital yesterday? I left feeling better. The adults with learning difficulties I teach on Thursdays? I laughed so much that I forgot all my anxieties. The homeless person whose face fell when I told him I lived on my own – then said 'Never mind, you've got us'?

The miracles, paradoxes and parables of the gospel come alive every day in our ordinary worlds, as if the letters and 'characters' have danced off the pages, to bring us healing and hope.

We pray for all who are sick, homeless and hungry,
those who are in despair,
for all who seek healing of mind and body.
God is near.

Old age

1 Reflections on old age: God is there

Notes based on the New Revised Standard Version by **Pauline Webb**

Pauline Webb is an octogenarian and still a Methodist local preacher. She retired after a lifetime of service and travel in the worldwide church as a writer and broadcaster. She lives alone and is in good health, but is well aware of the 'wear and tear' of old age.

Preparing for the week

I began my personal pilgrimage of faith in the optimistic years immediately following the Second World War. Youth movements, like the Methodist Association of Youth Clubs, reached out in imaginative ways to the younger generation; evangelists like Billy Graham attracted crowds and called for wholehearted commitment to Christ; many battle-scarred men and women returned from the armed forces determined to work for a better world. The worldwide church embraced a new ecumenical vision.

Now, over half a century later, in many churches people of my generation still make up the majority of the congregation. What has kept our faith alive, despite the difficulties of deprivation and sense of loss that old age can bring? In our readings this week we shall hear the testimonies of those who have discovered through the experience of growing old that faith can become stronger even as our physical powers grow weaker, and that when we have to face loss and bereavement, God's continuing presence can become more real to us, as 'the distant heaven becomes a home to our hearts'.

From generation to generation

Psalm 90:1-17

This is one of Israel's great psalms of lament for the nation's transgressions and the transience of human life. It spans the scale of God's eternity, in the context of which no earthly life can be said to be too short or too long. It is the hymn of a community, which gains its strength from remembering God's providential care through past events, and expresses its faith in God's continuing care through future generations.

Though we live in an age where, for many people in the West, life expectancy extends beyond the 'threescore years and ten' recognised as the norm by the psalmist, those of us who have lived beyond that age may echo the psalmist's regret that longer life does not mean that we keep the strength and vigour of youth! Yet however much old age may change us, it cannot change the nature of the God whose love has surrounded us throughout our lives. We cannot know what life beyond death will be like, but we do know that here in this world our life continues, not only biologically through the genes passed on from one generation to another, but also spiritually through those who have inherited the values by which we have lived.

What will be your best legacy to your family, your friends, your church, and to the wider community?

Lord, teach us not to be anxious about how long we shall live, but to be glad all our days.

Lifelong praise

Psalm 71:5-24

I confess that I sometimes grow weary of the jokes that are made about old age (even on birthday cards!). So I understand why in this personal psalm the poet is tempted to feel that in old age he has become an object of derision and has lost the respect people once showed him. But the psalm has two parts. First, we hear an old person praying for help, expressing a sense of being left at the mercy of others who seem to think the lives of the old no longer have much value. Then at verse 14 the prayer turns into praise as this same old person remembers that God's love surrounds us from the moment of our birth and enhances the whole of our lives. Faith in that love has brought us triumphantly through many changing experiences. So we older people have even more reason to celebrate life and should do all we can to help youngsters to realise that God's mercies will never fail them whatever life might throw at them in all the coming years.

What issues caused you most anxiety when you were young? If you have elderly parents or grandparents, what issues seem to worry them most? Give thanks for the ways in which God's continuing care through the years has enabled you/them to overcome both bad and good times.

God of all time, help those in old age not only to remember past blessings but also to forget past bitterness, through faith in your continuing goodness.

Old age   Pauline Webb

Days of trouble

Ecclesiastes 12:1-7

The preacher, the original author of Ecclesiastes, knew that it is no fun growing old. Nowadays my diary seems to record frequent appointments with the dentist, the chiropodist, the optician and the doctor, all helping to repair the ravages of old age. The preacher pessimistically describes what happens in the winter of life. The senses of hearing, seeing, even tasting, begin to fail and what once gave us pleasure no longer delights us. We become more fearful, not wanting to venture out at night. He compares an old person to a ruined house, where windows (eyes) have grown dim, and strong men (legs) have become weak. In verse 6 graphic metaphors of old age are presented in which it is seen as a time of snapping and breaking.

So what is there to look forward to? Old age, the preacher declares, is but the prelude to the time when the breath of our life returns to God. This was written long before the good news of Christ's resurrection had taken away the sting of death and opened up the hope of heaven. Nevertheless the preacher argues that the deprivations of old age should prompt even young people to remember the ultimate purpose and destination of all human life.

Reflect on what compensations old age brings for the losses we experience.

Lord, save me from being so concerned about my own physical wellbeing that I fail to appreciate the care and courtesy shown to me by others.

Old age

Respect for elders

1 Peter 5:1-6

In the earliest church the word 'elder' simply meant 'leader' without specific reference to age. Some of the elders were comparatively young apostles whose qualification was not their age but their experience of having known Christ during his earthly ministry. In time, many of the leaders of the church were becoming older in age too. The writer of this epistle is urging the young people to respect those who are older, and the elders to become good role models for the young.

When I was growing up, we young people used to complain that the church was full of old people, as though that demeaned its value. Young people today make the same complaint. I remember visiting the Soviet Union at a time when I was told that 'only old women' went to church, but throughout the long period of Communist rule and atheist propaganda, successive generations of old women persisted in church attendance and have remained the strength of the church today. So let us beware never to underestimate the strength of faith to be found among old people or devalue the contribution they can make, especially to all-age worship.

Reflect upon what older people can do to encourage and equip young people to take up the responsibilities of church leadership.

Thank you, Lord for the older people who have been our role models and have made your presence real to us.

Old age   Pauline Webb

Accepting the limitations of old age

2 Samuel 19:31-38

To one like me who has spent a lifetime in travel, it's hard to accept that in old age long journeys become daunting. So I find particularly moving this cameo of Barzillai, the wealthy landowner in Gilead who had been a loyal friend and generous host to King David at the time of rebellion in the land. After the tragedy of Absalom's death, the king's followers had been vying for the honour of accompanying David back to Jerusalem. But the king himself invited Barzillai to come with him to be honoured in the capital city. Barzillai, feeling that he can no longer fully enjoy such festivities, sadly declines the invitation lest his age make him a burden to the king. So he agrees to accompany the royal party only as far as the River Jordan where the king affectionately bids him farewell.

One of the sad results of the difficulty of travelling far when one is old is that one visits old friends less frequently. So I for one particularly welcome those who take the trouble to come and visit me and I like to be able still, albeit in limited ways, to offer them hospitality in my home.

Reflect on the many ways in which in old age we can still keep contact with old friends.

Lord, we thank you that difficulty of travel no longer need separate us from those we love, and for ways we can still communicate across the miles.

The special occasions which I most frequently attend now in my old age are the funerals of friends or of family members. They are always a reminder of how fragile all life is. Whether that life has been long or short, they always leave behind the pang of bereavement. Yet we are assured of the promise of the new life that comes out of death. I was inspired once by the comment of an African friend who suggested that we should think of every death simply as the opposite of birth – the passage into a kind of world we can never envisage until we enter it, but a fuller life than we could ever know here. The two passages we are reading from the book of Isaiah today stress the permanence of God's rule over our lives, continuing through our death and preparing us for that new creation in which there will be no more grieving or bereavement.

Reflect on what form you would like your own funeral to take – the hymns you would like people to sing, the readings you would choose and how you would want people to remember you.

Lord and Giver of Life, whether your gift be a life of many years or of only a few days, may we value every moment of life here on earth and anticipate with joy the life that awaits us in your new creation.

Solid joys and lasting treasure

Isaiah 40:6-8; 65:17-20

Old age

Pauline Webb

Old age

2　Old age: lived with God

Preparing for the week

This week's readings have a strong thread of looking forwards into our future as we age towards our dying, and also creatively backwards as we look over our life and try to sum it up. It's helpful to do this in a spirit of clear reality, no rosy spectacles but also no grim self-blame or pessimistic gloom. God can use a life examined honestly in this light. There will be causes for smiles and tears, hopes and forebodings.

Although Bible notes are often read when we're alone, this chance to look at your life and your ending may lead you to share some things with those closest to you, to check out your own self-estimate, to heal mutual hurts, to share your fears and probably to be surprised by love.

For further thought

- As you look back on your life, for what do you give thanks? For what do you feel regret? For what do you need God's grace and forgiveness?
- As you look forward, what do you fear? What do you hope for? What do you desire to give?

Notes based on the Revised Standard Version by
Geoffrey Herbert

Geoffrey Herbert is a retired priest of the Church of England and his main ministry now is in spiritual direction. Before ordination he was an educational psychologist.

Laughter runs like a ripple through this story, presumably from the name of the unexpected son, Isaac –'he laughs'. Abraham and Sarah are 'past it' sexually, so doing 'it' and, even more, actually conceiving, is wonderful ('wonderful' is the alternative to 'hard' in 'Is anything too hard for the Lord?').

So Sarah and Abraham look at one another as they set out to try to conceive. We can imagine some laughter in the making of Isaac! We aren't likely to have quite the same adventure in our old age, but there will be others. There'll be new discoveries, new friendships, new wisdoms, things in which we'll be surprised and laugh that this is happening to us. It won't all be loss. Part of it is being able at least sometimes to laugh at ourselves, to take lightly the way our bits wear out, fall out or get taken out, but another part is to become more free, less concerned about our standing and image, and ready for venturing.

I'm slowly coming to love the notion of the Holy Fool – someone who can laugh at self and its seriousness, and take a plunge or two. Isaac was born from laughter, and old age became new.

Lord, give me the gift of laughing at the good things with delight, at more of the hard things with a holy old fool's humour – and at myself.

The laughter of old age

Genesis 18:9-15, 21:1-8

Old age

Geoffrey Herbert

The land of lost content

Deuteronomy 34:1-12

'I have let you see it with your eyes, but you shall not go over there.'

(verse 4).

Even before the extreme end of life, we may look at all we might have achieved and now will not – that 'if only' feeling. I would like to have learned some modern languages to a good level; I wish I'd started writing poetry as a young man; I was too professionally ambitious to be a good dad and spend time just playing with my kids early on . . . and a lot more besides. Perhaps you too can see a lot of lands you'll never go into now.

The 'if only' feelings sometimes lead into bitterness or self-accusation. We can become bitter old fools instead of holy old fools. One antidote is to look for our legacy. Moses gave the law and would always be remembered. Jesus gave us the Last Supper, a living memorial. We aren't in their league, but we can all go 'good-finding' in our own lives. We can own our good bits, just as we must own our bad bits too. I recently held a big celebration of my 70 years of life and my 25 as a priest. I was enormously surprised to find that people had really good things, not just polite things, to say about me, despite all my 'if onlys'.

Lord, show me the good bits of my life, and help me feel good about them.

Geoffrey Herbert

Old age

My Muslim dentist tells me that his parents may well be the last in his family to be looked after by their own children. He can foresee a need for his own generation to have residential homes suitable for their own culture. At present his culture's custom is closer to today's reading than most Westerners are. My mother looked after her father in our house for years, including times when he had massive shaking strokes in the bedroom next to mine. Two years ago, aged 93, she asked to come into residential care near us. We visit her twice a week and I look after her affairs, mainly by internet banking, word-processed letters and phone calls. How do you see all this in Christian terms?

And how about us as we age? What are our hopes and fears and prayers? I know I'd be very bad at looking after myself. Also I hope I won't live alone, mainly because as a twin and then a married man I've never been alone for more than a few days. I'm afraid of being in the semi-solitary state of residential care, yet I certainly won't use 1 Timothy 5 as a moral weapon, and won't expect my children to take me in.

Lord, as I age, enable me to learn to be alone in your presence for longer than I can now, and to face my fears.

Facing a lonely future

1 Timothy 5:1-8

Old age   Geoffrey Herbert

Where we don't want to go

John 21:18-23

Jesus died a young man in years, but I do believe he knew old age. Back in chapter 12:1-7 he receives Mary of Bethany's anointing as being for his burial. In 12:27 we have John's echo of the agony in Gethsemane, Jesus handing himself over to his father: 'Now is my soul troubled . . .' Of course, a young man facing a terrible death would feel this way, but the whole hard journey of the Passion also contains within it an old person's entry into physical helplessness, being 'girded' (verse 18) – having our clothes put on and taken off for us? – and being led where we don't want to go. 'You will stretch out your hands . . .' reminds me of my mother holding out her hands to be led to her wheelchair.

I'm sure Christ's heart was open to feel the end-journey of old age, so we can see him as our Saviour sharing our end-years. Because it was the suffering of the Triune God, his three hours on the cross held all suffering, including the suffering of the really old, the end-time of each of us, as well as the end-time of our world.

Lord, be gentle with me in my helplessness, and walk with me in my last journey.

Geoffrey Herbert

Old age

Passing on the blessing

Luke 2:22-38

Simeon and Anna are old people who have remained faithful and who can in their own way take Jesus and bless him and his mother, like the bread of the Last Supper, the sign of love to be remembered and to nurture a huge and costly future. These old people are still open to the younger generations and will hand the future over to them. They are ready to 'depart in peace', knowing their work is done and must now be entrusted to those who come after them. This entrusting includes an acute awareness of the challenges and agonies this child and these young parents will carry, the swords that will pierce them as they share the travails and the joys (the 'falling and rising') of their own generation and those to come. Yet all the old can do is to entrust and bless, let the future go on to be itself without them, hoping they will be remembered and their love be held and carried onwards in young hands.

Lord, keep me faithful even if my soul seems to fail me, and pass on my blessing for love, endurance and hope.

Old age

Geoffrey Herbert

Handing ourselves over

Mark 12:41-44

At our end we may be at peace and full of faith, richly surrounded with loving care and gratitude. Or we may be alone in an impoverished darkness of fear, pain and forsakenness. These are the extreme ends of the spectrum of dying. Where our own dying will be is beyond our control. We can, as it were, rehearse a little and prepare, but we cannot tie it up. We're not all called to make 'good deaths'. Forsakenness has a Christ-precedent.

I remember a sermon by Basil Moss, then Provost of St Philip's Cathedral, Birmingham. He said something like, 'I've already given God some bits of myself – some hair, a few teeth, an appendix, some flakes of skin . . . One day I'll be able to say, "There you are, Lord, this is the whole of me."' A sister I know says just, 'I'm ready to entrust myself into this darkness.' What can *you* say at this moment?

The widow's little gift was all she had. We may be rich in assurance and hope when we die; we may have only a tiny chink of light left or none at all. The call is to give all of ourselves, our wealth or our poverty, into the cloud of unknowing which is God.

Lord, just be there to receive me, please.

Geoffrey Herbert

Old age

Consider a legacy

Help us to continue our work of providing Bible study notes for use by Christians in the UK and throughout the world. The need is as great as it was when IBRA was founded in 1882 by Charles Waters as part of the work of the Sunday School Union.

Please leave a legacy to the International Bible Reading Association.

An easy-to-use leaflet has been prepared to help you provide a legacy. Please write or telephone (details below) and we will send you this leaflet – and answer any questions you might have about a legacy or other donations. Please help us to strengthen this and the next generation of Christians.

Thank you very much.

International Bible Reading Association
1020 Bristol Road
Selly Oak
Birmingham
B29 6LB
UK

Tel. 0121 472 4242
Fax 0121 472 7575

Micah

1 What angers God

Preparing for the week

The prophet Micah lived in challenging times. The prevailing belief in the Ancient Near East two and a half thousand years ago said that the deity one worshipped was only as good as his last victory. Defeat by another nation or tribe meant that one's deity had failed and the conquerors' deity should be worshipped instead.

In common with the other prophets of Israel and Judah, Micah put forward a new vision of the one invisible God who rewarded and punished. Micah demanded that the vanquished people of the kingdom of Israel and their vulnerable neighbours in his homeland, Judah, should not seek to blame God for failing to protect them against the invading Assyrians. Rather it was the people who were to blame for having let God down: the destruction of Israel and the threat against Judah and her capital, Jerusalem, were punishment for the people's failure to observe God's laws of righteousness and justice.

All quotations are from the Liberal Judaism Daily and Sabbath Prayerbook *Siddur Lev Chadash* (1995) unless otherwise stated.

For further thought and action

- How far do you believe in a God who rewards and punishes?
- What angers God today in the world?
- Are you called to share God's anger in any way?

Notes based on the *Tanakh: The Holy Scriptures* (Jewish Publication Society, 1985) by

Pete Tobias

Pete Tobias is rabbi of the Liberal Synagogue, Elstree, in Hertfordshire. He has two published works: *Liberal Judaism: A Judaism for the Twenty-First Century* (2007) and *Never Mind the Bullocks: a 21st-century exploration of the Torah for bar-/bat-mitzvah students* (2009) as well as many articles. Pete can be heard regularly offering a 'Pause for Thought' and other reflections on BBC Radio 2. He is a devoted fan of Watford Football Club!

Who's to blame?

Micah 1:1-7

We are never short of news telling of some disaster or other, as a consequence of natural or human activity. Images of earthquakes, floods, wars and bombings seem to flow endlessly across our television and computer screens and the pages of our newspapers. When human beings are involved, attacking fellow human beings, there is usually a political or religious distinction that is the basis of dispute. Even when a natural disaster occurs, people invariably look for someone to blame.

How easy it is to pass judgement on the suffering of others, to assign to them some failing that must have brought upon them this 'act of God'. In Micah's time, human wickedness was blamed for natural disasters like the destruction of Sodom and Gomorrah or Noah's flood. And he similarly justifies Assyria's assault on Samaria.

With our modern scientific and political awareness, simplistic ideas of cause and effect no longer work. And yet we like to assign explanations to such catastrophes. Even though war and disaster may not specifically be a form of divine punishment, they cause us to examine our consciences and past behaviour in search of an explanation. Micah may be closer to the truth than we realise – perhaps this is how God works in human life.

Do we do right to regard the suffering of others as a form of punishment for their failings?

Keep us from making judgements that serve only ourselves, and from the urge to rise by our neighbour's fall.
Siddur Lev Chadash, p.297

Micah   Pete Tobias

'Was it something I did?'

Micah 1:8-16

If it is wrong to apportion blame to victims of human or natural catastrophes in places distant from where we dwell, how shall we cope with disasters closer to home? How shall that same aspect of human nature that impels us to seek explanations for the misfortune of others be accommodated when the misfortune befalls us?

Rabbi Harold Kushner tells how he once visited a member of his community who had suffered a terrible personal tragedy. The rabbi was greeted at the door by a person who said to him, 'This happened because I didn't go to synagogue on Yom Kippur, didn't it, Rabbi?' A simple explanation was needed to justify the tragic event, as though the individual was receiving some kind of divine punishment.

It's important that we consider our faults at all times, not just when events force us to do so. The real tragedy is that it so often takes a horrific incident or catastrophic situation to occur in our own community or to us as individuals to make us reflect on our responsibilities.

Think of a time in your life when you perhaps viewed a difficult situation as a punishment for something you did wrong. Then think of the times you did other wrong things that weren't 'punished' in this way.

Enable us, O God, to behold meaning in the chaos of life about us and purpose in the chaos of life within us.

Siddur Lev Chadash, p.302

Being aware of our own faults is a vital step towards creating a responsible and compassionate society. Only by identifying the failings of which we are capable and to which we succumb can we place ourselves in a position to challenge the behaviour of those amongst whom we live. And there is much in our society that needs to be challenged. So many of the things in our lives that we take for granted are produced through the exploitation of others. The clothes that we wear – have they been produced by individuals who receive a fair wage for their labour and work in healthy conditions? The food that we eat – do those responsible for farming and producing its basic ingredients live and work in an environment that values and properly rewards their efforts?

It sometimes seems that in our haste to extract wealth from our planet and the individuals on it by forcing them to serve the needs of the wealthy, we betray our very humanity. Religion is not religion if it does not demand that we speak out against those who exploit, and seek justice for those who are exploited.

Make the effort to be more aware of the source of basic items in your everyday life and try to consider the circumstances of the people who worked to bring them to you. How does your life compare with theirs?

The earth has enough for everyone's need, but not for everyone's greed.

Siddur Lev Chadash, p.285

'It's not my fault!' (1)

Micah 2:1-11

Micah

Pete Tobias

'It's not my fault!' (2)

Micah 2:12-13, 3:1-4

The structure and nature of the societies in which we live are dictated by our leaders. Power is a difficult and dangerous phenomenon, for those who wield it often become mesmerised by the ability they have to manipulate others. What might have begun as a genuine wish to work for the benefit of any society or group of people can quickly turn into a desire to wield power for its own sake rather than in the interests of those whom leaders claim to represent or serve.

And it is so easy to ignore the actions of our leaders or to convince ourselves that there is nothing we can do to influence or change their behaviour! How important it is that we remind ourselves that those who lead us and speak for us are, in fact, just like us – ordinary people who breathe and eat and bleed, just as we do. And it is even more important that we remind them of that also!

Do those who hold positions of leadership in your life respect you? And do you respect those people over whom you exercise influence or power?

Eternal God, make our leaders conscious of their responsibility and teach them to exercise it in accordance with your will. May we all help to fashion a society that excels in freedom and justice, tolerance and compassion, so that it may be a force for righteousness and peace in the life of humanity.

Siddur Lev Chadash, p.484

Pete Tobias

Micah

Let us be wary too of those who seek to deceive us with false promises and impossible dreams. In our time as in Micah's, there are many who try to persuade us of the authenticity of their view of the world and of their solutions for its ills. How shall we distinguish between those who speak truth and those who spread falsehood, and how guard ourselves against prophets and peddlers of untruths?

A century after Micah lived, the prophet Jeremiah warned the people of Judah of impending disaster at the hands of the Babylonians. This was not what the people wanted to hear – they were frightened of what this mighty empire might do to them. Jeremiah's unpopular views were challenged by so-called prophets such as Hananiah who told the people what they wanted to hear and promised that there would be no sword and no famine and that God would grant them unfailing security.

It is easy to block our ears against those who tell us things that we do not wish to hear, while consoling ourselves with opinions and predictions that offer us safety and refuge. But at critical moments in our lives and the lives of our societies, it is often necessary to face up to uncomfortable truths.

What measures can you use to distinguish between false and true prophecy?

Prefer the truth and right by which you seem to lose, to the falsehood and wrong by which you seem to gain.

Moses Maimonides

Micah   Pete Tobias

'It's not my fault!' (4)

Micah 3:9-12

Micah has painted for us a picture of a damaged society. The neighbouring kingdom of Israel has been destroyed by the Assyrians; his home country, Judah, is under threat from the same empire. The destruction of Israel has raised frightening questions for the people of Judah. How can the God of Israel – who is their God also – have abandoned their neighbours, their cousins, to this terrible fate at the hands of the Assyrians? Will they suffer the same fate?

Micah's answer is unequivocal. Yes, they will. 'Jerusalem will become a heap of rubble,' he predicts (verse 12). And he is equally clear about the reason for this. With typical biblical zeal, he points to the corrupt religious and political leadership of this small kingdom as being to blame for the impending and inevitable catastrophe.

Micah's brutal assessment of the woes of his time should encourage us to be critical of the world in which we live and challenge its failings. Only if we are honest about our world's failings – and our own – can we hope to move forward, avert catastrophe and begin to build a society worthy of God.

Be with us, O God, when we strive to do your will. Teach us to see that the men and women about us are our brothers and sisters; and fill us with an ardent love for all your creatures, that we may never wrong them, or exploit them, or take advantage of anyone's weakness or ignorance.

Siddur Lev Chadash, p.344

Micah

2 What does God require and promise?

Notes based on the
*Tanakh: The Holy
Scriptures* (Jewish
Publication Society,
1985) by

Pete Tobias

For Pete's biography
see p.280.

Preparing for the week

Having made clear that the responsibility for the defeat of Israel and the grave dangers being faced by the people of Judah lie in the nature of the society in those kingdoms and those who play a leading role in it, Micah now guides the people to an understanding of how they should live their lives to avoid God's wrath. Although our view of divine reward and punishment is, perhaps, somewhat more refined than that put forward by Israel's prophets, individual and collective responsibility for the fate of a society is a factor that speaks as loudly in our twenty-first century as it did in the eighth century BCE.

A society is made up of individual people. Although events that take place on the national and global stage affect all of us, it is how we behave in our own lives that will truly shape the ethos of the society in which we live. Micah's demands for peace, his message of hope and acknowledgement of God's goodness are set against the geopolitics of his time, but their message demands that we each bring those aspects of God into our own lives in order to better ourselves as individuals, thereby influencing our wider environment.

Only through self-improvement can the world in which we live truly become a better place: the place that God wants it to be and the place that we need it to be, for ourselves and for those who will come after us.

For further thought

- In what ways do you consider yourself responsible for the values and actions of your society?
- How can you help those around you to choose the ways of justice and peace rather than their own narrow self-interest?

Bringing peace to our world

Micah 4:1-7

The first prerequisite for peaceful living is the abolition of weapons of war. This famous vision of Micah's, echoed by the prophet Isaiah, has its concluding words of nation not lifting up sword against nation engraved outside the United Nations building in New York.

But there is so much more to peace than simply the removal of weapons, the absence of war. In order truly to live together in peace, human beings must first be at peace with themselves. The Bershider Rebbe (a Chasidic rabbi of the eighteenth century) suggests a structure for the establishment of peace in the world which goes something like this: You should work for peace in yourself, then in your household, then in your street, then in your town, then in your country and then in the world.

The establishment of peace in the world does not begin with the breaking of swords into ploughshares and spears into pruning hooks. It begins with individuals working to reject violent or aggressive tendencies within themselves.

What can you do to find peace in your own life?

It is not enough to *pray* for peace. We have to *work* for it: to challenge those who foster conflict, and refute their propaganda; to ascertain and make known the truth, both when it confirms and when it runs counter to conventional views; to denounce injustice . . . and to build bridges of respect and understanding, trust and friendship, across the chasms that divide humanity.

Siddur Lev Chadash, p.293

Bringing hope to our world

Micah 5:1-15

In Micah's time, as in our own, the prospects for peace among nations seemed a distant dream. But just as the road to world peace begins in our own homes and our own hearts, so too does hope.

Here's a story that one of my teachers, the late Rabbi Hugo Gryn, once told. It was winter 1944, though he and his father, in a concentration camp in Silesia, didn't know the actual date. He tells how one evening his father took him and some friends to a corner of their barrack and announced it was the eve of the festival of Chanukkah. He produced a curious shaped clay bowl and began to light a wick immersed in his precious, but now melted, margarine ration. Young Hugo protested at this waste of food. Hugo's father looked at his son, then at the lamp, then said: 'You and I have seen that it is possible to live up to three weeks without food. We once lived almost three days without water, but you cannot live properly for three minutes without hope!'

If we look at the troubles of the world and despair of their ever being resolved, we actually contribute to them. We owe it to ourselves and to God to hope for a brighter future, even in the darkest of times.

Do not abandon the hopes you cherish.

When evil darkens our world, give us light.
When despair numbs our souls, give us hope.
Siddur Lev Chadash, p.220

Micah   Pete Tobias

Remember God's guiding hand

Micah 6:1-5

One of the ways to find hope is to look to moments in our past when prospects have seemed bleak or desperate and recognise that we have managed to come through these challenging and difficult moments. Micah reminds his audience – who are, let us not forget, facing the prospect of an assault from the Assyrians similar to that which destroyed their Israelite cousins – of moments in their history when they have overcome seemingly insurmountable obstacles.

Just as the Israelites were able to look back on their history and recognise God's influence, so too should we be able to find comfort in our personal experience that will encourage us not to despair. Each of us as individuals can recall instants when we have felt lifted or guided by an unseen hand. Such moments do not necessarily have to take the form of miraculous encounters such as those referred to by the prophet as he encourages his listeners not to give up hope. Each of us has our own Egypt – a sense of liberation or release from something that held us trapped, our own Balak, who wished to curse us but could not do so, our own journey from Shittim to Gilgal, crossing a boundary to a new and longed-for place.

Look for such memories from your own past and let them give you courage, comfort and hope.

This I call to mind, therefore I have hope. Surely your love, O God, never ceases, your mercies are everlasting.

Lamentations 3:21

Now we have understood the need to search for peace as individuals as well as in the wider world of which we are part, and have replaced doubt with hope based on our personal experiences and trust in God, it is time to begin to live our lives more fully and with renewed confidence. The question – perfectly posed by Micah – is how shall we live our lives? What does God require of us?

We live in a world that seems constantly to bombard us with advice about how we should live our lives. A world of so many choices, such a variety of options, seems to have removed all certainty and filled us with doubt. One type of food is bad for us so we must eat another type – until someone tells us that one is bad as well and we are obliged to think again. Choices of clothing, of lifestyle, or of practice and belief can bewilder us and leave us lost and confused.

Living in a world that encourages us to think of our individuality and which suggests that individual needs and expectations are the sole measure of human happiness, we would do well to remind ourselves of Micah's famous words – the answer to his own question about what God requires of us, so simple and yet so profound that the words deserve to be repeated here today – and every day: 'Seek justice, love mercy and walk humbly with your God.'

Walk humbly with God

Micah 6:6-16

Micah

Pete Tobias

Turn to God for help

Micah 7:1-13

It might seem, then, that if we are surrounded by disaster and catastrophe on the one hand, and shallow, meaningless claims for our attention on the other, there is nowhere we can turn, no one we can trust. Without the humble faith of our biblical ancestors and their belief that God rewards and punishes with mighty acts of nature, how shall we find a place of safety in our world?

Micah saw that there was much confusion and conflict in his world – and ours is certainly no better than his. We understand all too easily the misery he feels when he sees the world around him and the fact that he feels unable to trust in anyone.

We all experience such moments of complete isolation and despair. In the wake of a terrible accident or catastrophe, we turn to God for understanding. And in times of bewilderment, we turn to that same God for compassion and consolation, guidance and hope.

Perhaps there have been times in your life when you have imagined God to be punishing or judging you. Do not forget also to look for God as a comforter and healer.

Some lose their way in the trackless desert, unable to find their way to others; they are hungry and thirsty, their spirits are low. Let them cry out in their trouble to God, who will rescue them from their distress.

Psalm 107:4-6

Pete Tobias

Micah

In the end Micah recognises, as must we all, that power wielded by unworthy leaders and unrighteous nations will finally come to nought. The solution to the problems of the world and of the individuals who live in it can be solved if only people pay attention to the voice of God.

Micah offers us a way of confronting the world and its challenges. We can seek to read into every setback, personal or global, the hand of God bringing punishment to those who suffer. This is a harsh view of the world, for we know that not all evil is punished – nor, indeed, is all goodness rewarded.

We need then to find other ways of measuring God's presence and involvement in our lives. The fate of nations and their leaders is something for which we are all responsible, directly or indirectly, though sometimes it is hard to have a sense of our influence as individuals. The real test of locating God in our lives occurs in our everyday behaviour, in the way we treat those closest to us, how we function as responsible members of our communities and how we respect our world. Our actions can either bring the world closer to God – or take it further away. It is up to us.

It is up to us

Micah 7:14-20

Individuals are judged by the majority of their deeds. Happy are those who perform a good deed: that may tip the scales for them and for the world.

Talmud

Micah

Pete Tobias

Reconciliation

1 Be reconciled to one another

Preparing for the week

Reconciliation is one of the key metaphors for what God is about in the world. Sometimes when words are so familiar to us that we may no longer reflect on their meaning, I like to check out dictionary definitions. One dictionary gives the primary meaning of the verb to reconcile as 'make friendly again after an estrangement'. Reading that, I immediately think of Jesus' words 'I have called you friends' (John 15:15). These words come in a context where Jesus is speaking of a new way of relating – we are no longer servants or slaves but friends, loved by God, in return loving God and each other even as we are loved.

While we often come to reconciliation from a personal viewpoint, our individual stories and experiences are part of God reconciling the world to Godself in Christ. The readings this week provide different stories of reconciliation from the Old and New Testaments, frequently illuminating the frailty of humanity who nevertheless are loved and nurtured by their Creator.

For further action and thought

- Look up the word 'reconciliation' in one or two dictionaries and ponder what you find.
- How do Jesus' words about friendship challenge you in a context of estranged or broken relationships?

Notes based on the New Revised Standard Version by
Fran Porter

Fran Porter is a theological and social researcher and writer with particular interest in socially engaged theology and feminist engagement with theology, church culture, biblical studies and hermeneutics, including the need for reconciliation in gender relationships. Now based in the Midlands, England, she spent many years in Northern Ireland where reconciliation was a contested matter.

The reunion between Jacob and Esau comes after years of separation and individual journeys by both men.

However, we know very little of Esau's story. We know he was deceived out of his birthright and blessing (27:35-36), that he took wives that displeased and distressed his parents (26:34-35), which he later realised and addressed by taking a wife who would be more acceptable to them (28:8-9). The blessing he received from Isaac in lieu of his birthright blessing was about luck, strife and how he would serve his brother until he grew restless and throw his brother's yoke off his neck (27:38-40). We are told he held a grudge against Jacob and plotted to kill him following Isaac's death (27:41). But we are told nothing of what occurred after that and before his reunion with Jacob many years later. Hence the anticipation in the story – as readers we share Jacob's perspective of fear at the news of Esau's approach.

Scripture gives us the story of Jacob – the younger brother, blessed, prosperous, both deceitful and then himself deceived – and his journey over many years and, before the brothers' reunion, Jacob's encounter with God. While Jacob seeks to influence Esau, he can only control his own demeanour and behaviour.

How can separation make reconciliation possible?

God of Esau and Jacob, may my life be a transforming journey on the path of reconciliation.

Surprised by reconciliation

Genesis 32:1-8; 33:1-10

The bigger picture

Genesis 45:1-15

The parental favouritism that Jacob had experienced himself, he reproduces towards his son Joseph (Genesis 37:3). The resulting sibling rivalry saw Joseph end up a slave in Egypt. Only after many years of mixed fortunes does Joseph meet his family again and, in contrast to the experience of his father and uncle, the reconciliation results in ongoing contact and continuing relationship. The generosity Jacob received from Esau is now given by one of Jacob's sons to his other sons.

Perhaps the most perplexing part of this reunion story is the suggestion that God planned Joseph's downfall (verse 5). That God would provide is a more comfortable thought than that God would inflict suffering. Jesus set his face towards Jerusalem (Luke 9:51) in a way that Joseph did not set his towards Egypt. However, perhaps it is more that what others meant for harm, God intended for good, as Joseph puts it in Genesis 50:20. This verse also tells us that the family reconciliation of this story has far-reaching consequences – to preserve or safeguard numerous people. It is not that all things are good but that all things work together for good for those who love God (Romans 8:28). It is Joseph's ability to grasp the bigger picture that enables him to move to restore relationship rather than exact vengeance from his newfound position of power.

Dear God, as I struggle with the hurts of broken relationships, help me to see if there might be a bigger picture.

Safeguarding the enemy

1 Samuel 26:6-25

The story of Saul and David is set in a time of bloody wars and violent skirmishes between competing tribes in the region, most notably the Philistines. Saul's personal fondness for David (1 Samuel 16:21) competes with his growing jealousy and paranoia about his own public position and power within Israel (1 Samuel 18:7-9).

Like the relationship of Jacob and Esau and of Joseph and his brothers, David's fraught and volatile relationship to Saul is understood within the realisation that God is Lord of Israel and, in this case, that Saul is the Lord's anointed (verse 9). It is this knowledge that contributes to David sparing Saul's life a second time, having been evading his pursuer and escaping from attempts on his life – with 'but a step between me and death' (1 Samuel 20:3). On the first opportunity David had to harm Saul, Saul sums up the extraordinariness of this: 'Who has ever found an enemy, and sent the enemy safely away?' (1 Samuel 24:19). Yet David does so – twice. Saul's moment of awareness and lucidity results in his repentance (verse 21).

The future, however, is uncertain, and resolution on this occasion comes by David staying out of Saul's reach (1 Samuel 27:1). These adopted family members-cum-enemies are unable to share land and space together.

What does it mean to safeguard enemies today?

Help me to love my enemies and pray for those who persecute me.

Reconciliation   Fran Porter

It takes more than a lifetime

Psalm 85:8-13

This psalm begins by looking back to what God has done in the past for the people of Jacob. It is a prayer for God to restore the people again – to put away divine anger, forgive their sins and grant them salvation. It reminds us that reconciliation has to be sought by each generation in turn, that they cannot rely on the experience of others, and it reassures us that salvation is possible.

Such hope and promise (verse 10)! Yet the reality is that God's steadfast love and faithfulness do not always mean our immediate wellbeing. In our experience, righteousness does not always go with peace. For the work of reconciliation in the world is an ongoing task, one that is not fully realised in the span of a human lifetime.

The belief that human existence does not end with death, but that there is eternal reality, has often been used by the powerful to impose acquiescence in their situation on people facing poverty, injustice or oppression, thereby protecting a privileged status quo. But, when not so abused or manipulated, the idea serves as a source of hope that human endeavours to live in right relation are never wasted or meaningless but are participation in God's eternal work of reconciliation.

Reconciling God, show this generation your steadfast love and grant us your salvation.

Can you see the join?

Luke 19:1-10

How are we to understand the connection between our relationship with God and our relationships with each other? We might talk about a person's relationship with God ultimately being more important than their material welfare and social justice. Spiritual reconciliation may be prioritised over social reconciliation. Or we might say that reconciliation with God leads to right relationships with others – for 'those who love God must love their brothers and sisters also' (1 John 4:21), and indeed, must love their enemies (Matthew 5:43-44). Even to phrase the question this way – as about two distinct sets of relationships – influences us to talk in terms of priorities or consequences.

Could it be, rather, that our behaviour towards others (on a personal or societal level) is the embodiment of our right relationship with God? These are not separable into two distinct sets of relationships but rather form an integrated whole. While we may be able to identify various elements of the whole, sense and right meaning only come by holding onto and understanding the whole.

This seems to be what happened for Zacchaeus. His story is particularly compelling because his purse was affected – and money and greed is one of the most seductive forms of comfort and power.

May my knowledge of you, O God, transform my relationship with others, and may my relationship with others speak of my love for you.

Reconciliation   Fran Porter

The resentful son

Luke 15:11-32

We don't earn God's grace. It comes to us as a gift. Yet in practice, those of us who have been good, responsible, sensible, prudent, self-giving, helpful, dutiful, long-suffering – perhaps over many years – can find it hard not to begrudge God's grace in the lives of those who have acted irresponsibly, unkindly, selfishly, or who have done harm.

Even more, when there is no expression of regret or repentance in evidence, we may find it really difficult to act gracefully to those whom we do not consider have shown the remorse of the younger prodigal brother in our story. Truth and justice can cry out for a withholding of unmerited and undiscriminating grace. Are not truth and reconciliation processes named as such for good reason?

In the opening section of John's gospel, Jesus is described as being 'full of grace and truth' (John 1:14). The author continues, 'From his fullness we have all received, grace upon grace. The law indeed was given through Moses; grace and truth came through Jesus Christ' (John 1:16-17). Part of the Christian claim about truth is that it belongs with grace; in John's gospel the two are personified as part of an integrated whole, in Christ. A Christian concept of grace speaks of divine generosity towards humanity in our struggles to discover and live by what is true.

Gracious God, reassure me of your love. May I be generous towards others in my thoughts and behaviour.

Reconciliation

Reconciliation

2 Called to be reconcilers

Notes based on the New Revised Standard Version by
David Porter

David Porter is Canon Director for Reconciliation Ministry at Coventry Cathedral. A native of Northern Ireland, he has long experience in the peace process there where he was co-founder of ECONI (Evangelical Contribution on Northern Ireland). His commitment to reconciliation and peacebuilding involved working with both republican and loyalist leaders in the transition from violence to a political settlement. Now based at Coventry Cathedral, he is responsible for developing its ministry as a centre for reconciliation, including the international network, Community of the Cross of Nails.

Preparing for the week

This series of readings begins with the text most often thought about when considering the call to be reconcilers. But as the week progresses it is evident that reconciliation is more integral to Christian discipleship than simple obedience to a single command. Christian character and vocation find their roots in the character of God. Therefore to be formed as reconcilers and to sustain our commitment to this calling takes us to the heart of all Christian formation – worship. For it is in worship that we grow in our knowledge of God and knowing what God is like impacts on our being and behaviour. The readings sweep us towards a climax in a song of worship in which we find our vocation in a broken and hurting cosmos – 'be reconcilers because I am a reconciling God'.

For further thought

- Meditate on the character and being of God – in what ways is this the source of all human reconciliation?
- How does your worship of God show itself in acts of reconciliation with others?

New perspectives

2 Corinthians 5:16-21

At times when reading Paul we can get caught up in the relentless logic of his argument. He makes powerful statements about the faith and follows up with a series of consequences, using his much loved word – 'therefore'. This passage comes in a sequence of closely argued beliefs and behaviours which flow from the defence of his ministry.

This defence is passionate and rooted in what God has done for Paul and for the world. The focus is always on God and in these chapters we have some amazing reflections on what the gospel means. The radical transformation of being a new creation leads into his charge to us to be reconcilers.

That God was in Christ reconciling the world to himself changes everything: our view of ourselves, our view of others and our view of what ministry is about. Without such a change in perspective, reconciliation becomes almost impossible. Human instinct is to count people's trespasses against them. It is only when we grasp that this is precisely what God did *not* do in regard to us that we can invite others to share in reconciliation with God. This is the first step in changing our outlook that equips us for the ministry of reconciliation.

Lord God, in the face of the hate and injustice of others, help us to remember that when we were still your enemy you loved us.

David Porter

Reconciliation

Offensive teaching

The outrageous nature of what Jesus is suggesting in this passage lies at the heart of the challenge of making peace in many conflicts in our world today. The nature of sectarianism, nationalism, tribalism and racism engulfs whole communities and societies in decades of fear, suspicion and hostility. When some of those caught up in such struggles turn to violence, the consequences for all are devastating.

Matthew 5:21-26

Yet the painful search for peace often suffers from the failure of communities to take responsibility for the systemic nature of their division. The majority who do not resort to physical violence against the other, recoil at any suggestion of shared responsibility both for and with the so-called 'men of violence'.

Jesus reminds us that to point the finger makes us as culpable for war and division as those who pull the trigger. Stopping the violence in many of the world's endemic identity conflicts will prove in most cases the easy part. Getting a society to acknowledge mutual responsibility for the source of the violence and therefore its inevitability is a step too far for most. Yet it is this step that is the first on the journey to reconciliation in any post-conflict society. And it begins as Jesus suggests, not in waiting for those who have hurt us to come to us, but in us going to those who have something against us, whether or not it is real or perceived.

Father, forgive me my sins as I forgive those who sin against me.

Reconciliation   David Porter

Revolutionary relationships

Philemon 10-21

Clearly Onesimus has caused great offence to Philemon and is in fear of returning to him. It is implied that the relationship between them was one of slave and master. This being the case, the story and Paul's intervention expose the challenge that injustice presents, particularly in the form of economic exploitation.

The request to Philemon tests not only his relationship to Paul, but whether or not his new faith has transformed him where it most matters. Is Onesimus simply an economic unit, a symbol of his status and wealth? Or does he now see a brother in whom there is dignity and worth of a different order?

For Paul, Philemon's acceptance of Onesimus is nothing less than his duty. But his goal is voluntary consent and not a forced obligation. Reconciliation cannot be forced. To this end Paul himself is willing to take responsibility for excising the debt that may be owed. He personally becomes the bridge across which master and slave walk to find each other as brother. It is as if nothing should be allowed to get in the way, and every effort must be made, even at personal cost, to make reconciliation possible.

This is the practical outworking of his reconciliation ministry between two close colleagues. Its success will refresh his heart. And despite the demands it puts on us, being reconcilers has its own reward.

Father, help me to see where I can assist those I love to live in harmony as brothers and sisters, with respect and joy.

David Porter

Reconciliation

Ending hostilities

How easy it is to forget the favour we have received of God! The temptation to take the vantage point of privilege is not new. Throughout their history the people of Israel were constantly tempted to forget that they enjoyed the blessings of covenant not because of something inherently special in them, but because of God's choice and promise. Those customs that marked the boundaries which kept them special as a testimony to God, over time became the barriers which kept others at arms' length and marked the other out as different. A lifestyle that was meant to keep Israel set apart as a witness, over time became the high walls of exclusion and hostility. The thought that those outside, the gentiles, could share in this rich inheritance was difficult to accept.

Ephesians 2:11-22

For Paul, Christ is the one in whom all this changes – utterly and for ever. As in Corinthians, the emphasis is again on a new creation, one new humanity in place of the two. Together Jew and gentile are now reconciled to God. Hostilities are at an end.

But are they? The church in its history has also succumbed to the temptation. Most of us being gentiles have reversed the roles. We have forgotten that we were far away, and with no merit on our part have been brought near in Christ. Whom do we now exclude? With whom do we need to end hostilities?

Lord God, reconciled in Christ, let me not betray your grace by failing to embrace those who are still far away.

Reconciliation   David Porter

Pursuing peace

Romans 14:7-19

'Do not, for the sake of food, destroy the work of God' (verse 20). With this plea Paul cuts to the heart of a debate that was causing great offence and hurt in the church in Rome. Feasting and feast days were an important part of Roman religious life. For these new Christians the simple meal of bread and wine that now replaced these elaborate and extended festivities must have seemed rather tame in comparison. And as many of the Roman feast days were civic as well as religious occasions, participation at meals and benefiting from the general largesse of the ruling class at such times would have been an integral part of the calendar. So this was no trivial matter. It brought plenty to poor homes and demonstrated participation as a citizen of the city.

Where you stood on the food debate quickly became a test of orthodoxy. Judgements were passed, injury was caused, even faith itself was at stake. Such sharp conflict caused disarray in the life of the community and whatever good there was had become spoken of as evil. Paul calls not only for an end to distracting quarrels, but for a new preoccupation. He had strong convictions on this question; it *did* matter. However, they had lost perspective and a new orthopraxy was required. (Orthopraxy, or right action, is a term coined by liberation theologians to contrast with orthodoxy, right belief.) It was time to demonstrate the real family character of the children of God – as peacemakers.

Father, help me as your child not to forget, in holding true to my convictions, that your kingdom belongs to those who make peace.

David Porter

Reconciliation

Cosmic concerns

Colossians 1:9-23

Here we have a profound statement of Christ not only as the Progenitor, Creator, Ruler and Sustainer of the universe but as the reconciler in whom the fullness of God was pleased to dwell. Reconciliation is a fundamental dynamic in God's relationship to the universe.

It is costly, requiring God to become embedded as part of the created order as a human being. And in entering fully into the human story through death, estrangement and hostility are in turn put to death. Without the concept of reconciliation we cannot understand God, and without knowing the fullness of God in Christ we do not truly understand reconciliation.

Reconciliation has become something of a buzz word in international relations. We need to recognise that it is the Christian worldview that gives particular meaning to this word in human affairs. As alternative terminology around peace-building and just peace find their rightful place in our lexicon, they only serve to highlight the competing demands imposed by our broken relationships if peace is to be found. Truth and justice increasingly stand alone without reference to reconciliation.

This is never the case with God. The demands of truth and justice are met, peace is made and mercy is extended. This is the true art of the reconciler.

Lord God, who reconciles all things in Christ, may we be merciful in pursuit of truth and justice.

Reconciliation   David Porter

Women of the New Testament

1 Women disciples

Sunday 31 October

Notes based on
the Good News
Bible by
Glory Befeke Anye

Glory Befeke Anye is an
ordained Presbyterian
Cameroonian. She is currently
serving as parish pastor of
a new town airport parish
and is chaplain to the Douala
colleges. She is also a New
Testament teacher at the
Ecumenical Bible Institute,
Douala. She is married with
two children.

Preparing for the week

The cultural situation at the time of Jesus by and large did not permit women to engage in societal affairs, due to gender and class differences. Yet their contributions in society remained enormous. Similarly, in most tribes in Cameroon such as those known to me in the North-West Province, women remain insignificant as far as decision-making is concerned. Yet both within and beyond such contexts their contributions to society and to family growth remain invaluable.

In this week's study we shall journey with the Jesus tradition – a tradition which accepts everyone without exception who is prepared to engage in the perspective of God in bringing about justice and wellbeing for all. In the perspective of this model, we will consider prominent women as paradigms of true disciples whose contributions were remarkable not only for their generation but also for subsequent generations. Theirs is is a continual call for a global confrontation and challenge to contemporary practices, cultures and traditions which do not practise the inclusivity of the Jesus tradition.

For further thought

- Reflect on the women who have been inspirations to you in your faith journey. Give thanks for them and consider the qualities you admire about them.
- In what ways is gender justice still required in the contexts you are familiar with through work, church, community involvement and the wider national and international scene?

In my primary school days, when the student achieving the top mark in the class was a girl it was announced thus: 'The first boy in this class is a girl'! In other words, it was considered impossible for a girl to do well and, when she did, she was regarded as a boy!

Mary, chief of the chief shepherd

There is nothing impossible God cannot do (verse 37). On this basis it was not impossible for God to have chosen a man to accomplish the task for which Mary was elected, and indeed, contemporary assumptions at the time would suggest that the divine could not be so closely associated with a woman, seeing that women were to be identified by their inferiority, sexuality and ritual uncleanness. However, because Mary was ready with great determination and faith (verse 38) to engage willingly in the work of God and to share God's perspective, the story as we know it came to pass. As the chief of the chief shepherd she bore in her own body the good news of salvation, Jesus Christ (the chief shepherd) to the world.

Luke 1:26-56

When equal opportunities are given to everyone without segregation in terms of gender, class or race, then justice and love can find their way to the entire world.

If God's choice to save can be hindered by our prejudices and barriers, what conditions and parameters do I set that may hinder God's love and justice?

Lord, liberate us so that the parameters set by society do not hold us back or cause us to hinder your work on the basis of our sexuality, gender, race or class.

Women of the New Testament

Glory Befeke Anye

Mary Magdalene, evangeliser

Luke 8:1-3; 24:1-11

In most tribes in the North-West Province of Cameroon, when the political or social situation becomes unbearable, the men go underground while the women (the 'ntangubengs') go out to bring calm. So it was in the New Testament. After Jesus' arrest, the female disciples, spearheaded by Mary Magdalene, did not flee like the male disciples who went underground and fled back to Galilee. Rather, they stayed in Jerusalem for his execution and burial, as loyal disciples who were prepared to remain with their beloved friend until the bitter end. The 'ntangubengs' will not sleep nor slumber until the future is guaranteed.

Within the historical setting of the time, one might have thought it was easier for the women to go underground than the men since *they* were considered the 'stronger race', and the patriarchal tradition did not consider the women as real disciples. What they said was 'nonsense' (24: 11). Yet the 'nonsense' had some kind of impact on the runaway 'sensible' men. Mary Magdalene evangelised the Twelve with the 'nonsense'. However, we see that even within the New Testament period itself, the honour of resurrection is accorded to the male disciples by Paul and presumably others in the early church. 1 Corinthians 15:5 quotes only men to whom the risen Christ appeared, and names not one of the women. No matter what the 'ntangubengs' do, they are still considered insignificant by the men.

Lord, let neither racial nor gender differences deter us from recognising the works of others, but enable us to pay tribute where it is due.

Glory Befeke Anye

Women of the New Testament

Reading this passage within the context of Cameroon, I'm conscious of two settings: what happens when someone dies, and what happens in an educational context. First, only the ancestors go to the shrine to confront death and to invoke life when someone dies. Second, only a loyal and committed student will always remember what the teacher teaches and will also remind the teacher of his duties.

In this story, Martha behaves as both an ancestor and a loyal student, showing her teacher Jesus the way forward. Like Simon Peter she confesses Jesus as the Messiah, as life confronts death and brings restoration to Lazarus. Her preparedness, determination and zeal to engage Jesus challenges the patriarchal society of death and champions rather the shrine of life. Her risking of overstepping the mark and entering the male preserve of death enables the other to gain life.

Can women play the role of ancestors in cultures that limit them on the basis of gender or sex?

O Lord, raise up women and men who will go out of their way and risk their lives for the sake of the other.

Martha, the ancestor

John 11:1, 17-27

Women of the New Testament

Glory Befeke Anye

The Samaritan woman, an insider

John 4:1-30

Considered as a stranger by tradition, the Samaritan woman (known only by the name of her town) played a primary role in the beginnings of the Christian community in Samaria. Through this nameless woman, Jesus was compelled to reveal his true identity to the world – even though, up until this point in John, he had hidden his identity from his male disciples.

Secrets are generally not disclosed to strangers, but are shared with those 'on the inside' – such as members of one's family or close circle of friends. Jesus in fact treats this woman as an insider. In friendly and intimate conversation, Jesus gives her courage, certainty and assurance to take her mission to others with conviction. In this way, Jesus and the woman together call for an inclusive discipleship of equals.

How can we mission for Christ when society seems to shut us out?

Our all-embracing God, in the midst of barriers empower us to witness to you and to share the good news of the gospel with others.

This unnamed woman launched a theological argument for table sharing and fellowship with gentiles. In the theological discourse with Jesus she counters the argument that the children (Israel/men) should be fed and their food should not be taken from them and given to the dogs (gentiles/women). In the debate she breaks the chains of all those in bondage and sets free all those in any kind of prison – and by doing so she participates in Christ's mission to the world. For the graciousness of the God of Jesus is abundant enough to satisfy not only the Jews or men of one race but all races, and both gentiles and women.

How can we seek to transform structures and situations that deprive others of their rights, future, food and basic needs?

God of all grace, providence and abundance, help us to participate in your power that breaks all chains of oppression, so all can experience fullness of life.

The Syro-Phoeni-cian woman, chain breaker

Mark 7:24-30

The unnamed woman

Mark 14:3-9

In most companies the workers who do the hard jobs, often with considerable sacrifice, earn very little and are generally considered insignificant, quickly forgotten by those in power. Those who are considered significant and are remembered often do more congenial tasks yet earn considerably more.

In love, the unnamed woman prepared Jesus for his death. Her excessive generosity and sacrificial service as a loyal disciple called forth Jesus' prophetic commendation of her behaviour (verse 9). As far as we know, Jesus never asked his disciples to write anything down or himself wrote anything, yet he made a prediction that *her name* would be remembered. What an irony, then – even, we might say, blasphemy – that her name is not remembered despite this divine decree. Even this story is frequently passed over in church lectionaries – it does not feature prominently in Holy Week, for example, though stories of male betrayal do.

How can a forgotten memory be remembered?

Help us, dear God, to remember those whose sacrificial love has been offered as a generous gift for you and for the world.

Women of the New Testament

2 Women in the early church

Notes based on the Good News Bible by
Glory Befeke Anye

For Glory's biography see p.308.

Preparing for the week

In this week's readings, we will come across women who were not only evangelists but also apostles in the early church movement, although it is debatable how far they were regarded as apostles in their time. Nevertheless, we may now regard them as apostles, since they performed apostolic functions and pioneered the spreading of the word.

None the less, evidence about these women is pretty scant, and mostly consists of passing references to them in epistles or in stories where the focus is on the exploits of the men. Quite a lot of detective work has to be done to unearth the significance of these early women leaders. Few or none of these passages appear in lectionaries of most churches, and this contributes further to ignorance of their lives and work amongst contemporary Christians, and may even contribute to the ongoing oppression of women.

Similarly the patriarchal system in Cameroon does not consider women as heads of families, even though they generally shoulder all that a man does in the family and more. Although their efforts rarely earn them dignity and recognition, nevertheless they keep thriving and supporting both their own families and the wider nation.

For further thought

- Why is there so little reference in the New Testament to the roles of women in the early church? Why have the women's stories been largely written out?
- What can you do to ensure that the testimonies of women today do not get 'written out' of the account?

Mary, the mother of Jesus

Acts 1:12-14, 2:1-4

Mary of Magdala was the most prominent of the Galilean disciples, because according to tradition she was the first one to receive a vision of the resurrected Lord – although patriarchal tradition holds that it was Peter (see 1 Corinthians 15:5). As in many families in Cameroon, the women may work hard to train their children, both at home and in school, but society gives the honour to the man of the household.

Mary, the mother of Jesus, is another women whose significance and function within the early church is frequently disregarded. As the chief of the chief shepherd, Jesus, Mary held a primary place in New Testament tradition. She was with the disciples in the upper room and filled with the power of the Holy Spirit on the day of Pentecost. In icons of Pentecost, she is always shown with the eleven disciples, usually at their head, as the Spirit descends in tongues of fire, testifying to her status as first amongst the apostles, or even as the mother of the disciples (and therefore the mother of the church). She mothered the apostles as Cameroonian women shepherd and shelter their families and children. She shows us that all may receive the Spirit and may nurture the faith of the church and build the broken world – women as well as men. We are called, like her, to mother faith where it is young and weak, and to continue the work begun by Jesus even if tradition may hinder us as a result of differences in our gender or sexual orientation.

Lord, help us to continue with you and to walk in your footsteps when the path seems dark.

Philip's daughters

Philip the evangelist (so called to distinguish him from Philip the apostle in John 1:43-46) proclaimed the message with his daughters, who were his successors. As evangelists of Christ, they proclaimed the word with their father, attending to the church not only as helpers but as leaders. As what we might nowadays term 'ordained ministers' in the church, Philip and his four daughters gave up all for the service of God. Yet despite holding such prominent positions in the church their names are only known through their father's. Once again we see the process whereby women's gifts and names quickly become forgotten in church tradition and where the glory of women is given to men. For whatever a woman does it is believed a man is behind it and thus it has been done by the man.

Acts 21:7-9

Although their names have been lost, these daughters of Philip inherited and shared in the prominent role and work of their father. This story therefore challenges those who still prohibit and inhibit women from inheriting their father's rights – as many in Cameroon do.

How can traditions which still hinder the leadership role of women in the church or society be transformed and duly give honour where it is due?

Lord, raise up women who can work with their mothers and fathers to move society forward without being diluted in the process.

Women of the New Testament   Glory Befeke Anye

Priscilla

Acts 18:1-3; Romans
16:3

Priscilla is here referred to as a 'fellow-worker' or 'co-worker' of Paul. She is ranked in the same category as an apostle. No one is refered to as a colleague who is not in the same rank. And the fact that Priscilla's name is mentioned first, before that of her husband, is an indicator that Priscilla did most of the work as an apostle and was very prominent and an influential character amongst the other apostles. This counters the tradition that women should be silent in church and public places which we find echoed in Paul's letters in other places, a tradition powerfully used by many churches and authorities as a weapon to subdue and oppress women. Here respect is given to Priscilla as the mover, rather than to her husband or father.

How can this picture of Paul working as a colleague with women transform traditions that see women as always in the secondary roles?

Lord, even when the world does not recognise our calling, let that not hinder us from doing your will and playing the primary roles you have called us to.

Women of the New Testament

Phoebe

Romans 16:1-2

Phoebe was a prominent leader of the church at Cenchreae, as is clear from the prominence Paul gives her in this list of greetings to significant members of the church in Rome. As a spiritual administrator and overseer of the church, like Paul she exercised apostolic functions in preaching the word and administering the sacraments. Yet she is known only as an appendage. Her works are not made prominent like the other male disciples. Had it not been for Paul's greeting to her in this chapter, this significant woman leader would not even be known, like many women in Cameroon whose credits usually go to men.

But if Phoebe was such a co-worker why did Paul not write to her as he did to other fellow workers like Timothy? We will never know the answer to this question. Perhaps he did, and these letters have not been preserved or considered worthy of inclusion in the canon. And if Phoebe is one female leader in the early church movement about whom we know little, how many more women were there about whom we know nothing?

Lord, give us spiritual eyes to discern your hidden truth as we read scripture, and wisdom to notice the clues you offer, so we can become empowered and withstand all that would prohibit us from playing our full part in your work.

Women of the New Testament   Glory Befeke Anye

Lois and Eunice

2 Timothy 1:3-5

My aunt-in-law was abandoned, with her children, by her husband. Single-handedly she nurtured, educated, trained and brought up her children. Then, rather belatedly, her husband reappeared on the scene, to take all the credit for the fine children he had largely neglected during most of their upbringing – while my aunt was pushed to the background.

Timothy's grandmother and mother, Lois and Eunice respectively, not only possessed faith but had sincere faith. They were Timothy's mentors, tutoring him in the path of faith in Christ. In other words, Timothy was a mirror of these two women's faith. As role models, masters and teachers, they shaped him in the faith from childhood onwards. Yet it is Timothy's name that is prominent in later tradition, and the names of Lois and Eunice are hardly well known. It is significant that there is no mention of Timothy's father or grandfather, suggesting that they played no key role in the development of his faith and ministry. As Abraham is regarded as the father of faith, so we can celebrate Lois and Eunice as mothers of sincere faith – not only of Timothy but of all those who have come after him. Many well-educated and well-cultured children are usually the product of their mothers.

How can mothers and grandmothers ensure their children and grandchildren gain true credit in our contemporary world?

Lord, help us to have sincere and genuine faith like that of Lois and Eunice, and to nurture the faith of successive generations.

Women of the New Testament

'The Lady'

2 John 1:1-13

Although the appellation 'Lady' here probably refers to a church rather than to an individual, the question that comes to my mind is: Why was this letter not addressed to the leader of the church, as the same writer addresses his third letter to Gaius, the leader of the church? Could it be that, since the name of the leader of this church is not mentioned and it is addressed merely to 'the Lady', this church was in fact headed by a woman? If so, why is her name sacrificed for the anonymous name of the church? What is her crime? Nothing more than being female! As in the case of many of the women we have read about this week, 'the Lady' has lost her identity and her status and we know her only as a rather shadowy figure subsumed under the characters of her children – even in this case her spiritual children, the members of the church, rather than her biological offspring.

Are we sometimes ashamed to honour those who have played a significant part in our own nurture and growth in faith?

Lord, help us to shake the dust off our feet and rise when insults and hurts are aimed at us.

Women of the New Testament

Glory Befeke Anye

Readings in Luke

8 Living in the kingdom

Notes based on the Revised English Bible by
Alec Gilmore

Alec Gilmore is a Baptist minister, Senior Research Fellow at the International Baptist Theological Seminary in Prague, and author of *A Concise Dictionary of Bible Origins and Interpretation* (Continuum).

Preparing for the week

Think of the kingdom (of God) as a way of living here and now rather than some non-identifiable world past or future. Think of a world that could be, here and now. Try not to think of what Jesus said as 'commandments – 'do this and the kingdom will come'. The kingdom cannot be achieved by our efforts. Think of it rather as something in the mind of God, which Jesus has a unique way of penetrating, and into which he shares his insights with us. Like a botanist walking through a very ordinary garden where most of us simply smile and nod, he stops us in our tracks with, 'Hey, look at this,' and then opens our eyes to what we are missing. The botanist helps us to see life in nature. Jesus helps us to see life in the kingdom. Call such a revelation a 'kingdom moment'. Jesus invites us to identify kingdom moments for ourselves. The kingdom is a given. Our privilege is to recognise it, practise its virtues, encourage its development and tell others.

For further thought

- Think of five situations where the Golden Rule ('Do to others what you would have them do to you', Matthew 7:12) is absolutely crucial and unquestionable. Think of another five where it could border on disaster.
- Make a list of your assets other than financial, evaluate your attachment to them and re-evaluate your priorities.
- When you next have a time of prayer with friends, spend at least 45 minutes sharing your kingdom moments before you pray.

The Golden Rule

Avoid Bibles with sectional headings as if to tell you what to find there. Practise reading the text for yourself. See it in relation to what went before and what happened next. Such interconnections often carry their own message. These verses, for example, raise tough questions about the ways we treat one another which go far beyond those we normally think of as 'enemies' and suggest how different life would be by a simple observance of the Golden Rule. Allowing truth to strike us in different ways can teach us a lot not only about the world but also about ourselves.

Luke 6:27-38

Recall an occasion when somebody got the better of you, damaged your reputation, hurt you or someone you love. What was your first reaction? To strike back? To call for justice? To seek compensation? All fairly natural and (depending on the circumstances) not necessarily unreasonable. Then think of someone you know, personally or from film, theatre or fiction, whose attitude instinctively would have been softer and shown more understanding. Which in the long run is likely to be more beneficial to the offender, to society and to your health? To find the answer is to glimpse the kingdom. To practise it is to participate in the kingdom.

Thank you, Father, for opening my eyes to a new world and a totally different way of living. Keep me always mindful of how I treat others and especially those who have offended me.

Readings in Luke

Alec Gilmore

Catching the mirror

Luke 6:39-49

A strange collection of aphorisms here which don't immediately connect too readily with one another. Begin with questions. What might have led Jesus to make that remark about the blind leading the blind or the disciple who rated himself about his teacher? Did he have somebody in mind? And whatever caused his outburst in verse 42? Try recalling something in your own experience which might have led to any one of them.

Notice then the change of tone. The first two sayings (verses 39-40) are fairly objective. You know people like that. The third (verse 41) is different. It is addressed directly to me. I know because when I hear it I begin to feel uncomfortable. By verse 43 the window where I am looking out has become a mirror. I see myself. But which tree am I?

I pause. The mirror penetrates. This is not the doctor assessing a few external symptoms. This is an internal examination. It is a challenge to get a better understanding of myself and my relationship with others. Everything I say and do reflects what is inside. I see what he is driving at. Good people are not good because they do good things. They do good things because they are good people – inherently at peace with themselves and with God.

Kingdom bells are ringing – too loud for comfort. I turn the volume down and go away. 'Fine,' says Jesus, 'but don't forget the man who built a house without adequate foundations.'

Dear Lord, now I understand.

Learning to pray

Luke 11:1-13

When the disciples asked to be taught to pray, what do you think they were asking for or expecting? If you asked your minister the same question, what would you be expecting? If a member of the congregation asked you, what might they be looking for? Learning words, phrases, sentences, liturgy maybe? A list of set times, how to stand, kneel, sit or hold your hands? Places to visit, perhaps. All may be helpful, some more than others, depending on the person asking the question, but they are not what Jesus goes for.

Luke's shortened version of the Lord's Prayer and the accompanying story get down to basics. Prayer begins with attitude and relationship – first, with God (a recognition of who God is and how you see God); second, with life (food is vital for living and basic food for healthy living, as also is living a day at a time); third, with our fellow human beings (relationships and a proper sense of forgiveness for our failures which matures as we experience what our forgiveness of others means to others).

Simple basics maybe, but already we begin to wilt at the thought. More like weariness and hard work than immediate excitement which leads to exhilaration. Much easier to close our eyes and say the words. But that's what Jesus says it is, and the story seems to underline the point.

Dear Jesus, teach me first to think what to ask for, then give me the persistence to work at it.

Readings in Luke

Alec Gilmore

Signs and blindness

Luke 11:29-36

Begin with the request for a sign. What did they want and what would have satisfied them? What sign could anyone have given that would not leave further space for doubt, question and argument? Better to ask a different question. Why were they asking? Recall any moment when you have caught yourself asking for 'proof' when the most you could only ever hope for was 'evidence' and how convincing would even that be, especially if you didn't want to believe it?

Underlying this question is a demand for certainty about something where certainty is not really possible. Precisely what led the Queen of the South to come from the ends of the earth to sit at the feet of Solomon nobody knows, but certainly something did, even if it was only her surmise that he had something of value to offer. Nor do we know what led the people of Nineveh to repent, save for the sharp realisation that what Jonah was going on about had about it the ring of truth. In both cases something grabbed them, and once hooked like that they really had no need or desire to go hunting for signs.

Jesus sees himself as holding up a lamp (just like any preacher). See it and your whole life may be transformed. Asking for signs may be an indication that you don't, in which case any number of 'signs' will make no difference. Kingdom moments don't come to order.

Lord, help me to see, especially when I find seeing difficult.

Two key words here are 'anticipation' and 'expectation'. We are never going to see the kingdom if all we are engaged in is question, argument and discussion. Of course there are always going to be doubts and differences of opinion among believers (in all faiths) and exploration, discussion and even confrontation at times are appropriate responses. Sometimes they produce a kingdom moment of their own, provided we are not so engrossed in the argument that we fail to spot them.

Some of the best kingdom moments, however, are a by-product of people faithfully knowing what they are about and getting on with it, always prepared to admit that they may be wrong, and therefore prepared to change and adjust according to needs and circumstances, but always (and especially) alert to that moment when the light flashes, the drums roll and you suddenly become alive in a new way. It can happen any time and anywhere and if Peter wanted to lay claim to the experience for the elite he was doomed to disappointment – it can happen to anybody, and does.

It is a hard saying and a tough gospel. It makes sharp divisions between those who see and those who don't, and has been known to split families down the middle; but it is a sad day if we can read the runes of the weather, the environment and the economy and be blind to the kingdom moment.

Please God, keep me ever humble, ever faithful, ever watchful.

Light your lamp, read the signs, be ready

Luke 12:35-53

Readings in Luke   Alec Gilmore

Lose your assets

Luke 18:18-30

This is more than a hard saying about the penalties of wealth. Riches are not the only asset. Look more closely.

This man is 'a ruler'. He knows something about power and control. He needs to know where he is, and where other people are. His strength comes from his position (as a ruler) and from the fact that he has kept the rules – always. So why is he worrying about eternal life? Either his life is not fully satisfying or he wants Jesus to be more specific. Jesus plays along with him and the ruler knows the stock answers. So Jesus tries another line. Literally, it is a statement about wealth, but Jesus might have meant at least two other things.

One, forget your assets and embrace a totally different way of life. Sell up. Take off. Start again somewhere else. A challenge to people who have nothing as it is to those who have much, as the disciples knew only too well. Peter says as much. 'We have – so what?'

Two, consider whether you are looking in the wrong place for what it is you are hoping to find. Don't look for fresh fish in the depths of the ocean or tigers in Africa – they are not there. What you are looking for may not sit comfortably with what you treasure. Jesus had hit the nail on the head and the ruler knew it.

Father, it is time for a stocktaking, and please help me to surrender without waiting to discover the rewards.

Readings in Luke

9 Stories of the kingdom

Notes based on
the Revised English
Bible by
Alec Gilmore

For Alec's biography
see p.329.

Preparing for the week

Having opened our eyes to kingdom moments, Jesus proceeds to tell stories of kingdom values. Stories about what it is like living in the kingdom; about the qualities which need to be cherished, similar to those later noted by Paul as the fruits of the spirit (Galatians 5:22-23).

Kingdom values are universal and honoured in different ways and to varying degrees in most if not all religions. Most of them need little defence, though the devil as always is in the detail and there is room for wide diversity in application. If kingdom moments identify the kingdom, kingdom values tell us where to spot it. As with moments, their very nature takes us by surprise and there may well be some slight twist which pulls us up with a jerk, making us think again and possibly leading to adjustments in our attitudes or lifestyle.

Some stories also have more than one kingdom value. Just because you are familiar with a story, don't imagine you know everything it is saying before you begin. Try writing down what you feel the kingdom value is before you read the notes. The notes try to focus on one. See if it is the same. Perhaps you can spot others.

For further thought

• What values are reflected in the story of the Good Samaritan? How many are genuine kingdom values?

• Consider the price paid by those around you to enable you to believe and do the things that you are committed to.

Knowing myself

Luke 8:1-18

Taken out of context, verses 5-8 lend themselves to allegorical interpretation and most preachers have taken advantage of this, identifying the crowd variously according to their readiness to believe. In context it may have a wider interpretation. This tour (verse 1) is not an evangelical campaign or a comfort zone for believers, and the parable may be taken as a comment on life. It is how people are – how we all are.

Imagine a stranger with an odd collection of followers suddenly arriving in your town. The locals all react in very different ways, and it's the same everywhere. His entourage can't understand it and he knows it. He, on the other hand, sees very clearly what is happening and shares it with them, possibly to enlighten, possibly to see how perceptive they are. Apparently they aren't, so he has to spell it out for them.

Try reading it not as a story about believers and unbelievers but about all of us. And not only about faith but about everything we touch. Some see, some don't. Some start, some finish. Some cop out, some struggle to stay in. It doesn't have to be a judgemental parable, though it does suggest that those who hear and persist are likely to make the most of their lives and this does represent a challenge to his immediate hearers (the disciples) to sort themselves out.

Thank you, Jesus, for opening my eyes to see myself and others in a different way.

Basic humanity

Instead of beginning with the lawyer, begin with the disciples returning from a preaching mission (verse 17), overwhelmed by their success, not by numbers but by the sort of people they have picked up. Not 'the learned and the wise' but the 'simple' – people whose capacity for seeing and hearing outshines that of the clever and the bright. The lawyer just doesn't get it, and if he does he is not happy about it. It doesn't fit in with his expectations. How does it relate to eternal life? Living and working on a different planet, he listens on a different wavelength. And there are 'lawyers' in all professions and none with similar emotions and queries. Think of some.

Luke 10:25-37

Next, instead of spotlighting the Samaritan, with the familiar dig at the faithful and the statutory medal for the outsider, the rejected and the marginalised, reflect on other basic human attitudes in the story. In a tight spot, where do you find kingdom values and where are they missing? Ask people who collect for charity where it is easiest and hardest to knock on doors and with what result. Identify stories of people who willingly share resources and people who find good reasons for not. Ask yourself questions about the exclusive defensiveness and self-protection of religious people when it comes to faith and customs. Preserving purity usually gets more votes than costly redemption.

Dear Jesus, never let my determination to protect what I have prevent me hearing the cry from those in need.

Readings in Luke

Alec Gilmore

Justice and fairness

Luke 12:13-34

Possessions need not be a problem. The desire to hang on to them, to control them and to use them to control others is. The kingdom is not about claiming divine authority for what we want. Jesus refuses to get involved and turns our attention to the underlying sense of greed and power. Forget the negatives here (verses 22ff). We need food, we need clothes, and you can't start afresh with everything every morning. There are other issues and going down that road may be a useful way of avoiding them.

Think of tensions, which may be inevitable and necessary and can also be creative, rather than black and white, right and wrong. Many tensions lurk here. Tension between possessions themselves and our attachment to them is only one. There is the tension between having enough to live reasonably and an over-reaching grasping mentality; between what we would like and what we really need; between reasonable concern and unreasonable anxiety (verse 29). You can no doubt think of others.

Justice is both a kingdom value and a human right, and at all levels includes basic fairness, sensible rationality and human understanding. Commitment to kingdom values is not the same thing as getting what you want or advancing your cause. It is more about recognising and appreciating those fundamental qualities of life that never wear out, last for ever and (as values) can never be taken away.

Thank you, Jesus. Your stories so help me to keep kingdom-centred.

Ho! Ho! (verse 15). If the kingdom is so great let's make sure we get a front seat. 'Oh dear,' says Jesus, 'they still don't get it.' Another story needed.

These people don't know a bargain when they see one. It's a generous invitation. A free gift. Well worth having. Great on a Sunday when it comes. Who could not respond? Nothing changes and there's nothing wrong with it by the time they get to Wednesday or Thursday – just that it gets low priority when the time comes and it has to compete with everything else that has to be done. A side effect is that kingdom values then turn up somewhere else as the householder's overwhelming generosity breaks through. He turns his attention elsewhere. First the second eleven, then all the people he had never even thought of befriending or co-operating with. Those on the far horizon are suddenly centre stage with an opportunity to enjoy something they never thought would come their way, and the absentees are left to work it out for themselves without a word of encouragement.

But then there is no such thing as a free lunch. A price has to be paid (verses 25-27), and often not only by those who enjoy the feast. So we must think before we jump. Pause to count the cost, to ourselves but also to others.

A free gift but no free lunch

Luke 14:15-35

Father, keep me ever mindful of the people who pay a price for my commitment. May I never take it for granted.

Readings in Luke   Alec Gilmore

Crisis time

Luke 16:1-17

References to dishonesty and an 'unjust steward' can be misleading. As in a stop-and-search operation this man is under suspicion (verse 1) and feels the dice of justice loaded against him. He knows and fears the worst, and in a tight spot turns to his friends. They may not save him but he will need them when he comes out. You may be able to identify him, not very far away.

Begin with his emotions. What if he knew he had done wrong and had been rumbled? What if he knew he hadn't but feared he was being victimised? And what about his master? Is he honourable, is he being got at, is he genuinely seeking truth or has he already made his mind up?

Avoid the issues of right or wrong. There is not enough evidence to make a judgement and Jesus doesn't go down that road either. The Greek translated as 'dishonest' (verse 8) can simply mean 'to do wrong'. Similarly avoid the argument as to whether the master is the householder or Jesus. Both may well have agreed that his handling of the crisis was 'wrong' but the master applauds him 'for acting so astutely' (verse 8), and in the second half of the verse Jesus seems to wish that all God's people were a bit more like him.

Please God, help me not to rush to judgements on others until I have entered into their emotions, established the facts and worked out what I might have done in their shoes.

The ceiling and the sky

Luke 16:19-31

In Brecht's *Galileo* there is a reference to the need to look not to the ceiling but the sky. In Tennessee Williams's *Stairs to the Roof*, we have an office clerk working in a sweatshop on the top floor of a 12-storey building. He doesn't fit the system, rebels against the rigidity and tells his boss he wants to go higher. His matter-of-fact boss explains that since they are already on the top floor there is nowhere higher to go. 'But there is,' says the man, 'there are stairs to the roof.' Nobody had ever found them, but he often retreated to enjoy the sky. His boss was content with the ceiling. Kingdom people are sky-people.

Ceiling-people know what they want, are single-minded and preoccupied with the satisfaction that comes from the fulfilment of their dream. Dives is a 'ceiling' character. He was not unaware of Lazarus. He instantly recognised him and knew his name (verse 23) but Lazarus was not part of his world until Dives was in dire straits and even then he only wanted him as his lackey. Dives lives in a closed world, his mind closed to God and his heart to compassion. He is sensitive to his brothers to a point (verse 28) but still fails to appreciate that they were well aware of the teaching and if they were not convinced on moral grounds they were highly unlikely to be changed by Lazarus.

Thank you, Father, for the warning. Keep me always reaching for the sky.

Readings in Luke

Alec Gilmore

Treasures of darkness

1 Are your wonders known in the darkness?

Notes based on the New Revised Standard Version by

Lori Sbordone Rizzo

A native New Yorker, Lori Sbordone Rizzo has been a 'journeyman-teacher' preparing at-risk youth to pass their high school equivalency tests. Theologically, she describes herself as a revolutionary evangelical lesbian mystic. In 2010, she hopes she will be doing more preaching, writing and fishing.

Preparing for the week

Darkness is a rare commodity in the inner city. I realised this when I tried to take a group of students outside one evening to view the exploding nebula in the Orion constellation. I was confident as I marched them to a nearby empty lot, borrowed telescope in hand. Surely anyone could find Orion! It wasn't until that moment that I realised we had no sky of stars; a few stars make it through the haze of the city's reflected light, but not enough to constitute a constellation. We just don't have sufficient darkness. This haze of artificial light obfuscates the night sky, and as a result we have lost all sense of the galaxy surrounding us. Small wonder then that in the midst of this bustling metropolis, people feel so isolated and alone.

Darkness in spiritual vocabulary is synonymous with the absence of God, or at least the absence of divine favour. St Bernard of Clairvaux, in his classic treatise, *On Loving God*, differentiates between loving God for what God does for us, and loving God simply for who God is. I don't know if we get there without a dark night or two. As Jesus said to Thomas, 'Blessed are those who have not seen and yet have come to believe' (John 20:29).

For further thought

- What are your own personal associations with darkness? Are they largely positive or negative? Why?
- What have you learnt about God through the dark times?

Keeping it real

Psalm 88

Some of the best advice on prayer I was ever given is that we should always speak to God with words that are both honest to who we are and honest to who God is. The psalmist is in misery, and he does not spare God the details; 'My life is a train wreck, and it is all your doing.' Honest to God: You are the creator and sustainer of the universe. You can do all things. Honest to me: I am overwhelmed with sorrow; I cannot bear the weight of my life another minute. The conclusion is inevitable: God could help, he just won't.

The psalmist holds God personally responsible for his suffering: and yet, is there any doubt that he will return to prayer tomorrow? Of course not. He returns, and we return because, honestly, God is faithful. He allows evil to co-exist with us, this is true. Oftentimes God's call on our lives necessitates pain, causing us to cry with the psalmist, 'Your wrath has swept over me' (verse 16). I remember a night where I felt as if I was beating my fists against God's chest until I punched myself out and collapsed. When I awoke, nothing had changed, except an edge had been ground off my anger. More than this, there was a confidence borne from the assurance that God could take my worst, and still be there. Because honest to God, he is faithful. He won't make suffering go away, but he does keep it all good.

Faithful God, there is so much I need to say to you.

Treasures of darkness   Lori Sbordone Rizzo

Sweet

Psalm 18:6-16

There is a story about a young monk who set out into the woods to try to find a quiet place to be alone with God. He walked far into the forest until the monastery, with all its distractions, was far from sight, then he took out his prayer book and his Bible and began his devotions, but before he finished the office, he had fallen fast asleep. When he awoke, it was night. He had no light, no trail map, no way that he could find his way back to the safe confines of the monastery, and in the gathering darkness, every sound became the footsteps of ravenous wolves. In terror, he cried out, 'Jesus! Dear Jesus, please help me. Jesus!' He noticed that this seemed to work. The wolves, or whatever they were, seemed to keep their distance so long as he continued to shout the Lord's name. Morning came, and he found the path again and returned to the monastery. When he arrived, he told the brothers, 'I had the best night of prayer in the woods!'

A second-century shepherd proclaimed, 'The name of Jesus is great and wonderful and upholds the whole universe.' Shepherds also know a little something about lying in the darkness listening for threats. There is something about darkness that makes the name of our Saviour especially sweet.

Jesus, Jesus. Help! Help!

I used to have little sympathy for Job's friends. Then I worked as a chaplain in an AIDS ward. When you sit at the bedside of someone whose body is being possessed by cancerous sores, it is impossible to say anything that makes sense. Of course, sense is exactly what they are looking for: they want you to make sense of what is happening to them. And you can't. There is no sensing it, not with our little minds. Part of the human condition is that we do suffer, and often the why of it is beyond our grasp. Still we shoot that 'why?' question into our consciousness like a pinball, enduring the torture of its incessant bouncing because we think that as long as we can keep the question in play, God will address himself to it. We'd have better luck setting out wind chimes and expecting to hear Bach.

Martin Luther King Junior insisted that unearned suffering is redemptive. Forcing white Americans to watch as peaceable black folk were beaten for the right to ride in a bus allowed us to see the sin of racism within us and repent. Job's suffering is unearned; God is very clear on this point. Through it all, Job affirms, 'I know that my redeemer lives' (Job 19:25). Martin Luther King shouted to the faithful, 'I have a dream.' How is that possible, given all they suffered? There's no sensing it!

I cannot imagine what it must be like to suffer without any hope of redemption, and thanks be to God, I don't have to.

Dear God, through all darkness, let there be hope.

Beat down

Job 38:1-21

Treasures of darkness   Lori Sbordone Rizzo

Cheating and not cheating

Isaiah 45:1-7

My godson Andrew has been obsessed with video games from an early age. Before he was allowed to use the internet, he would call and ask if I could look up 'cheats' for the games he was playing. Cheats were essentially inside jokes written into the software by the game's creators. Some of them provided life-saving help for your virtual hero in his quest for ultimate glory – a secret store of energy to help you evade the killer snowmen or a doorway out of a room full of ghosts. In one virtual world, we discovered that if you threw a bomb at some random chicken, a million chickens rained down vendetta from the sky and pecked you to death. It was a source of endless amusement for us.

Virtual worlds exist as maths equations stored within microchips. In the real world, our one life is all we have. We stumble forward often blindly in an environment so merciless that there isn't so much as a reset button or an undo key. If a higher power wants to step up and offer me a way out of darkness, I'm taking it. So long as I (and my tribe) get to the other side alive, relatively unscathed, reasonably sane, I will have no problem giving that God all the glory. Some folk might call that cheating. To me, it's common sense.

For waking me up today, and sustaining me all my days, O God, I give you all the glory.

There is a prayer in the Anglican Communion called the Collect for Purity; it is an ancient one, dating back to AD800, and translated into English by Thomas Cranmer in the very first Book of Common Prayer. The address is terrifying; 'Almighty God, unto whom all hearts are open, all desires known and from whom no secrets are hid'. You say this with your arms open and your hands up, almost as if someone has just pulled a gun on you, almost as if you were saying to God, 'OK, you've got me.'

Hold up

Psalm 139:7-18

How did God get to create a set-up like this? He knows everywhere we hide, and everything we creep around hoping to avoid. It's a seriously uncomfortable truth about God, so much so that most preaching I hear avoids it. The problem is that when they strip God of omniscience, they leave him with very little power to save because you can't fix what you don't know. As a fearless preacher, Paul Tillich proclaimed, 'God is inescapable. He is God only because He is inescapable. Only that which is inescapable is God.'

It's hard to cosy up to the inescapable God. Imagine someone put a mirror in your bedroom that reveals everything. Get that thing out of here! What would make anyone embrace such torture? Someone would have to promise that as a result I would love God with more of my heart.

Pray the closing plea of the Collect for Purity: 'Cleanse the thoughts of our hearts by the inspiration of your Holy Spirit, that we may perfectly love you, and worthily magnify your holy Name, through Christ our Lord.'

Treasures of darkness   Lori Sbordone Rizzo

Bragging rights

Psalm 91

The psalmist brags of God's almighty, all-encompassing protection. He claims that no evil shall fall upon those who dwell in God. The testimony of saints in our lives and in scripture seems to tell a different story. What's up here?

Satan used a verse from this psalm when testing Jesus in the wilderness, inviting him to throw himself from the temple and see if God would send angels to the rescue (Matthew 4:6). Jesus didn't have to go looking for trouble; his whole life is about revealing the power of unearned suffering, but if God did not spare his Beloved from suffering, what are our chances?

The question is way bigger than this page, but I will point to that wonderful biblical verb, 'abide'. Trust in God's protection is given to those who abide in him. A stone which abides in the sun is warm; an iron that abides in fire can burn almost as hot as the fire itself. Each takes on the characteristics of what they abide in. Job, Jesus, Martin Luther King – each took on the characteristics of the one they abided in, and each displayed confident trust in God's protection, even in their darkest moments. To stand in the face of trouble and brag on God's promises demands a confidence which belongs only to those who abide in God. Otherwise you're bragging on nothing. Whereas for those who abide in God, who are taking on God's own character and bringing it everywhere they go, evil may come knocking, but it can't come in.

Dear God, give me courage to abide in you.

Treasures of darkness

2 God leads the Israelites in darkness

Sunday 5 December

Notes based on the New Revised Standard Version by

Michael N Jagessar

Michael N Jagessar is the Secretary for Racial Justice and Multicultural Ministry for the United Reformed Church (UK). Born in Guyana, he describes himself as 'Indo-Guyanese Caribbean'. He has lived, worked and studied in Guyana, Jamaica, Grenada, Curacao, Switzerland and the Netherlands. He formerly taught at the Queen's Foundation for Ecumenical Theological Education, Birmingham.
His blogsite can be found at http://www.caribleaper.co.uk.

Preparing for the week

The readings this week invite us to continue our exploration of the positive valuing of darkness, and to reflect on the mysterious ways and movement of God or the Divine. Various biblical testimonies either overtly or subtly point us to a sense of the holy that embodies both light and darkness, while at the same time underscore that the Divine is beyond both. However much we human beings try to bring closure on the ways of God, the reality is that God finds mysterious, mischievous and surprising ways to subvert our intentions, speaking, revealing, accompanying and leading us in multiple ways and places.

Light and darkness, black and white – or whatever the binaries we offer – these will always remain limiting human constructs in our efforts to 'image' the extravagant love, expansive generosity and borderless compassion of God, the Divine Lover.

For further thought

- Reflect on a story (or stories) from your own life journey where you have had to trust God when you did not know what the final outcome would be. What insights (about yourself, your faith and God) have you gleaned in retrospect?

- Reflect on ways that our positive imaging of darkness is a counter-cultural act. How do our recognition and positive experience of darkness enable us to acknowledge the holy in new ways? Can we miss an experience of mystery and the Divine because of our fear of and prejudice against darkness?

God speaks to Abraham in the dark

Genesis 15:12-21

We can all share stories of the ways through which God has spoken and continues to speak in our lives. Our scriptures are replete with examples of a calling and speaking God. And the Divine does surprise us human beings with when, where and how such encounters happen! They may happen in extraordinary ways, but most likely God comes to us in the ordinary and mundane circumstances of our lives.

In today's reading God speaks to Abraham and a covenant is made when the sun is set and darkness falls. Here is subversion at work – God speaking to Abraham in the darkness. Experience of the holy and the Divine comes in the darkness. God is there present! But, how do we know that it is God who is speaking and is really present? This remains a troubling question as history is replete with examples of the Divine being hijacked to suit our selfish inclinations. Do you think that Abraham heard everything the Divine whispered? Or did his aural receptacles filter the message?

We know that the Divine is speaking when we have an experience that changes us. The experience can be as small as a new feeling or insight, or as grand as a vision. We measure the experience, not by its depth, but by the extent to which it changes us. And, to experience the empowering dimensions of God's covenant, we must relate covenant to justice and peace in our calling and practice as people who walk the way of God in Christ. The key here is relationship and what lies within one's heart.

Give us ears, eyes, minds and hearts, O Divine Lover, so that we may hear, receive and live your purpose for us and the whole of creation.

Jacob crosses the Jabbok by night

Genesis 32: 22-32

There is something unpredictable and even dangerous about encountering the Divine. For being changed by such an encounter may bring about some pain. Can there ever be transformation without pain? Jacob's wrestling match is understood as a significant turning point in his life, though not without a degree of ambiguity, ambivalence and pain. In the encounter with a mysterious figure near the Jabbok, there is no true victor, though this does not mean that nothing has happened.

Jacob gains a new identity (name change). With that identity he moves on to meet Esau, making a kind of peace with him. Jacob's new name was not just for himself. The encounter here embodied a whole people, becoming a 'corporate personality'. Jacob also comes limping away from the conflict. Given the complexities of life, we are aware that sometimes when we emerge from our own 'wrestlings' we may do so transformed yet wounded.

In Jacob's case, meeting God did not lead, as so much of our theology tends to imagine, to reconciliation, forgiveness, healing. It may be that Jacob's crossing of the Jabbok by night and his encounter is a reminder of what relationship with the Divine really looks like once we get past our worn-out and neat religious vocabulary.

Before we can meet the other, reconcile with our enemy, find peace and acceptance, we must find that space apart from others to come to know ourselves better. And this may be the most unlikely of places.

Be it on the banks of the river or in the crossing, help us, O Compassionate Companion, to understand that reconciliation involves struggle within and without and that our spirituality is shaped in the midst of wrestlings with the demands and trials of life.

Treasures of darkness   Michael Jagessar

A darkness that can be felt

Exodus 10:21-29

Meditate on the following:

There are those who seek to penetrate the immensities and to see God. One ought rather to sink into the depths and seek to find God among the suffering, erring and the downtrodden. Then the heart is free from pride and able to see God.

Martin Luther

'Total darkness covered Egypt for three days', so the story goes. We, of course, have been conditioned to think of darkness as frightening and as representing a host of evils. Darkness frequently evokes what is not of God. We tend to forget that God created both darkness and light, and that God's Spirit moves mysteriously over the face of the deep. Our liturgies and hymns reinforce the myth of fearing darkness and not associating any movement of the Divine in darkness. Absence becomes the operative word.

Look again and closer at this event. Whereas the invasion of locusts strips power from Egypt, the ninth invasion of darkness actually buoys Israelite faith. This subversive act effectively blanketed Egypt with dense darkness to immobilise the Egyptians. Yet, it is within this darkness that the oppressed Israelites found an opportunity for release. Immobilising the oppressor in a darkness that can be felt, and allowing a temporary respite to Israelites within that darkness, the Divine opened up the possibility of liberation.

Here was a foretaste of the freedom to come in subsequent events. The darkness here strengthens confidence and renews faith in God. God is right there in the darkness, leading and opening up multiple possibilities for release and for self-perception. For to be truly free, individuals need faith in their identity as free people and the assurance that the Divine is always near – whether in darkness or in light.

Michael Jagessar

Treasures of darkness

Crossing the Red Sea by night

There is always a point beyond which an oppressed people will not put up with their oppression. They will do anything to get out of their situation – even daring a dangerous crossing in the night with the oppressor's war machine not far behind. St John of the Cross writes of 'the dark night with its aridities and voids' as 'the means to the knowledge of both God and self'. I am also reminded of what the mystics refer to as the 'darkness of unknowing' and being enveloped by an expansive graciousness which one cannot see, feel or touch.

Exodus 14:19-31

Do you suppose that the Israelites had a transforming encounter with the Divine which propelled them to cross the Red Sea? Or was it more a case of getting up and taking their destiny into their own hands? In retrospect we may wish to call it 'putting faith into action'!

Rabbi Abraham Heschel suggests that we do not take leaps of faith, but rather leaps of action. What would have happened had the Israelites not taken that first step into the water – that leap into action? Those who would have survived the might of Pharaoh's war machine would have remained enslaved in Egypt and this enslaved people would have disappeared from the pages of history.

When we respond to our own prayers with an 'amen' that is characterised by action, such a response can change everything. This is when the miracle begins.

Create in us and stir up among us, O Subtle One, faith and courage to leap into action in response to your call, be it day or night.

Treasures of darkness   Michael Jagessar

God gives the law out of darkness

Deuteronomy 5:22-27

Many years ago the hymn writer J G Whittier, in a hymn that is still sung today, images God as a 'still small voice of calm' speaking 'through the earthquake, wind and fire'. He may not have had a passage such as that of the book of Deuteronomy in mind (as his focus was more on the practices of Hindu India), yet his words connect very well with our selected verses for today's reflection. God speaks and moves in unlikely places. By now this is such a well-established idea that we need to ask why we still make the mistake of looking for the Divine in the *likely* places.

Here is Moses reminding the Israelites of their history and emphasising that the commands of God did not originate from him (Moses), but from God who spoke out of the midst of fire, cloud and thick darkness. What are now received as commands to live and walk by come from the Divine, all of which have been attested to by the assembly of Israelites. This covenant, embodied in the commands, is about the prioritising of relationships with the Divine. Remembering this is critical.

Indeed, God speaks and works in what we human beings will consider 'wrong' or unlikely places and ways. The implications here are numerous. Among them we may wish to consider the following questions: What does this say of God? What does it say of these places? What does it say of us, our understanding of God and our faith?

Work your yeast of surprise, O still small voice of calm, in those unlikely places and corners of our lives and our world. May we see and be your work of goodness by walking your way of love.

Michael Jagessar

Treasures of darkness

The glory of the Lord in 'thick darkness'

1 Kings 8:1, 6, 10-21

Where is the dwelling place of the Divine? Imagine Moses right at the top of Mount Sinai, there in the dense darkness where God waited for him. The Divine finds unlikely places to dwell. In today's reading the Ark of the Lord's covenant (carrying the two stone tablets that Moses had placed in it at Horeb) is brought to and placed in the inner sanctuary of the temple. This is the temple that Solomon built, overflowing with such opulence and grandeur.

Was the glory of the Lord in the Ark? Or was it in the temple? What happens next is significant. As the priests withdraw there is such thick smoke that they are unable to carry out their rites, for God's glory fills the temple in thick smoke or darkness. Solomon takes the initiative (and priestly role) and notes that God has said that God's dwelling place is in the dark clouds. He then blesses the gathering and praises God. Solomon the great king, after all his efforts towards his magnificent building project, has to concede that the presence of the Divine cannot be contained in any human-built structure.

Solomon realises that the Divine cannot be contained even in the highest heaven and that God's expansive generosity has space for all – even foreigners. Here is a profound theological truth: nothing in heaven and on earth can sufficiently contain the glory of God.

Help us to perceive so that we may understand; help us to believe so that we may perceive; help us to attend to your way of love, O Divine Lover, so that we may believe.

Treasures of darkness   Michael Jagessar

Treasures of darkness

3 Darkness in Jesus' life, death and resurrection

Notes based on the Revised English Version by

Jan Sutch Pickard

Jan Sutch Pickard is a poet and storyteller living in the village of Bunessan, on the Isle of Mull. A member of the ecumenical Iona Community, and formerly warden of the Abbey in Iona, she comes from the Methodist tradition, at the moment worships and leads worship in the Church of Scotland, and was trained and supported by the Quakers as a volunteer with the Ecumenical Accompaniment Programme in Israel and Palestine.

Preparing for the week

The days before Christmas are often filled with preparations and practicalities. In the British Isles (particularly as far north as Mull) the days are also short, with darkness closing in. So it is possible to feel pressured by time and oppressed by darkness. But night is a time for healing sleep, and darkness can be solace to the soul. Here are some Bible passages, from seasonal and challenging sources, to help us explore that theme. Although we may be used to the images of light and darkness for good and evil (for instance in John's gospel, and the letters of John) there are many passages in the Bible that remind us that God is in all things, including the natural alternation of night and day. There are also points when, lacking language to describe the mystery of God's being, we may glimpse it in the depths of the night sky.

For further reflection and action

- Try to look at the night sky, this week.
- And take time before dawn, or after nightfall, to sit with a single reading lamp, maybe lighting a candle, too, to read, reflect and pray.

In a dark, safe place, a child is growing, becoming a distinct and viable human being.

Elizabeth feels her baby (who will be John) stir in her womb, as she is greeted by Mary (who will be the mother of Jesus). Luke has also given us a picture of Mary, learning from Gabriel that she would bear God's child: troubled, fearful, questioning ('how can this be?') then accepting and then – singing the Magnificat – joyful, praising God.

The mysterious moment of conception is described thus: 'the power of the Most High will overshadow you' (verse 36). The image is not of menace, but of shelter. And then, in the shelter of Mary's womb, in the safe darkness, the child grows.

Charles Causley's poem, 'Ballad of the Breadman' (in *Collected Poems 1951-1975*, London, Macmillan, 1975, pp.165–7), reminds us of the harsh light of popular perceptions, as neighbours gossiped about Mary's pregnancy:

> *Mary never answered,*
> *Mary never replied.*
> *She kept the information,*
> *Like the baby, safe inside.*

God's wisdom was to use the down-to-earth human experience of pregnancy, and the nurturing darkness of the womb, to bring love into the world.

The baby in her womb

Luke 1:30-41

O God, fathering and mothering us,
we thank you for the mystery
of the moment when life begins,
and for the long months of caring and growth
within the womb, in the gentle darkness –
afloat in the waters of creation –
when each of us lies close to your heartbeat.

Treasures of darkness   Jan Sutch Pickard

Keeping watch through the night

Luke 2:8-20

'Suddenly an angel of the Lord appeared to them, and the glory of the Lord shone round about them. They were terrified'

(verse 9)

Why would shepherds be afraid of darkness? They were used to the night shift, lived in a land without electricity, were too poor for oil lamps. Living half their lives by firelight and starlight, they found their way about without fear, knowing the hill paths like the back of their hands.

It wasn't the darkness that scared them, but sudden light that filled the sky, dazzling, in-explicable, overwhelming.

And they saw an angel. What does an angel look like? The gospel writer will have imagined something powerful, not sweet like a Sunday school child with tinsel in her hair – maybe a figure like a warrior. Or a non-human phenomenon, like the Northern Lights – hard to describe: a presence suffused with 'The glory of the Lord'.

Yet (like Gabriel to Mary) the angel says to the shepherds, 'Do not be afraid.' Darkness is familiar territory. This light is strange – but it's also a sign of God's presence. Setting their fear aside, they can hear the Good News. So can we experience God in both the familiar and the unexpected; in the darkness and in the light – and in the place where they wonderfully co-exist?

Henry Vaughan's poem 'The Night' includes this line: 'There is in God (some say) a deep but dazzling darkness.' Take time to reflect on these words.

Treasures of darkness

A day in the life of Jesus. At daybreak, gathering his disciples, he chooses a leadership team of twelve. Imagine a large crowd listening intently to the names Jesus calls out. Each stands for an individual, with abilities and flaws. Each face is now looking to Jesus for guidance and reassurance as they're given new responsibilities – which not all can sustain.

Spending the night in prayer

Luke 6:12-19

They move to a large open place, with little shelter from the noonday sun, where a crowd has gathered: more followers, and folk who've never seen Jesus before, but have come to listen to his teaching or to seek help. They call out his name. He sees their need as hands reach out to touch him. 'Power goes out from him' (verse 19). This, in the gospels, is a day in the life of Jesus. Where does he find his strength?

Look back to verse 12. Jesus went out into the hill-country, 'and spent the night in prayer to God'. Alone in the silence of the hills; in darkness, except for the remote light of the stars; away from the clamour of the plain, the demanding detail of life under the sun, Jesus takes time in the presence of God, drawing the strength that he, his followers and the crowds, will need. Like the months of growing in Mary's womb, the night of prayer nurtures him.

In these busy days before Christmas, how can we find space like this to pray? Henry Vaughan wrote:

Dear night! . . .
The stop to busie fools; care's check and curb . . .
my soul's calm retreat which none disturb!
Christ's progress, and his prayer time;
The hours to which high heaven doth chime.

from 'The Night' by Henry Vaughan,
1621–1695

Thank God for precious moments of calm retreat!

Treasures of darkness Jan Sutch Pickard

Darkness over the whole land

Luke 23:33; 44-49

This is a very different kind of darkness: a terrible darkness at midday, an eclipse overthrowing the natural order, 'over the whole land', inescapable. What does it mean? It's as though God is dead. To the friends of Jesus, including the women watching helplessly as he dies on the cross, this is the death of all their hopes. The place is called The Skull – and the darkness in the sky seems to reflect the darkness in the minds of torturers, politicians, soldiers. We see that human beings, though made in the image of God, can deny God and destroy each other.

Is this an appropriate reading for Christmas time? Yet it was Christmas two years ago when the bombs began falling on Gaza – in a conflict with both fear and violence on two sides, but also complex politics, a history of long and deep injustice, and a world that stood by while children died and black clouds of homes burning covered the sky. Darkness over the whole land – indeed, the world.

And where was God in all this? In the broken body of a child. In the human compassion that wept helplessly or worked to save lives. On the cross, and at its foot: there in the darkness.

Where are you, God, in the darkness?
Have we lost you? Have you lost us?
(silence)
For our complicity in violence – forgive us;
For our apathy about injustice – forgive us!
(silence)
Can you hear us? Are you near us? Can you bear us?
(silence)
We are people walking in darkness:
Give us courage to go on; hope that light will dawn.
(silence)
Is it you, God, walking beside us, bearing our sorrows?
God-with-us!

Jan Sutch Pickard

Treasures of darkness

It was not yet evening. The eclipse had passed. The sun beat down again on the rocky hills around Jerusalem, the place called The Skull, the city walls. The body of Jesus was taken down from the cross, carried to a cave-tomb nearby, and laid out on a rock ledge in the cool shadows.

Joseph of Arimathaea helps take down the body and carry it to a safe place, away from scavenging creatures. In this hot country, funerals happen as soon as possible – though, because Jesus died on the eve of the sabbath, there wasn't time to observe all the rituals of burial. That's why the women planned to come back and lay out the body properly later. Their careful preparation, and Joseph's practical intervention, show respect both for tradition and for the battered body of a man executed as a criminal.

Some of Jesus' followers – the disciples he named and called to follow him – had gone into hiding. Imagine them spending the sabbath in secrecy, overshadowed by fear, shame, disappointed hopes, distress at their loss. Joseph's action, though, could not be secret. He was known as a member of the Council; the crucifixion was on a hilltop; he had to ask permission from Pilate. So his response happened in the light, in public view – as did the women's presence on that execution ground, in the heat and glare of the day.

On that day they experienced the black hole of bereavement; the welcome darkness of the tomb.

The darkness of the tomb

Luke 23:50-56

God, give us courage for the things that we need to do today, and when we need to rest, or to hide, may we find your healing darkness.

Treasures of darkness   Jan Sutch Pickard

While it was still dark

John 20:1-18

This chapter holds the story at the heart of the Christian faith, taking us, with the disciples, to encounter the empty tomb, the possibility of life after death, and then, face-to-face, the risen Christ. It is a complex story and the experience is not the same for everyone. It is still unfolding as darkness falls on the road to Emmaus, having begun before dawn, in a garden, at the mouth of the tomb.

The story of the Resurrection has been told many times, put under the glare of the world's questioning, lit in different ways by what people believe. This weekend, as we read and reflect in the different season of Advent, we will not rush on to all that happened on that first Easter Day, all the running to and fro, all the sharing of rumour and eyewitness accounts. Instead, let's stay with Mary in the garden, in the darkness before dawn.

Let us stay with the mystery: in the place of baffling absence, and of God's presence everywhere. In darkness, we can often be more aware of that.

Henry Vaughan's poem 'Night', has this compelling image:

God's silent searching flight:
When my Lord's head is fill'd with dew, and all
His locks are wet with the clear drops of night:
His still, soft call;
His knocking time . . .

from 'the Night' by Henry Vaughan

For Mary, God's 'knock' came when the man she took to be the gardener called her by name.

Close your eyes, imagine the smell and touch of that Easter garden, still dark, full of mystery and possibility; listen for God's 'still, soft call'. What does it mean to you?

Treasures of darkness

4   Riches hidden in secret places

Notes based on the Revised English Version by

Jan Sutch Pickard

For Jan's biography see p.350.

Preparing for the week

It has been challenging for me, working on these particular readings. Yet, like many things we don't choose, it has been a blessing. The first challenge was to be given a passage from the Book of Daniel to comment on. I don't know about you, but the story of the prophet Daniel is not one I turn to often. It's been a closed book to me! I couldn't get my mind round its apocalyptic imagery. But there is something very here-and-now about the story of the ruler with power of life and death over others, who's afraid of something as insubstantial as a dream, and needs help to understand what it means in his life. And how moving and relevant is the story of the courageous visionary who 'speaks truth to power' – and brings about change. This bit of the Bible, which I've been avoiding, helps me to reflect on living my faith today.

The problem with the parables is quite different. They are so familiar – and so compressed. We may think we've got our minds round them, know what they are all about. But imagine being told these stories for the first time. What new and surprising insights would they bring?

We are reading these passages together just before Christmas. So the image that came to me was of an Advent calendar, in which day by day one opens a window to reveal religious scenes, or secular images such as a wrapped present, a sledge, a snowman, a Christmas pudding! The parables Jesus told are like windows showing us many things which we may not think of as 'religious' – but which help us to see God at work in our lives.

For further thought

• What are the objects that you touch, the everyday things that you do, that could be parables of 'God with us'?

Dreams

Daniel 2:1, 17-30

What is more secret than someone's mind, richer than the symbolism of dreams? Although the complex drama in this passage has several characters – the king, his executioner, the wise men, a prophet – the most significant action happens not on stage, but inside the heads of Nebuchadnezzar and Daniel, the prophet.

In the darkness of the night, the king has been sleepless. He wants to know the meaning of his disturbing dreams. Who can read another man's mind, or interpret his dreams? Yet the penalty for failing to do so, for the wise men, will be death. Daniel prays to God, who helps him (in the depths of his mind) to find a meaning, which will enlighten Nebuchadnezzar, though not put his mind at rest.

Before telling the king, Daniel prays again, praising God, whose power is seen both in the natural order (the cycle of the seasons) and in surprising interventions (the overthrow of tyrants). God, above all, 'reveals deep mysteries [and] knows what lies in darkness' (verse 22). Then the dream is interpreted, and the death sentence lifted.

This is one small scene in the story of salvation. It reminds us of the depth of God's understanding: of us, the most complex beings in creation, and of the meaning of our experiences, our lives.

When have you looked for a meaning, and felt 'in the dark'? What happened when you prayed?

O God, you know what lies in the darkness; you know the dreams we fear most. We believe that you walk with us, through the valley of the shadow; and that, in the depths of your mystery, we can safely let go, and not be lost.

Jan Sutch Pickard

Treasures of darkness

Like the windows in an Advent calendar, the parables of Jesus reveal small pictures – not of preparations for Christmas amid familiar scenes, but glimpses of farmers, merchants and housewives going about their daily lives in first-century Palestine. Each parable is a little glimpse of the way God works, of God's coming kingdom. For the next three days I invite you to open a few of these windows.

Seeds, yeast

Matthew 13:24-33

The field

Wheat and weeds grow together – God lets them grow.
Right and wrong in our lives – which is which? God knows.
'Good is stronger than evil' – in God's time it shows.

A favourite slogan in Nigeria is 'God's time is best'. Does this make sense to you?

A seed

A tiny seed, the smallest thing:
plant it and watch it grow tall.
This is the way God works, changing
the whole world – and starting small.

Look around you – where are the mustard seeds?

Yeast

A woman in her kitchen with a great lump of dough
mixes in living yeast – so it warms and begins to grow.
This is the way God gets to work in hearts that are cold and dead:
the stodgiest church can rise again – becoming like living bread.

What could help you and your church community to be lifted out of the concerns that weigh you down, to be changed in a way that will nourish your neighbours and the world?

God of growth and goodness, on this shortest day, help us to see you at work in the smallest beginnings; open us to be changed by your love; and, as light comes back into the world, may your kingdom come.

Treasures of darkness

Jan Sutch Pickard

Hidden treasure

Matthew 13:44-48

Open more windows in our Advent calendar. What surprising pictures – a man digging, a fishing crew, a merchant cradling a pearl.

Buried treasure

A man digging in a field finds treasure under the earth.
So he runs and shows it to others in great delight?
No! He hides it again, then bids for the land outright.
He's sold all he owned to buy it, knowing the field's true worth.

Jesus isn't encouraging underhand dealing, but reminding us that sometimes we need time to value an experience before we start sharing it with others. We need to live with it, reflect on it, 'own' it. Is this true of the way you learned and are still learning about God's love embodied in Jesus?

The net

Fishermen anywhere in the world (on Ghanaian beaches, going out from jetties in the west of Scotland, or on the Sea of Galilee) know that their nets will bring in a variety of fish: some delicious and nutritious, some bony, some even poisonous. We too need to exercise discernment with what the world brings to us: what's worth keeping, what to throw overboard. How easy do you find this?

The pearl

This merchant knows what he's doing:
who wouldn't sell everything, to buy the best?
But you need to recognise it, first.

God of grace, in Jesus you were born into a world of power politics as a small and helpless child. We thank you for those who recognised you and welcomed you in the baby: his life in their hands, a pearl of great price. Help us to recognise you in things and people that are small and often overlooked. Help us to desire your love above all, and to cherish what you have entrusted to our human hands.

Jan Sutch Pickard
360

Treasures of darkness

Here's a woman sweeping her home. She's lost something tiny, but much valued. It could simply be small change, in a household where every penny counts. Or it could be part of her bridal headdress the equivalent of losing a wedding ring. She searches hard, sweeping in every corner, and when she finds it she shares the good news with all her neighbours.

Think of a time when you lost something that you valued greatly, and how you felt when you found it. Have you ever felt that you lost touch with God – and then found meaning again?

I remember visiting the Church of the Nativity, in Bethlehem. The only entrance to that ancient building is through a door so low that only a small child can enter without bending – so adults have to humble themselves, becoming like little children. Sadly, religious buildings in the Holy Land are sometimes the scene of military occupation or of adult wrangling. But on that day a Palestinian woman my own age was preparing the place for worship. She made me think of Mary and all the other ordinary people whom God has entrusted with carrying, and protecting, concealing and revealing his love in Jesus.

Finding our heart's desire

Luke 15:8-10

Church of the Nativity

Here, through an open door, becoming like children,
we enter a warm place.
Sunlight slants through high windows and
dust-motes dance,
light as the human spirit.
A woman, sweeping the patterned floor with simple grace,
looks up, smiles, welcoming us
into a silent and expectant place.

God, help us to prepare a place for you. May this Christmas be a time of expectancy and simple joy; may we find you in the little, the least and the lost, and welcome you in other people.

Treasures of darkness · Jan Sutch Pickard

361

Readings in Matthew

1 Emmanuel, God is with us

Notes based on the New Revised Standard Version by **Jim Cotter**

Jim Cotter is an ordained Anglican who ministers in the parish of Aberdaron in north-west Wales to house-holders and to visitors. He also writes and publishes as Cairns Publications. See www.cottercairns.co.uk.

Preparing for the week

No, my name is not Matthew, but I did give shape to the short book you refer to as the gospel according to Matthew. Thank you for asking me to help you understand what it was my community and I were trying to say two generations after the time in which Jesus lived.

I grew up in the port of Alexandria in Egypt. We lived in uncertain times: we often felt all at sea ourselves! For it seemed as if the very heart of our Jewish faith had been torn from us. The Romans had destroyed the temple in Jerusalem. Could our faith survive without it? We had already begun to be dispersed through the empire, but the aching hole of what you tell me you call 'ground zero' was an agony and a bewilderment.

The members of my particular Jewish community had been captivated by Jesus of Nazareth. In himself and in his message we were finding a new focus for our faith. We were convinced that he was the promised liberator, or Messiah, God's anointed one who would, like Moses of old, bring us freedom. Indeed, the book you have in your hands could be subtitled 'The new Moses: the renewal of our freedom'. We wrote to our fellow Jews to convince them that our future was with Jesus, God-with-us, Emmanuel.

For further thought

- Do we expect to read directly from the pages of the Bible handy spiritual and moral advice? Or do we wrestle with our ancestors, expectant of being changed by the encounter with them and with the God who turns us inside out in the very midst of the struggle itself?

Your ancestors link you with all your people. You are related to each and every one, right back to the very first forebear. You know the stories of a few. Most have been forgotten, but the obscure in their day were as important in God's eyes as the famous – as you are in yours.

Embrace Jesus. This is what I was inviting my contemporaries to do. And I was showing them his credentials, right back to our forefather Abraham.

It's encouraging to remember that even the most famous were imperfect, even the most obscure were important, even the lowest of the low were high in God's purposes, even the morally suspect played their vital part, and even the foreigners were welcomed, to remind us that we can't rely on our supposed pure bloodlines.

I knew the rumours, that Jesus had been born to an unmarried mother and nobody was quite sure who the father was. So I reminded my readers that there were some very doubtful women among their ancestors whose parts in the story were blessed by God – Tamar who disguised herself as a prostitute and Rahab who was a prostitute, Ruth a Moabite and Bathsheba a Hittite, all foreigners. They used their wits, they showed loyalties beyond what might have been expected. They found a place, and the story continued. Among the insecure and the unnoticed, Jesus was born.

What is your place in the story? Who are your immediate ancestors in the genealogies of flesh and of faith?

A disreputable family tree

Matthew 1:1-17

Readings in Matthew

Jim Cotter

363

A disruptive dream

Matthew 1:18-25

An exceptional life. An exceptional destiny. That is what we have come to believe about Jesus. When people in my time, Jewish or Greek or Roman, came to write stories about the birth of such a special person, we wrote about the direct intervention of a god in the life of a woman who did not expect to conceive because she was virginal or sterile or elderly. You mustn't think that the divine conception of Jesus marked him out, because that was a unique event in history. What marked out this 'son of God' was that he wasn't powerful in a worldly way, that he wasn't born in a palace, and I haven't written this gospel to claim that he is really the emperor. His rule was different, and the God whose son he was, was showing us again that his heart was with the vulnerable and insecure.

There is something else about this story of his birth that may help you understand what I was trying to say. 'Holy Spirit' and 'in a dream' are both indicators that God is experienced as being specially close at critical moments in a person's life – or in the history of a people. If you saw a vision or heard a voice in a powerful and vivid dream, you 'woke up', trembling or in a sweat, every nerve ending alert to the presence of the divine.

Christmas Day can be lonely and disturbing for many people. If that's true for you, accept that you are indeed disturbed and ponder, perhaps in a daydream, what God may be saying to you.

Jim Cotter

Readings in Matthew

There's an important clue in the last line of this story. The exotic visitors returned to their own country 'by another road'.

The outer journey had been disturbing enough: a particularly bright star in the sky, an unknown road into a foreign country, a courtesy call to the king's court that clearly threw their hosts into a panic, silky words of diplomacy that they must be sure to return and let the king know the whereabouts of the child. The city palace was not the destination after all, but a village home.

Disturbing, too, for a peasant family. Enough equipment in the house to get by, maybe a family heirloom, certainly no hoard of gold, no temple that needs incense, no myrrh. No worldly king here, despite the gifts that would have been more at home at the court of Herod. There are clashes in this story, nothing is quite right, nothing you might expect.

And they were warned in a dream – that other clue to the unexpected God being unexpectedly present, guiding you in unexpected ways – not to go via Herod, not by his assumptions and paths, but to return home by a very different road.

Think of somewhere you have visited, memorable but in a way you weren't expecting. How did your life change as a result? How are you being challenged here and now by stories that still have the power to disturb?

Disturbing visitors themselves disturbed

Matthew 2:1-12

Readings in Matthew

Jim Cotter

A dislocating tragedy

Matthew 2:13-18

When he became a public figure, Jesus was never far from controversy, criticising and upsetting our religious and political leaders. Not only in emergencies were women and children put first by the rescuers: Jesus taught and practised that they were always first, the least powerful at the heart of God's domain.

So, in the overture to my gospel I needed a stark story to show how trouble followed Jesus. Again, a crisis. Again, a dream. Again, a journey along a road. And because I'd had the vision of Jesus as the new Moses, I wanted part of the prologue to be a journey to and from Egypt, much as our ancestors had taken. It was as if God was saying again, 'Out of Egypt I have called my son'. So Jesus had to escape the danger he was in from King Herod – as the infant Moses had escaped from Pharaoh's decree.

Herod panicked under the threat of a usurper – which is how he must have thought of Jesus from the visit of the wise men. He had the young boys of Bethlehem killed. But Joseph and Mary and Jesus had already fled. Jesus lived – at the cost of slaughter and grief for many. But one day he would give hope to the oppressed and bereaved, and pay the cost himself.

Ask yourself about the people you meet today. Is this person more powerful than I am or more vulnerable than I am – here and now, in the details of this encounter? Who has the responsibility of being Christ to the other?

A distilled journey

The question still lingers: Who is the king of the Jews? Another Herod now, but much like his father – and the same question. And two more dreams for Joseph: God is very near, with us, Emmanuel. And, in the second dream, the same warning: do not go Herod's way. He is yet another violent lord. You have come out of Egypt, the old story resonating still: flee from the Pharaoh's wrath. The task of the new Moses will be in the promised land, not to lead the people of old to that land. There he will transform people's lives and put the power in their hands to share their substance with others, and to bring God's healing to one another. Do not go the centre of power, give Jerusalem a wide berth.

Matthew 2:19-23

So I have given you five dreams in this prologue – and five quotations from scripture. Read on in my gospel and you will find five long addresses, the first being the new law from a new mountain, (chapters 5–7), the others being about mission (chapters 10–11), parables (chapter 13), the community (chapters 18–19), and the last things (chapters 24–25). But for the time being, it is obscurity – growing into early adulthood in Galilee, in Nazareth. The overture is over.

Think about your own journey. When has power been exercised against you? When have you been most free? How have you used your own power? When have you been able to say, 'Yes, we have known the Spirit of Emmanuel, God here and now with us'?

Readings in Matthew

Jim Cotter

A disquieting prophet

Matthew 3:1-12

So the main story begins, with a revival of the old tradition of the fiery prophet speaking unwelcome truths, calling people to repentance. But we haven't forgotten the story of Moses, and of Egypt, and of the journey to the promised land. For John the Baptist is gathering people, not to any old river, but to the Jordan. The very name stirs the heart of my people: our ancestors crossed it to their new home.

The new Moses would have to make this journey too. John's task was to make the people ready for him, to clear the way through the wilderness, to create an atmosphere of expectancy of a new kingdom when we would no longer be ruled by the latest imperial power, that of Rome. But what kind of struggle would ensue? What kind of God would intervene? Violence or non-violence? Impatient destructive force or patient persistent power? A world turned upside down with the ones at the bottom now at the top, and the powerful overthrown, or a new kind of society and community, fair shares for all, justice in a commonwealth, and compassion towards those that needed help?

So a 21st-century voice has come in to replace the late first century Matthew. Ask yourself about the way John is predicting. Are some human beings worthless chaff fit only to be burnt? Or is there chaff in each human being, needing not to be burnt but to be gently sorted by a discerning presence, and simply blown away and forgotten?

Jesus was baptised by John, a fact that the early church was uncomfortable with. It seems to make John superior and Jesus needing to repent of sins.

Mark is straightforward in his account but emphasises the heavenly vision and the intimate relationship of Jesus with his Father. It is similar with Luke, with the addition that Jesus was praying. Here in Matthew, John objects and has to be persuaded to baptise Jesus. And if you read the first chapter of the fourth gospel you will find John witnessing to Jesus, and describing the descent of the Spirit, but all mention of a baptism has vanished.

Perhaps Jesus at first joined John's movement. We may wonder if he shared John's fierce view as an apocalyptic prophet expecting destruction. Maybe, maybe not. Later in Matthew, in chapter 11, he defends John the desert prophet over against the third Herod in his life, Herod Antipas who had John executed. But immediately afterwards he demotes John, for the least in the kingdom of God is greater than John, even a powerless child. And that implies that Jesus' God is very different from John's.

Matthew might well say to us that he really did believe that Jesus was the new Moses, that people were being called to follow the one who proclaimed and lived God's justice, that Jesus more profoundly revealed the true nature of the one God, but that this was no new God but the same God of Abraham more profoundly understood and more accurately lived.

What do you think?

Have a go at continuing the conversation with Matthew begun this week. Take your part in the ongoing dialogue with our ancestors of faith.

A distinguishing light

Matthew 3:13-17

Readings in Matthew

Jim Cotter

All about IBRA

IBRA readings

The list of readings for the whole year is available to download from www.christianeducation.org.uk/ibra. You are welcome to make as many copies as you like.

IBRA books

Both extraordinary value at £8.50 each in the UK, with writers from around the world and many different Christian traditions.

IBRA samplers

From time to time IBRA publishes samplers using notes from *Light for our Path* and *Words for Today*, suitable for introducing new readers or for use with Bible study groups. Please contact us at the address below for availability.

IBRA Rep discount

If you live in the UK and purchase 6 or more copies of IBRA books, you can sign up as an IBRA Rep which entitles you to 10% discount off all your IBRA purchases. Just tick the IBRA Rep box on your order form and we'll do the rest.

IBRA International Fund

The IBRA International Fund enables the translation, printing and distribution of IBRA Bible notes and readings. For more details, see page 158. You can make a donation when ordering your books.

IBRA, 1020 Bristol Road, Selly Oak, Birmingham, B29 6LB, UK

International Bible Reading Association

A worldwide service of Christian Education at work in five continents

HEADQUARTERS
1020 Bristol Road
Selly Oak
Birmingham, B29 6LB
UK

www.christianeducation.org.uk
ibra@christianeducation.org.uk

and the following agencies:

AUSTRALIA
UniChurch Books
130 Little Collins Street
Melbourne
VIC 3001

GHANA
Asempa Publishers
Christian Council of Ghana
Box GP 919
Accra

ymyesitso@yahoo.com

INDIA
All India Sunday School Association
Plot No 8,
Threemurthy Colony
6th Cross, Mahendra Hills
PB no 2099
Secunderabad – 500 026
Andhra Pradesh

sundayschoolindia@yahoo.co.in

Fellowship of Professional Workers
Samanvay
Deepthi Chambers
Vijayapuri
Hyderabad – 500 017
Andhra Pradesh

fellowship2u@gmail.com

NEW ZEALAND
Epworth Bookshop
157B Karori Road
Marsden Village
Karori
Wellington 6012

Mailing address:
PO Box 17255
Karori
Wellington 6147

sales@epworthbooks.org.nz

NIGERIA
David Hinderer House
The Cathedral Church of St David
Kudeti
Ibadan
PMB 5298 Dugbe
Ibadan
Oyo State

SOUTH AND CENTRAL AFRICA
IBRA South Africa
6 Roosmaryn Street
Durbanville 7550

biblereading@evmot.com

IBRA themes for 2011

God still speaks
God's word at work in the world
Pay attention!

Attitudes to suffering
From anger to trust
Your will be done

Readings in Galatians
One gospel for all God's people
Freedom with the Holy Spirit

Marks of a successful church
Five marks of a successful church

Readings in Matthew (4–10)
Proclaiming the kingdom
Kingdom living
Healings

Mercy for sinners
God wants sinners to come to him
God's forgiveness is for everyone

Conversion and change
Power to change
Life transformed

Readings from Colossians
Christ in you, the hope of glory
Do everything in the name of the
Lord Jesus

Living with Easter

Questions Jesus asked
Questions Jesus asked: in Mark
Questions Jesus asked: in Luke
Questions Jesus asked: in John

Imagination and creativity
Imaging the divine and the human
With the eyes of the heart
Jesus' imaginative teachings

Readings in Matthew (13–19)
Parables of the kingdom
Signs of the kingdom
Teaching of the kingdom

Marriage
Marriages good and bad
Marriage as metaphor

Readings in 1 Kings
Solomon and the temple
The demise of the kings
The prophetic ministry of Elijah

Openings and closings in the New Testament
Greetings and blessings

Readings in Matthew (20–25)
Going up to Jerusalem
Conflict
Signs at the end

Angels
Angels in the Old Testament
Angels in the New Testament

Prophecy of Jeremiah
Prophetic words in action
A prophetic life: memoirs
Chanting down oppressive nations

Trade between the nations

Gratitude
How to give thanks
What to give thanks for

Readings in Matthew (26–28)
Arrest
Trial

Salvation history
Salvation belongs to God
Salvation with a difference
Singing salvation
Salvation beyond boundaries

The good news